LEADING
with
CARE
in a
TOUGH
WORLD

Beyond Servant Leadership

Bob DeKoch & Phillip G. Clampitt

RODIN BOOKS™

Rodin Books 2022

RODIN BOOKS™

Hardcover ISBN 978-1-957588-10-0

eBook ISBN 978-1-957588-11-7

PUBLISHED BY RODIN BOOKS INC.
666 Old Country RoadSuite 510
Garden City, New York 11530

www.rodinbooks.com

Second Printing, March 2024

Book and cover design by Alexia Garaventa

Manufactured in the United States of America

BOB'S DEDICATION

To Debbie, who, for more than fifty years, has been my best friend and the love of my life. Her unwavering support has been my rock. Thank you from the bottom of my heart.

PHIL'S DEDICATION

To Laurey, who continues to dazzle me with her caring, wit,
and just the right amount of mystery,

and

Dr. Bert H. Clampitt, Dr. M. Lee Williams, and Dr. Cal
Downs, who taught me to think with rigor, imagination, and joy.

CONTENTS

FIGURES

TABLES

APPENDICES

PREFACE

Type the words *leadership book* into Amazon.com and you'll find over sixty thousand titles. That's good news, because it means that many people aspire to be better leaders. The bad news? You can't read them all.

Leading with Care in a Tough World differs from other books because we explain how recalibrating five core leadership beliefs (uncertainty, progress, values, learning, and caring) can transform your daily leadership behaviors in ways that will fulfill your career aspirations and propel your organization to new levels.

The first section of the book helps leaders grapple with some fundamental questions:

- How should you react to the inherent uncertainties of life?

- How do you define progress?

- What core values should guide your relationships, aspirations, and decisions?

- How do people learn and unlearn?

- How can you be kind in a tough world?

All leaders, regardless of experience level, could enhance their viewpoints on these questions. This book provides the framework for wisely responding to these fundamental questions.

Answers to these questions serve as a springboard to the second section of the book, which highlights specific visible and subtle practices of inspiring leaders. In this section we discuss issues such as coaching employees, communicating effectively, collaborating with others, establishing value-adding relationships, and managing pushback.

Other leadership books may deal with some of these issues, but few connect these issues to core leadership beliefs in the way *Leading with Care in a Tough World* does in terms of depth, insight, and practicality. We sought to go beyond the rich foundation of the servant leadership movement. Specifically:

- *Leading with Care* goes beyond a string of stories from accomplished executives. To be sure, much can be learned from leaders like Steve Jobs, Meg Whitman, Winston Churchill, Indra Nooyi, and others. Leadership books of this type often illuminate and may inspire readers. Yet these books often neglect to discuss the practical, strategic insights leaders need to use on a daily basis to achieve amazing outcomes. We tell our fair share of illuminating stories, but we also drill down into the specifics of the lessons learned and how to implement the lessons in the workplace. (Note: In some cases we used aliases and changed small details to protect a leader's identity.)

- *Leading with Care* highlights both the development of the leader's mind-set AND the leader's relationships with others. Many books devoted to the "softer" leadership side tend to focus on "me"; that is, development of the leader's personal emotional control and empathy. That's important but only part of the equation. The missing piece of the equation involves developing the proper "we"—the cultivating of proper relationships between leaders and others. Part One of *Leading with Care* highlights the core beliefs and thinking routines leaders need to develop themselves (the "me"). Part Two builds on this foundation and educates readers on how to cultivate the proper relationships (the "we") to create extraordinary outcomes. If you wade through all the leadership books, you would be unlikely to find any other work that skillfully integrates these two sides of the leadership equation.

- *Leading with Care* presents leadership principles that were tested, tried, and refined over decades of practice. Some leadership books tout trailblazing research. Others advocate ideas based on extraordinary personal experiences. Both approaches have merit. *Leading with Care* is based on both original research and professional experience. Yet we take it one step further: we've tested these practices and refined them based on the experiences and feedback of others.

The approach we take in this book allows us to answer some of the most tough and vexing challenges leaders face today, including:

1. How can leaders better respond to the great uncertainties of the day and make progress?

2. How do leaders translate admirable leadership ideas into everyday practices?

3. How can leaders transform pushback into a unifying consensus?

4. Why isn't emotional intelligence enough to succeed as a leader today?

5. How do caring leaders encourage others while avoiding toxic positivity?

6. Why do leaders need to adjust their leadership approach in a post-COVID world?

7. How do leaders transform the sentiments of servant leadership into tangible actions that produce extraordinary results?

8. How should caring leaders respond to political activism by employees?

9. How do caring leaders embrace diversity and inclusiveness to cultivate high-performance cultures?

Answers to these questions and many more emerge in the following pages. Enjoy. Learn. Explore.

INTRODUCTION

If you have ever received a package in the mail emblazoned with a "Handle with Care" label, what would you expect to see inside? Something fragile, no doubt. And perhaps something quite valuable. Your anticipation grows as you carefully unwrap the package and wonder about what might be hidden deep in the bubble wrap or buried in the shredded paper. After you solve that mystery, what happens next? You look for damage or if something is broken or missing. You wonder, if, in fact, the package was "handled with care."

Treating people (e.g., employees, colleagues, customers, and stakeholders) like they have "Handle with Care" tags affixed to their T-shirts, smocks, hoodies, sweaters, or lapels should be built into every leader's DNA. Likewise, treating the pursuit of outcomes like they were wrapped with "Fragile: Handle with Care" tape should be a fundamental dimension of every leader's passion.

This norm suggests an important question: What does "Handle with Care" actually mean to those in leadership positions? To many people, caring simply means expressing empathy, compassion, or concern. Fair enough. But we think it means much more—caring at a deeper level acknowledges the unique circumstances people face. Think of it this way: people, like packages, endure lots of jostling and bumping as they move through life. Likewise, well-developed plans get challenged and torpedoed, sometimes every step of the way.

Shallow caring rarely produces magical outcomes. Amazon would never have become a Fortune 50 company if it merely shipped packages with best wishes for a safe arrival. Rather, Amazon thinks more deeply about how to properly care for parcels. For instance, the packaging in the box protects the cargo, but so does the box's structure and the way the item gets packed. Using the right packing material (visible) is important, but it must be arranged in the right way (subtle). Amazingly, Amazon has now reinvented package delivery with Amazon Prime service to underpin the importance of deep caring in delivery. Likewise, we think of caring leadership as composed of visible and subtle elements. You might fool some people with shallow caring, but you can't lead them to extraordinary results by nodding concern and hoping for the best. You wouldn't treat a valuable package that way. So, why would anyone lead in that way? Sadly, many in leadership positions do exactly that.

Deep caring goes beyond short-term well wishes (see Table 0.1). We champion deep-caring leadership that focuses on long-term, proactive, and developmental relationships. The contrast between shallow and deep caring may not be immediately evident to people. Yet over time, deep-caring leadership supercharges people and their organizations while unleashing latent energy on scales few could imagine. It never ceases to amaze us what people will accomplish when they know leaders:

Table 0.1

DEGREES OF CARING

SHALLOW CARING	DEEP CARING
• Short-term	• Long-term
• Appeasement focused	• Development focused
• Excuse enabling	• Change enabling
• Comforting mind-set	• Transformational mind-set
• Empathy motivated	• Solution motivated
• Visible	• Visible & subtle
• Reactive	• Proactive
• Placating	• Empowering

- Commit their time to develop them

- Have their back

- Sincerely recognize and appreciate their contributions

- Display a genuine interest in them

- Lead with a sense of warmth and empathy

- Take time to listen to employees and make sure they feel heard

- Encourage them to do their best work

- Provide space for them to grow

In this tough, competitive, and high-expectations world, many leaders don't behave in ways that generate these instinctive feelings. Yet, when people sense these passions about their leaders, it magically awakens a visceral spirit of connection that engages people in wonderful ways. The passions, commitments, and sheer grit released by a caring leader springboards people to unseen and unparalleled heights.

WHY DO WE NEED TO LEAD WITH CARE?

Our businesses, our organizations, our governments, and our people are riddled with divisiveness. Consider five of the top concerns leaders across generations must address:

Concern #1—Employees lack engagement in their workplace. Gallup reported that only 15 percent of employees in the United States are truly engaged in the workplace.[1] Yet nearly 70 percent of employees say they would work harder if they felt more appreciated. Over 90 percent of the employees surveyed believed their leadership "lacks communication skills to lead." Another recent study estimated that low employee engagement costs US companies $450 to $550 billion annually.[2] We believe that estimate is too low.

Concern #2—Citizens lack trust in public-sector leaders. Public-sector leaders recognize that trust in their leadership is approaching historic lows. Citizens are resisting their public health advice. Pushback regarding the direction of public school instruction makes daily headlines. The lack of trust emerges, in part, from poor leadership skills by those who govern. Many political leaders are pushing people apart rather than pulling people together.

Concern #3—The workplace in a post-COVID world will be reimagined. Work flexibility offered by remote work is considered a perk by many. In fact, 54 percent of office workers say they'd leave for a job with more flexibility.[3] Envisioning an empowered workplace with a mix of on-site and remote workers represents an unprecedented leadership challenge.

Concern #4—Heightened political activism by employees has paralyzed many leaders. High-profile political protests represent sentiments that percolate throughout many organizations. Vocal employees often demand action by their leaders on their political issues, even as other employees directly or indirectly push back. Navigating these tricky waters requires a different and nontraditional leadership approach.

Concern #5—The sentiments behind servant leadership and emotional intelligence have proven to be a daunting challenge. A virtual flood of books, seminars, and podcasts about servant leadership and emotional intelligence cultivated some of the core sentiments advocated in *Leading with Care*. Yet, many leaders struggle with how to act on these ideas in a practical way.

Leading with Care directly addresses these concerns. It has broad, worldwide applications in both the public and private sectors. Leaders who practice this caring approach will bring about much-needed leadership change. It will unite people allowing them to accomplish the amazing.

WHO SHOULD READ THIS BOOK? (AND WHO SHOULD NOT?)

We wrote this book for aspiring leaders, practicing leaders, and seasoned executives seeking ways to unlock the untapped potential of others, their teams, and their organizations.

- Aspiring leaders often have the right desires but not the tools. If you are an aspiring leader, you will encounter an avalanche of leadership articles and books. By placing *Leading with Care* at the top of your reading stack, you can develop the fundamental sentiments of great leaders as you learn the specific practices to act on those sentiments.

- If you are practicing leader, you may have hit a rough patch because you recognize that meeting the organization's expectations is not enough on a personal or professional level. You may be seeking something more and want to invest in others in ways that produce magical results. At the root of your challenge may be the need to better understand the subtle skills of a caring leader. These are the ones that few researchers and practitioners ever speak about. This book will help you discover and develop exactly those skills.

- If you are a seasoned executive (leader of leaders) who wants to build a great place to work, you may be looking for a framework to inspire other leaders in your organization. Caring leadership can awaken deeper, more profound passions in people. Nothing inspires people more than seeing caring leaders in action every day.

So, whom is this book not for? It's not for those who are mired in self-deception and unwilling to shift their perspective and do the hard of work of deep caring. If you think you might fall into that category, then we would recommend reading *Leadership and Self-Deception* as your starting point.

WHY SHOULD YOU BELIEVE US?

Some authors' credibility flows from years of successful practice. Check. Other authors' expertise emerges from novel research projects. Check. And a few leadership authors offer a new twist on the extensive writing in the field. Check.

We offer all three:

- **Successful practice**—Collectively, we have over six decades of experience successfully leading organizations. Bob has held a number of leadership positions in a diverse set of high-profile businesses. In his previous role as president of the Boldt Company, he and the Boldt team transformed the company into a billion-dollar business with divisions all across the United States. This was accomplished totally through organic growth. Phil has been honored with multiple named and endowed professorships and has received numerous awards for his teaching and scholarship while acting as department head in Communication and Information Science programs. Both of your authors have mentored and coached leaders in for-profit and nonprofit organizations. And, yes, both of your authors have made mistakes, but we have used them as learning opportunities to refine our leadership approaches. We use these experiences to enrich the practices advocated in this book.

- **Novel research**—We have conducted numerous innovative studies about uncertainty management, communication satisfaction, progress making, organizational culture, clear thinking, safety practices, and employee empowerment with thousands of employees across a wide range of organizations. We routinely monitor employee engagement in a variety of companies. For example, over a recent six-year period at the Boldt Company, we found that 93 percent of over four thousand respondents agreed that "team members collaborate to solve problems," and the most frequent words used to describe their work environment were *exciting*, *collaborative*, and *team*. In another study we found that 98 percent of employees believed the "leadership team has responded appropriately to the COVID-19 virus." We used the insights from these various studies to formulate the sensibilities and key insights in this book.

- **New twist**—Our respective shelves are stacked with books on leadership and biographies of great leaders, accumulated over decades of readings and pondering the core practices of excellent leaders. The books range from scholarly tomes like *Sensemaking in Organizations* by Karl Weick to more popular books like *Emotional Intelligence* by Daniel Goleman to the softer but enlightening works like *Who Moved My Cheese?* by Johnson and Blanchard. Before writing this book, we scrutinized the heavily earmarked and highlighted passages from the stacks of books and articles that line our personal libraries. We sought to distill the core insights into our unique perspective on caring leadership. We even revisited and refined ideas from our previous books. No doubt, some readers will recognize updates to that thinking in this book.

In short, here's why you should carefully contemplate the ideas in this book: we've uniquely synthesized our collective expertise, novel research, and new twists on the leadership literature in order to provide you with actionable practices to enhance your leadership style. We don't claim to have all the answers, but we believe this book offers profoundly valuable perspective to aspiring leaders, practicing leaders, and leaders of leaders. Embrace a little uncertainty, read on, and let's find out!

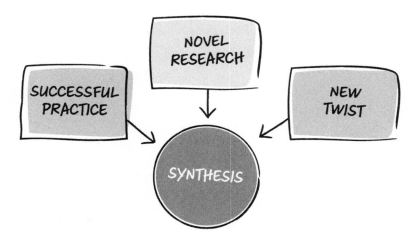

Figure 0.1

WHY SHOULD YOU BELIEVE US?

WHAT CAN YOU EXPECT?

Deep-caring leadership emerges from five core beliefs:

- Embracing uncertainty promotes growth
- Progress making inspires extraordinary performance
- Cultivating the right values builds a special sense of identity
- Lifelong learning fosters humility
- Acting with kindness is not being soft

These fundamental beliefs are captured in Part One, "The Beliefs of Caring Leaders."

Part Two of the book builds on these core beliefs and highlights nine key practices leaders need to master in order to deliver unexpected and remarkable outcomes. We start each chapter by defining the core practice and discussing why it is so important. Next, we share more specific techniques you should master in the quest to become a more caring leader. We divide these techniques into two categories: a) visible practices that people can easily observe and b) subtle practices that are not clearly visible to many but engage people on deeper levels.

Figure 0.2

WHAT CAN YOU EXPECT?

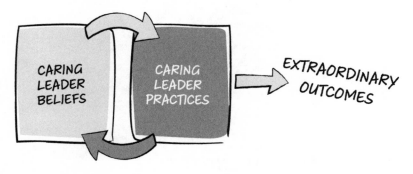

Parts One and Two are symbiotically related; strengthening one bolsters the other and vice versa. (See Figure 0.2.) As your commitment deepens to these core beliefs, so will your ability to act on those beliefs. Likewise, as you use more of the caring leader practices, your beliefs that support those practices will intensify.

Caring leaders embrace a deep, robust, and never-wavering commitment to their fellow human beings. Yet, sometimes caring leaders need to be tough to demonstrate that they care on a deeper level. In short, caring leaders are on a mission to inspire others to achieve even more extraordinary results than they ever dreamed possible for themselves and their organizations.

So, let's get right to the hard work. It starts with reexamining your core beliefs about deep caring. Read on. Reflect further. And grow!

PART 1

THE BELIEFS OF CARING LEADERS

This section spotlights five core beliefs that distinguish caring leaders from other types of leaders. Enriching your understanding, appreciation, and commitment to these beliefs profoundly enhances your leadership potential. Collectively, these core beliefs of caring leaders can generate greater passion, performance, and results.

It is better to know some of the questions than all of the answers.

—JAMES THURBER

CHAPTER 1
EMBRACING UNCERTAINTY ACCELERATES GROWTH

With open arms and high expectations, administrators, professors, and staff welcomed the new chancellor, Dr. Faux, to their midsize university. His friendly smile, amiable manner, endearing and inspired quips, and occasional *y'all*s endeared him to many—at least for a while. Some grumblings about his leadership style emerged about six months later. "Growing pains" was the refrain for some time as people adjusted to his priorities, proclivities, and style. During the summer break, the misgivings about his leadership seemed to dissipate, much like the winter chill.

As the fall semester progressed, the original concerns reemerged and became more acute. In November, Dr. Faux held a regularly scheduled brainstorming meeting with his direct reports.

This was the first occasion when Dr. Faux invited some faculty members to "expand the pool of ideas." Most of the faculty members were honored to be included and welcomed the opportunity. After Dr. Faux presented the problem to the group, he asked for ideas. The faculty, who were new to the group, waited for the direct reports to offer up the first comments. Crickets. Not a chirp. Time seemed to tick down like the clock on the final round of *Jeopardy!* When the time was just about to expire, Dr. Faux queried, "What about the faculty members? Do you have any ideas?"

One senior faculty member immediately heeded the opportunity: "What about ABC?" Dr. Faux grimaced a bit and declared with his most charming accent, "That dog don't hunt. Any other ideas?" Another faculty member suggested another approach. Dr. Faux's response: "That dog don't hunt, either, and here's why." Sensing the pattern, nobody else offered any ideas, even though Dr. Faux kept prodding the group for more input. His patience waned and he huffed, "Why do I have to do all the thinking around here?" and he disgustedly stomped out of the room.

The answer, of course, was painfully clear to everyone around the table: Dr. Faux was the only one with good ideas. By routinely shooting down every suggestion, he had stifled all input.

Dr. Faux's style vividly illustrates how someone—despite his queries—actually thinks he has all the answers. He demonstrates no tolerance for uncertainty because his analysis is always correct. He won't even explore the reasoning behind a suggestion that he disagrees with. At the most fundamental level, he leads by commanding others through his positional power rather than caring about the people and the university in a meaningful way.

WHAT DOES IT MEAN TO EMBRACE UNCERTAINTY?

Uncertainty can best be defined by its opposite (see Figure 1.1). Certainty means that something is fixed or settled. Every time we jump up, we come down. That's a certainty explained by the law of gravity. Ben Franklin's oft-quoted maxim cites two other certainties: "Our new Constitution is now established, everything seems to promise it will be durable; but, in this world, nothing is certain except death and taxes." So, we think of death and taxes as certainties because they are absolutely predictable knowns, even though we just don't know when or how much. But Ben's quote also offers some frequently overlooked advice about uncertainty. The first clause of this legendary quip cautions the founders; they should not take for granted that the constitutional principles will endure over time. In other words, don't treat something that is inherently uncertain as if it is a

Figure 1.1

UNCERTAINTY CONTINUUM

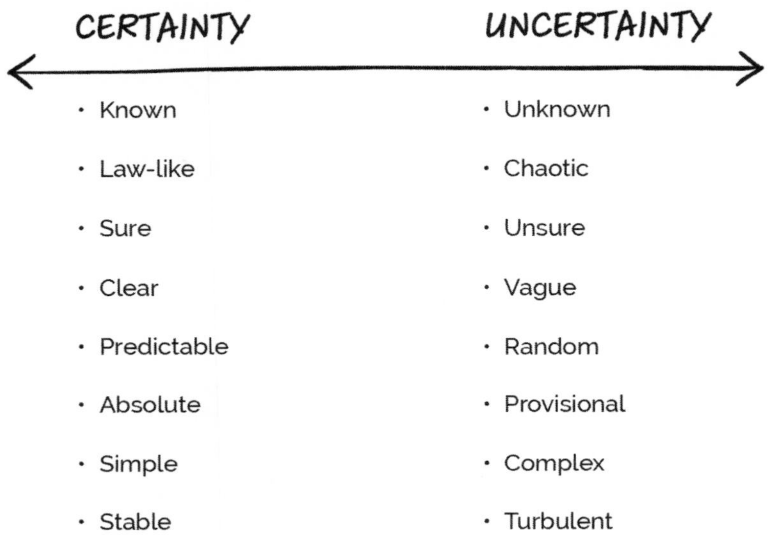

CERTAINTY	UNCERTAINTY
←	→
· Known	· Unknown
· Law-like	· Chaotic
· Sure	· Unsure
· Clear	· Vague
· Predictable	· Random
· Absolute	· Provisional
· Simple	· Complex
· Stable	· Turbulent

certainty. Those who are certain are free of doubt; they are sure of what they know—just like Dr. Faux.

Leaders who embrace uncertainty embrace doubt. They question what is fixed and settled. Are there places in the universe where people could jump up and never come down? Questions like this suggest an implicit tentativeness about our state of knowledge. Nothing is settled once and for all. Embracers of uncertainty hold even their most coveted knowledge as but a rough approximation. Physicist Richard Feynman described the impact of the theory of relativity in this way:

> The first discovery is, essentially, that even those ideas which have been held for a very long time and which have been very accurately verified might be wrong. It was a shocking discovery, of course, that Newton's laws are wrong, after all those years in which they seemed to be accurate … we now have a much more humble point of view of our physical laws—everything can be wrong![1]

If a Nobel Prize–winning hard scientist operates with this kind of humility, then why shouldn't world-savvy leaders succeed by acknowledging what they don't know?

Of course, there are degrees of uncertainty; this is not an either-or proposition. A continuum may be the best way to conceptualize uncertainty. Most people could mark a spot on the scale characterizing their level of certainty about the following statements:

- If a baseball player heaves a ball into the air, it will return to the ground

- The sun will rise tomorrow

- I'll have a job next year

- On the next flip of the coin, it will land on heads

- Elvis is dead

Even though embracing the unknown, the chaotic, the vague, and the random may not apply to all situations, it does dominate the mind-set of caring leaders. Why? Because the situations that command leaders' attention are fraught with uncertainty, such as envisioning the future, wrestling with novel circumstances, managing complex systems, and anticipating human behavior. Embracing uncertainty means not only accepting but welcoming fluidity, lack of explicit control, unknown variables, and new ideas into your everyday life.

WHY DO CARING LEADERS EMBRACE UNCERTAINTY?

Embracing uncertainty serves as a foundational belief for caring leaders for three mutually reinforcing reasons:

Important thing to do—If you are personally committed to deep caring, then embracing uncertainty could be viewed as one of your most important commitments. Why? Because caring leaders focus on the long-term development of others. If that's true, then leaders should allow others to learn, grow, and change in unexpected ways. Caring leaders let others surprise them.

For instance, one professor requires, on a weekly basis, that his students take a quiz on the reading material and then write a commentary about how the ideas relate to the student's professional or personal life. For grading purposes, he is much more interested in the quality of the commentary than the grade on the quiz. In fact, even if students correctly answer all ten quiz questions and write an acceptable commentary, they will earn ninety-five points.

Why ninety-five and not one hundred points? As one exasperated student expressed, "What do I need to do to get one hundred points?" The professor calmly replied, "Share an insight, a novel way of looking at an issue, a fresh, original thought in some unexplored terrain. Continue to push yourself. Wow me! And more importantly, wow yourself! That's the ninety-five–to–one-hundred-point range!"

And that's exactly what happened for this student and all the others listening to the exchange. This professor was embracing uncertainty in an educational world dominated by a checklist mentality.

Right thing to do—Ethicists liberally use words like *honesty*, *fairness*, and *truth* in their writings. These concepts directly relate to embracing uncertainty. After all, if leaders honestly evaluated almost any situation, they would admit that some situational dimensions remain obscure or unknown. In essence, the truth is often emergent over time. Acknowledging those unknowns produces a more honest appraisal of it and fosters more flexibility as new facts emerge. Humility in the face of the unknown and unknowable represents a fundamental kind of honesty (see Figure 1.2). Likewise, being fair to others requires caring leaders to acknowledge that there may be perspectives that have not been shared or issues not yet surfaced.

We believe all caring relationships are rooted in a healthy tolerance for uncertainty. This ethical imperative emerges from a core belief that leaders can only partially envision the potential of others because so much remains unknown and perhaps unknowable. Embracing uncertainty celebrates the emergent potential of people who are discovering their own potential with the help of a caring leader. That sounds like the right thing to do!

Smart thing to do—Several years ago we wrote a book, *Embracing Uncertainty: The Essence of Leadership*. The book was based on some groundbreaking research involving over one thousand employees working in organizations as varied as Fortune 100 companies to small businesses to educational institutions.[2] We developed a series of questions to gauge the degree

Figure 1.2

HOW UNCERTAINTY RELATES TO HONESTY AND HUMILITY

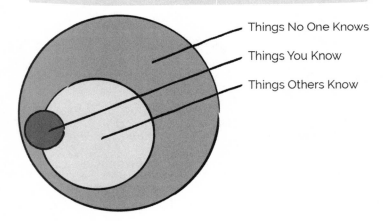

POTENTIAL UNIVERSE OF KNOWABLE THINGS

Things No One Knows

Things You Know

Things Others Know

to which employees and organizations embrace uncertainty (see sample items in Table 1.1).

The results of the study were revealing and somewhat surprising. We found that employees who worked in uncertainty-embracing organizations tended to be:

Table 1.1

DOES YOUR ORGANIZATION EMBRACE UNCERTAINTY?

1. My organization is always on the lookout for new ideas to address problems.

2. My organization flexibly responds to different situations.

3. My organization easily spots changing trends.

4. My organization doesn't need a detailed plan when working on a project.

5. Even after my organization makes a decision, it will reevaluate the decision when the situation changes.

6. My organization needs to know the specific outcome before starting a project.[*]

7. My organization encourages employees to discuss their doubts about a project.

8. My organization actively looks for signs that the situation is changing.

9. My organization doesn't want employees to admit that they are unsure about something.[*]

10. My organization discourages employees from talking about misgivings.[*]

[*] these items are reverse-scored

- More satisfied with their jobs
- More committed to their organizations
- More likely to identify with their organizations
- Less cynical about organizational life

The surprise? It didn't matter if the employees personally embraced uncertainty in their daily work life. Even if they personally tended to value certainty over uncertainty, they wanted their organizations to embrace it. This makes sense. Consider an employee who works in a placid, routine organizational environment. Some employees may well enjoy their daily stable routine, but they still recognize the ever-shifting, uncertain issues their organizations must deal with to stay relevant.

WHY DON'T LEADERS EMBRACE UNCERTAINTY?

So, let's assume that any or all of the above reasons for embracing uncertainty resonate with a leader's sensibilities. Well, why don't they do it? We've discovered three typical reasons.

Overconfidence

People often act with a certainty that only crumbles when the brute force of reality extracts its inevitable vengeance. Prior to World War II, the French generals defiantly insisted that the series of fortifications along the northeast border of France—the infamous Maginot Line—would protect the country from any Nazi attack. They were tragically mistaken. Perhaps if those in power had been a little less certain, the catastrophic and almost inexplicable human toll could have been diminished. But French generals were not alone. Many leaders suffer from overconfidence.

———————————————— **"** ————————————————

Humility is not the opposite of confidence. It's the freedom for learning. —SALLY GRIMES, CEO of Clif Bar

Success is usually the culprit. At one time, Sears, Roebuck was considered one of the best managed companies in the world and one of the nation's most admired organizations. No longer. Osborne Computers, Schlitz Brewing, and Schwinn Bicycles, to name a few, have similar histories. In fact, the typical company has half the life span that people do.[3] As one scholar concluded:

> ...there is something about the way decisions get made in successful organizations that sows the seeds of eventual failure. ..."good" management was the most powerful reason they failed to stay atop their industries. Precisely because these firms listened to their customers...carefully studied market trends and systematically allocated investment capital to innovations that promised the best returns, they lost their positions of leadership.[4]

The "something"? Overconfidence in established methodologies, markets, and modes of operation. Of course, companies need to listen to their customers. But not too closely. As Lee Iacocca once said, "No one ever told us to build a minivan." Of course, companies need to watch market trends, but not too carefully, because they can obscure new opportunities.[5]

Bottom line: the temptation to believe present success equals future success often proves too alluring, even when executives know better. Given this perspective, the philosophy of Andy Grove, the cofounder and chairman of Intel Corporation, that "only the paranoid survive," makes a lot of sense. Paranoids embrace doubt. Most people don't. In fact, most people overestimate the accuracy of their judgment.[6] In short, overconfidence leads to unrealistic expectations, overly aggressive goals, and a host of other miscalculations.

Frustration

Personal anxiety often intensifies when trying to control the uncontrollable, predict the unpredictable, or know the unknowable. Everyone has been in situations where they felt compelled to provide an answer to questions to which they didn't know the answers. Perhaps they didn't want to look stupid. Or perhaps they didn't want the boss to discover that they simply did not know. The result: an answer that provides temporary relief but in the long term creates frustration, embarrassment, and sometimes regret.

Consider the enormous pressure on law enforcement officials to produce a suspect when there is a serious crime. The grieving victim's family wants answers. Headline-seeking reporters demand answers as they thrust their microphones, recorders, and cameras in front of officials. Apprehensive citizens want action. It's tough to say, "We simply don't know yet." In fact, the pressure can be so intense that any suspect might do. After all, it creates certainty. The reporters go away, the public feels reassured, and the family starts the healing process. Unfortunately, the pressure can be so great that the wrong person is indicted. The public gets its certainty, but the officials must live with their doubts. In fact, officers of the court have been convicted for knowingly sending the wrong person to jail.[7] That kind of false certainty should trouble every citizen.

Expectations

Our culture often signals that leaders must know with absolute certainty. And it conveys to them in hundreds of ways, both large and small, that uncertainty is bad. Indeed, leaders are often ridiculed if they don't provide specific promises to deal with every conceivable problem. Consider the pressure executives feel to project next year's earnings to financial analysts. Woe to the company that misses the prediction because of unknown forces.

And when the COVID-19 pandemic struck, there were endless debates: What caused it? Did we act quickly enough? When will we be able to return to normal life? What will normal look like? When will the economy fully recover? The answers to these questions were uncertain; they were subject to speculation and opinion. Yet, often leaders were judged by their ability to provide accurate answers to unknowable questions. The models were all wrong. In fact, models are almost always wrong in some small or large way. Yet, if you use multiple models, it will help you keep uncertainties in mind by visualizing various potential outcomes.

SO WHAT?

Our beliefs shape our memories, fuel our actions, and influence our plans. Consider a prosaic belief like "Houseplants require watering." If one of your houseplants dies, your first thought might be, *I wonder if I watered it enough?* That question instinctively emerges from your core belief about how plants live and grow. Likewise, that belief explains why you routinely water your plants and even set up a watering schedule. Of course, your plant-growth beliefs are tempered by other beliefs and circumstances; you can drown plants with overwatering. Cacti don't need the same amount of water as your ficus tree, and so on. Likewise, easing up on the uncertainty watering jug makes sense in many circumstances.

In general, though, believing that embracing uncertainty accelerates growth shapes a caring leader's approach to learning, planning, coaching, communicating, and a host of other important tasks. We will more thoroughly develop this thought in Part Two.

For now, you can enhance your commitment to the "embracing uncertainty accelerates growth" belief by contemplating the following questions.

1. **Do you accept that there are questions that don't have answers and issues that are unknowable?** There is much more uncertainty in the world than ever gets acknowledged. Instead of wasting time and energy fretting over things that can't be known, caring leaders devote time and energy dealing with things they can impact.

We believe it is far better to plan and execute on the best available options that maximize the chances for positive outcomes instead of expending energy by asking questions and requiring answers for things that are unknowable. Situations are rarely one-dimensional. The best outcomes result from approaching problems on multiple fronts, addressing all the issues we know at the time. For example, during the COVID crisis, the CEO of United Airlines, Scott Kirby, abandoned any attempt to predict when the demand for travel would fully rebound. Instead, he formed a "bounce-back team" to envision slow, medium, and fast recovery scenarios. This insight about uncertainty allowed United to ride out the turbulence until the crisis abated.[8]

The unknown can be a source of motivation. Jacques-Yves Cousteau, the famed oceanographer, would never have plunged into the depths of strange waters without a love of the mysterious. Sir Edmund Hillary would never have scaled Everest without a willingness to face the unknown dangers of high-altitude climbing. But it is not only when exploring the heights and depths of our world that people need to make peace with their ignorance. Almost every important intellectual accomplishment starts with a willingness to embrace naïveté. David McCullough, the Pulitzer Prize–winning biographer, may have said it most eloquently:

> I feel that each project I've undertaken has been a huge adventure, a lesson in a world, a subject, a territory I knew nothing about. People will sometimes say to me, "Well, what's your theme?" as I start on the

—— **"** ——

[Genius has] the instinct to wait, and wait, and wait a little more, and allow dust to settle and thoughts to mature and truths to emerge. Hasty certainty tends to be a fool.
—LANCE MORROW

new book. "I haven't the faintest idea. That's one of the reasons I'm writing the book." "Well, you don't know much about that subject." "That's exactly right. I don't know anything about the subject—or very little. And, again, that's exactly why I'm writing the book." I think if I knew all about it, and I knew exactly what I was going to say, I probably wouldn't want to write the book because there would be no search, there would be no exploration of the country I've never been to—that's the way one should feel.[9]

In short, conquering any new geographical or intellectual territory begins by squarely facing our lack of knowledge.

2. **Do you transparently communicate about the knowns and unknowns?** This includes acknowledging that your current plans for managing uncertainty may not bear fruit. If you don't know, do you say so? If you have a point of view, do you let others know? Are you trying to create the aura of certainty where none exists?

When you say, "I don't know," others will not necessarily hear "I'm stupid" or "I'm ignorant." Instead, by admitting your uncertainty, you can inhibit hasty decision-making, thus encouraging further inquiry or deliberation. Interestingly, speakers may not even be aware that this conversational ploy stimulates more thoughtful inquiry and solutions to complex challenges.

A caring leader with a bit of a more whimsical spirit could even indirectly signal to others the power of uncertainty by prominently displaying the right artifacts and books in his or her office: an unfinished Leonardo da Vinci painting, an old LP record jacket of Franz Schubert's "Unfinished" Eighth Symphony, or the enticing book *Britannica All New Kids' Encyclopedia: What We Know & What We Don't*.

3. **Do you routinely applaud resiliency?** Reminding people of classic comeback stories—for example, the United States after the Great Depression—has a way of framing challenges in terms of resiliency rather than on immediate results. Tales of how obstacles have been overcome build members' personal confidence that they can get through the most demanding situations.

    Caring leaders can celebrate resiliency with a great deal of confidence because researchers have shown that over 90 percent of things most people worry about never materialize.[10] You could think of this anxiety as False Event Appearing Real (FEAR). Resiliency focuses attention on people's hopes rather than fears.

4. **Do you spin complex and uncertain issues 360 degrees around, by trying to see them from all sides?** Solutions to complex problems are rarely one-dimensional; rather, viewing an issue from many sides ensures better outcomes. For example, in shaping a response to the COVID virus, one organization's leader considered questions such as "What are the physical, emotional, financial, and social implications for our team members?" "How will the virus affect our suppliers? Customers? Family members?" "How can our expertise serve the national interest in innovative ways?" "How can we provide a sense of purpose and civic duty during this time?"

    In contrast, when employees experience pressure to "accept at face value the official rationale for organizational decisions," cynicism spreads virally in the organization.[11] Cynical employees often suspect that decision makers have not clearly thought about the real underlying problems from many different perspectives. Political expediency prevails. How do employees come to this conclusion? Experience. In particular, the experience of not having meaningful opportunities to share in decision-making or even being informed about what is happening.[12] In short, an organization that devalues contemplation naturally spawns cynicism.

5.   **Do you trust that, for the most part, people have the organization's best interests in mind?** Leaders often have to dig deep into their reservoir of faith in others during uncertain times. Thoughtful leaders will hear conflicting advice from experts and face pushback against their own ideas from others. This can be challenging, and leaders might be skeptical. Yet, resilient leaders need the support of their team to robustly respond to the inevitable setbacks and move the organization forward. Plus, leaders will need to rely on other opinion leaders to translate their vision and perspective to people beyond the leaders' immediate influence.

6.   **Does your language convey a sense of tentativeness rather than certainty?** Several Harvard University scholars investigated teachers who incorporated into their lectures a tolerance for new ideas and a respect for uncertainty. Students were put in one of two groups: Group One was taught a task traditionally, with an emphasis on the rote learning of steps, while Group Two was taught the same task with a greater emphasis on general principles and flexibility. The results were revealing. Both groups performed equally well on a direct test involving the task, however, Group Two performed significantly better when it encountered novel or slightly modified tasks. Group One had to rely on a memorized routine or a checklist.

Even subtle changes in language appear to produce this effect (see Figure 1.3). In a similar experiment, one group was instructed with the words "This is a..." while another

Figure 1.3

DOES YOUR LANGUAGE SIGNAL
A DESIRE TO EMBRACE UNCERTAINTY?

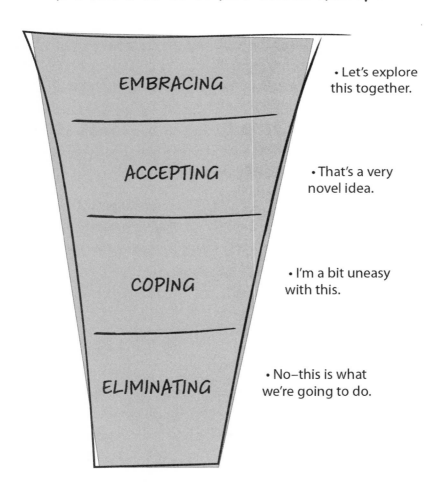

EMBRACING — • Let's explore this together.

ACCEPTING — • That's a very novel idea.

COPING — • I'm a bit uneasy with this.

ELIMINATING — • No—this is what we're going to do.

group was introduced to the task with the words "This could be a…" Note the tentativeness conveyed to the second group. The results were similar to those in the previous study. Professor of psychology Ellen Langer summarized her findings:

> The key to teaching this new way is based on an appreciation of both the conditional, or context dependent, nature of the world and the value of uncertainty. Teaching skills and facts in a conditional way sets the stage for doubt and an awareness of how different situations may call for subtle differences in what we bring to them.[13]

Caring leaders, like skillful teachers, learn to signal "we don't know" by the very language they use. The result: more creative and flexible students.

7. **Do you routinely ask for help?** The design company IDEO has a legendary reputation for developing innovative products. It has worked in over forty different industries, designing thousands of products ranging from baby food packaging to the Apple Watch camera band.[14] IDEO products routinely win international design awards for creating both functional and elegant solutions to knotty problems.

    The secret to their success: passionate curiosity, being open to new ideas, lack of arrogance, and commitment to collaboration. As one engineer explained, "At the first hint I don't know something, I ask, 'Does anyone know about this?' If you don't ask for help here, you're incompetent—you're useless to us."[15] Wow! What an unusual and refreshing way to demonstrate your competence. Yet, these sentiments reveal the underlying wisdom of fully embracing uncertainty.

CONCLUSION

Someday it may be fashionable to say, "I embrace uncertainty." We hope so! Currently, though, it's not a core, orienting belief of most leaders. In many organizations, affirmative answers to many of the questions above could be perilous to your career aspirations or professional standing as a leader. That's unfortunate.

Fortunately, you can make a difference. How? Thoughtfully embracing uncertainty represents a foundational belief. But that alone is not enough. We need to examine several other core beliefs in the following pages. Then we can create a wonderful tapestry of leadership beliefs and practices that will demonstrate the abiding value of caring leadership.

What is the use of living, if it be not to strive for noble cause and to make this muddled world a better place for those who will live in it after we are gone? How else can we put ourselves in harmonious relation with the great verities and con-solations of the infinite and the eternal? And I avow my faith that we are marching towards better days. Humanity will not be cast down. We are going on—swing-ing bravely forward along the grand high road—and already behind the distant mountains is the promise of the sun.

—SIR WINSTON CHURCHILL

CHAPTER 2
PROGRESS EMERGES THROUGH EXPLORING AND REFINING

What do people care about? Athletes want to get stronger. Runners aspire to run faster. Money managers seek to grow their portfolios larger. Teachers train their students to be smarter. Coaches want to be known as winners. Manufacturers try to make their products better and cheaper. Doctors treat patients to help them become healthier.

Caring leaders should pay particular attention to the powerful two-letter suffix -er at the end of these sentences: people care about getting better. They want to make progress. Caring leaders help others get better, teams stronger, organizations healthier, and businesses richer.

If making progress dwells at the core of most people's desires, then caring leaders should squarely address a seemingly simple but thorny question: How do we make progress? This chapter focuses on just that issue.

WHAT IS PROGRESS?

Progress means deliberately advancing forward. A college student makes progress by successfully passing a series of courses in a curriculum. A football team makes progress by advancing toward the goalposts in a series of short plays. Entrepreneurs make progress by creating new businesses like Facebook, Airbnb, or BioNTech.

On the surface, the concept of progress seems pretty simple. A deeper look into the concept reveals three observations:

Progress is not inevitable. People grow old. Some people grow wise. Growing old is inevitable, but it's not progress. Growing wise is a deliberate choice—that's progress! Likewise, caring leaders never assume that experience equates with competence. It should, but it might not. That's a truth that wise leaders choose to learn.

Progress always creates new challenges. Progress often takes the form of solving problems. The automobile resolved the problem of horse manure in the streets that fouled the air. Of course, the automobile created a different kind of air pollution. Electric cars will help solve that problem but will generate other challenges we will discover more fully with the passing of time. Nevertheless, caring leaders champion people and organizational programs even as they seek to prepare them for the inevitable challenges of progress.

Progress comes in two forms—evolutionary and revolutionary.

———————————————— **"** ————————————————

When we think about the future, we hope for a future of progress.　　　　　　　　　　　　　—PETER THIEL

Making something better, faster, or cheaper characterizes evolutionary progress. People who embrace this kind of progress are masters at refining and tweaking; they are the editors who sharpen a memo to better clarify the meaning of a key phrase or the technicians who squeeze steps out of a manufacturing process to get the product to the marketplace faster. They are the financial analysts who figure out ways to deliver quality service more cheaply. They are, in short, the people who try to improve or upgrade what already exists or what we already do.

The other kind of progress is game-changing and revolutionary. People who embrace this kind of progress are gifted at leaping to new ideas or exploring new territories. Declaring independence from Great Britain in 1776 was a revolutionary and world-shattering event. Building a telephone system transformed how people communicated. Most recently, using messenger RNA to create a viable COVID vaccine was, quite literally, a world-changing innovation in the fight against the deadly pandemic and others that will emerge in the future.

These observations imply unique challenges for caring leaders. For instance, caring leaders resist the subtle lure of inertia, because they know progress is not inevitable. Likewise, they help people grapple with unexpected difficulties as they make progress, because they know all progress has unintended consequences that must be mitigated. The two forms of progress represent a particularly unique challenge.

THE CARING LEADER'S CORE CHALLENGE

To understand the core challenge, we need to start by explaining the idea of a platform. Any relatively stable, underlying form or structure is considered a platform. Homes, trucks, iPhones, direct mail marketing, and even educational classes represent platforms. The old home signifies a well-developed mature platform; the new home symbolizes a fresh new platform. These examples imply that some platforms are well established, like the internal combustion engine; others are less developed, like the electric-powered truck engine. Older platforms yield more reliable results, at least for a period of time. Newer platforms tend to be less stable and may not survive competitive pressures.

To have a fuller understanding of progress, we need to add two other concepts: exploring and refining. Exploring means to make progress by creating something new or doing something novel. Explorers make things better through invention, innovation, or discovery. Exploring leads to revolutions in thoughts and practice. Exploring results in new platforms.

Refining means to make progress by improving platforms that already exist. Refiners make things better by increasing the efficiency of a process, adding a new feature to an existing product, or improving the quality of something. Refining leads to evolutions in practice and thought.

Refiners swap out light fixtures in their homes; explorers buy new homes. Refiners increase the gas mileage of trucks; explorers imagine and create electric trucks. Refiners improve their seminars with new PowerPoint slides; explorers develop new classes about subjects never taught before. In short, refiners tweak and explorers leap.

We believe a fundamental quandary leaders must tackle involves the tug-of-war between exploring and refining.

Figure 2.1 highlights how exploring creates more uncertainty because leaders are trying to develop a new platform, moving from platform 1.0 to 2.0. Refining builds more

———————————————— ❝ ————————————————

Key Ideas in Progress Making

Platform—Any relatively stable underlying form or structure.

Exploring—creating something new, novel, or revolutionary.

Refining—improving what already exists.

certainty because the aim is to improve on platform 1.0, with subsequent versions 1.1 to 1.2 to 1.3 and so on.

Caring leaders know the idea of progress appeals to almost everyone. The core challenge: What kind of progress do people, teams, and organizations really want? Do they want evolutionary progress or revolutionary progress? Should progress emerge from refining or exploring? Tweaking or jumping? These questions represent competing desires. These conflicts represent one of the central challenges facing caring leaders. The next section explores the deeper reasons why.

Figure 2.1

THE PROGRESS MODEL

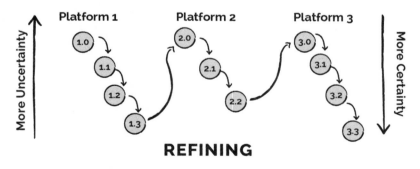

WHY IS THERE A TUG-OF-WAR BETWEEN EXPLORING AND REFINING?

The two types of progress pose three unique challenges.

First, Team Members' Talents, Fears, and Comfort Zones Differ

Most people have predominant tendencies toward either exploring or refining. Their talents, comfort zones, and, perhaps, unstated fears orient them in one direction or the other.

Explorers

Explorers gravitate toward the unknown, chaotic, vague, random, and complex. When confronted with uncertainty, they don't try to minimize it or chop it down to size; instead they investigate and seek to understand it. They are invigorated by it but not daunted. Sometimes explorers possess a whimsical streak. Consider, for example, the Nobel Prize–winning physicist Richard Feynman, who conceived of the unconventional but exceedingly influential Feynman diagrams that visually displayed the paths of subatomic particles. One day he opened an atlas and blindly put his finger on a random spot on the map and promptly planned a journey there. His exploits were wonderfully chronicled in a delightful book, *Tuva or Bust!*[1] Perhaps Professor Feynman captured explorer sentiments best in this revealing statement: "I feel a responsibility to proclaim…that doubt is not to be feared, but that it is to be welcomed as the possibility of a new potential for human beings. If you know that you are not sure, you have a chance to improve the situation."[2]

For explorers, uncertainty almost mysteriously energizes them, beckoning them forward; that's their comfort zone. They love tough, big, and unconventional questions. They are not afraid to ask them and tenaciously pursue the answers. By necessity, an explorer relies on a well-honed intuition because any exploration into the unknown involves unanticipated contingencies. Explorers recognize that waiting to get all the facts straight or a plan for every possibility is simply impossible; mountaineers scaling the highest peaks know that all weather forecasts are fraught with unknowns, yet they climb on.

That said, successful explorers do not recklessly dash into the unknown completely unprepared. Intuition works best when sharpened by extensive experience.[3] Intuition is the name we give to sensibilities that are beyond our awareness or cannot be easily articulated. These sensibilities emerge from gleaning essential patterns behind a wide variety of related experiences. These sensibilities are not easily communicated to others. A bullet-point list of insightful instructions on a PowerPoint slide will never hone intuition like a sustained string of good and bad learning experiences. The stories that emerge from the experiences serve as profound life lessons for all involved.

Refiners

In contrast, refiners often possess a heightened sense of orderliness and tidiness. They are agitated by clutter and incompleteness. They love order and everything in its proper place or space, particularly when completing a puzzle. In fact, they are often enamored with precision and clarity. Rosalind Franklin has belatedly received much deserved recognition for aiding in the discovery of the structure of DNA. It was Watson and Crick who received the Nobel Prize, but that would not have happened without Dr. Franklin. She took the exquisite X-ray diffraction pictures that led to the unraveling of the DNA mystery.[4] Her method tells us much about the qualities of great refiners. She made numerous pictures while making tiny adjustments to her equipment. Her quest was to make the clearest, most detailed pictures ever. And she succeeded by almost every measure. In fact, one fellow scientist put it this way:

> As a scientist, Miss Franklin was distinguished by extreme clarity and perfection in everything she undertook. Her photographs are among the most beautiful X-ray photographs of any substance ever taken. Their excellence was the fruit of extreme care in preparation and mounting of the specimens as well as in the taking of the photographs.[5]

Dr. Franklin's story reveals qualities that define the essence of great refiners. It shows how refiners take the existing equipment (or process) and push it to the extreme in a quest for greater clarity. It reveals the enormous power and influence that can emerge from more precise information—in this case, it was Watson and Crick's Nobel Prize. It also demonstrates how refiners often have a natural passion for their craft. In Rosalind Franklin's case, she went to the university over the strong objections of her father, who believed women did not belong in college. She, of course, proved him wrong. And, like any refiner, she had the precise facts to back her up.[6]

Refiners lean toward the predictable, known, and stable. They enjoy making what already works better. They improve the world from the solid ground of proven laws and established principles. They improve fuel efficiency by decreasing the weight of our vehicles (law of energy conservation). They increase the speed of customers through the checkout lane by changing the layout of the grocery store (principles of time and motion). They enhance your odds of winning at blackjack by teaching you about probabilities (law of probabilities). They make progress incrementally, not with revolutionary (and uncertain) notions. The refiner believes that if you fit all the pieces of the puzzle together, the correct answer emerges. (Of course, the problem is that you may not have all the pieces.) Unlike the explorer, they are not heavily reliant on intuition or hunches. That's why refiners are constantly tinkering with their procedures and processes to improve accuracy. Most refiners would agree with Voltaire's aphorism "Perfection is attained by slow degrees; it requires the hand of time."

Second, Measures of Success Clash

Measuring progress while exploring fundamentally differs from measuring progress while refining. The trajectories and probabilities of success vary greatly over time. Professor James March began his groundbreaking article on this tension with the following, almost benign statement: "A central concern of studies of adaptive processes is the relation between the exploration of new possibilities and the exploitation of old certainties."[7] This plainly expressed notion set off a vigorous wave of debate, research, and commentary in business schools throughout the world. And it should be a central concern of every leader of every organization. Why? Because leaders, whether they acknowledge it or not, confront the tension between exploration (exploring) and exploitation (refining) on a daily basis. How they resolve that dilemma profoundly influences the effectiveness and viability of their organizations.

How do these seemingly incompatible approaches to progress stack up against each other? In the short run, refining trumps exploring. In the long run, it's just the opposite.[8] For example, learning to make better, faster, and cheaper newsprint (exploitation) to the exclusion of other paper products made perfect sense in a newspaper-crazy world. But this capability rapidly became irrelevant once the world shifted to the electronic transmission of news stories on Kindle, Nook, or iPad-like devices. In the long term, it makes more sense to pursue other paper-related products that will be less threatened by information technologies.

Therefore, progress-making leaders care about both refining and exploring, even though those modes inevitably clash from time to time. They want people, their teams, and organizations to evolve through refining and transform through exploring. Leaders who champion these two progress-making modes recognize that some teams operate best in the leaping mode and others in the tweaking mode. Caring leaders educate others about these differing measures of success, thereby increasing tolerance for differing methods, perspectives, and people.

Third, Barriers to Success Vary

The influential philosopher and mathematician Alfred North Whitehead once noted, "The art of progress is to preserve order amid change and preserve change amid order." This one sentence packs some powerful wisdom that caring leaders should ponder.

Consider this example involving a senior leader who coaches a young and promising new manager. The senior leader recognizes that the new manager has a variety of improvement areas (e.g., platforms) like time management, team dynamics, and delegation. The new manager has adequate platforms (e.g., integrated skill sets) in each of these areas. Some could be tweaked for improvement, while others need to be totally reinvented or revolutionized to maximize the manager's potential.

The caring leader has two basic options:

- **Option one**: The senior leader could start the coaching process by tweaking existing platforms that need minor improvement, such as improving delegation.

- **Option two**: The leader might start by helping the manager in an area that needs total revamping, such as building an entirely new personal time-management system.

Both approaches have merits and drawbacks. Tweaking builds the new manager's confidence and has a high probability of success (Option One). The downside? It leaves intact an issue that needs major improvement. In short, this option preserves order through incremental change.

Helping the new manager revolutionize her time-management platform could yield extraordinary gains in productivity and influence (Option Two). The downside? The probability of success is lower than tweaking the other platforms. There is a high likelihood that there will be setbacks and a reversion to the inertia of the old time-management platform. The manager will need to devote more mental and emotional resources to making such a significant change. In short, Option Two fosters major change with the possibility of undermining order in other parts of the manager's skill set.

So, which option makes the most sense? The option that makes the most sense depends on the team member being coached. Caring leaders sense the momentum and proclivities of those they coach. Some people need incremental changes before they tackle a big reconstruction, while others want to dive right into the deep waters of change and learn how to swim, regardless of the waves of inertia pushing against them. The caring leader discerns which approach makes the most sense for the person.

SO WHAT?

Being pro progress resembles being pro love. Everybody is for it, even if they don't know how to make it happen. That's often because people don't take the time to delve more deeply into the meaning of progress (and love) and how to inspire extraordinary performance through that commitment. You can test your own level of commitment to this core belief of caring leaders by reflecting on the following questions:

1. **Can you explain the differences between explorers and refiners?** Sounds simple. In theory, it is. In practice, well, maybe not. Why? Leaders can overestimate their own explanatory

skills. They may reason, "If it makes sense to me, then it will make sense to you." Possibly. Possibly not. Here's a simple test to mitigate overconfidence: Can you explain to refiners the nature of explorers? And do that using an example, an image, and a metaphor? How about describing to explorers the nature of refiners?

We once asked one astute team leader this question. She eagerly ripped out a sheet of paper from her coiled sketchbook and drew a simple grid labeling three rows with the words, *example*, *metaphor*, and *image* (see Figure 2.2). She used this comparison to explain the differences between explorers and refiners: a musically inclined explorer would delight in making the jump from mastery of one instrument to learning a new one. On the other hand, a refiner just wants to get better and fine-tune her cello virtuosity; she would be wary of trying to learn the trumpet. Both instrumentalists love music, but they define musical mastery in different ways. Both make progress, but in different ways. Jumping from point A to point Z captures the essence of exploring; making incremental, smaller steps from point one to point two, from point two to point three, and so on, illustrates the objectives of the refiner—getting a little better every day.

The team leader took our question one step further by noting, "It's not enough to just know and explain the differences. You must be able to spot them in real time, like a Hall of Fame quarterback reading the defense." She enlightened us further: "That's when you know you fully understand the difference between exploring and refining." During a contentious team meeting, she asked, "Are we exploring or refining now?" That's the cue that the team members have reverted to their exploring and refining comfort zones. The conflict dissipated as the team laughed off the digression

Figure 2.2

EXPLAINING REFINING AND EXPLORING IN THREE MODES

	REFINING	EXPLORING
Metaphor	Walking from point 1 to point 2, from point 2 to point 3, etc.	Jumping from A to Z
Example	Practicing to improve mastery of a musical instrument	Learning a new musical instrument
Image	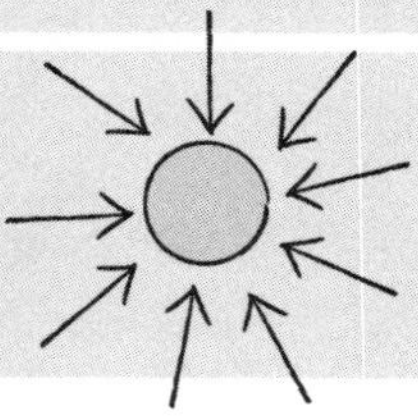	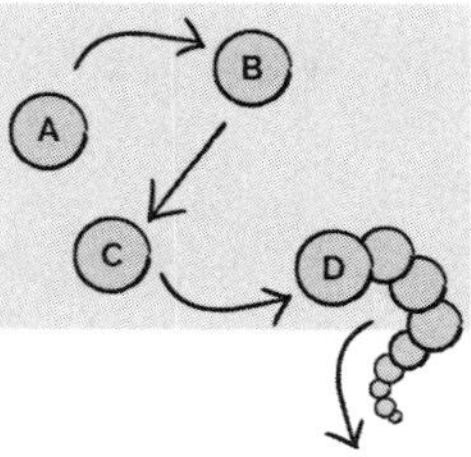

and decided to move in one direction. That's exactly the way a caring leader gently guides the progress-making process.

2. **Can you identify people who lean in one direction or the other?** Caring leaders genuinely understand people: their comfort zones, thinking styles, and natural inclinations. Some people naturally lean to refining; others to exploring. A select few might exhibit both styles, depending on the situation. Thoughtful leaders learn to discern the signs of these tendencies (see Table 2.1).

   Equipped with these insights, they sense how best to inspire progress in everyone they lead. Refiners, for example, would be more comfortable tweaking existing practices. Explorers prefer big, robust challenges that require rethinking of the conventional. That does not necessarily mean that refiners should always be assigned tweaker-like tasks. A skilled coach might work with some refiners, helping them build explorer-like skills or, at least, gain an appreciation for others with those proclivities. And, of course, there are plenty of explorers who could better appreciate the tweaker's talents. Wise leaders weigh all these factors when devising professional development plans.

3. **Do you select the right blend of people to make progress?** Caring leaders thoughtfully use the explorer/refiner typecasts when assembling teams to tackle projects. A team composed entirely of explorers could veer into spectacular disasters, while teams comprised entirely of refiners may lack the boldness to tackle the challenge.

   Refining activities often undercut efforts to explore a new path. Likewise, a host of exploring activities would undermine attempts at refining. Equally weighted teams of explorers and refiners may well brew up synergistic solutions,

Table 2.1

POTENTIAL SIGNS OF UNDERLYING TENDENCIES

REFINER SIGNS	EXPLORER SIGNS
o Enjoys order	o Appreciates a little chaos
o Values certainty	o Welcomes uncertainty
o Loves perfecting	o Cherishes discovery
o Frets about the incomplete	o Ponders possibilities
o Scrutinizes the details	o Ignores minutiae
o Systematically analyzes	o Jumps from issue to issue
o Relishes puzzles	o Delights in creative activities

but they could also stir up an elixir of contentious conflicts. Once again, wise leaders weigh these possibilities, both good and bad, when selecting team members. Caring leaders ensure that the voices of both explorers and refiners are heard. Therein lies the art of caring leadership.

4. **Can you put an expiration date on all your key platforms?** All platforms go through developmental phases that determine their stability, utility, and relevancy. By necessity, a freshly established platform, such as a new social media platform, experiences a lot of growing pains as it ripens into maturity through continual tweaking. At some point, platforms assume a middle-aged degree of stability, which brings high levels of efficiency and reliability. For instance, think of how efficient and reliable today's internal combustion engine is compared to the gas-guzzlers of yesteryear.

   Middle-aged platforms represent perplexing dilemmas, because it's difficult to determine how long they will continue to deliver reliable results before becoming irrelevant. Unlike milk bottles, most platforms are not imprinted with expiration dates. Social media platforms, for instance, are eclipsed by new social media tools far faster than the internal combustion engine. So, if platforms lack embedded expiration dates, then leaders who care about progress need to make the estimates. That means confronting some thorny questions:

   • How long do we stay with platforms that are working?

   • When should we start building a new platform?

   • What can we learn from the old platforms that will benefit the new ones?

   Progress makers in different industries answer these questions in different ways depending on circumstances.

Chairman Mike Cowen of Sportable Scoreboards knows how to refine a platform and, when necessary, how to jump to a new one.[9] In 1986 he discovered a need for a portable scoreboard for youth sports. At that time, most facilities had no such scoring devices. His company developed a battery-powered scoreboard that used solid-state electromechanical number displays that were controlled by a wireless, handheld electronic keyboard. His staff improved the reliability and performance of these products. But like a true progress maker, Mike realized that the company could continue to grow by developing new and larger, permanent scoreboards for their school and park customers. These scoreboards utilized incandescent light bulbs to display the scores. They worked brilliantly, however, the bulbs frequently burned out and needed to be replaced. So, his leadership team once again sought out a new platform. The result? They discovered how to replace the energy-hogging incandescent light bulbs with energy-saving LED lights. There was an added bonus: decreased maintenance costs. Today, the multimillion-dollar company provides scoreboards to many NFL and NBA teams, "as well as major colleges and universities, high schools, park and recreation departments, youth leagues, corporate recreation leagues, military bases, and thousands of other organizations."[10] The company will soon be the largest in the market. Mike personifies the caring leader that recognizes the importance of affixing expiration labels on his platforms, even if they might be hidden underneath his scoreboards!

5. **Can you sense momentum in people and the team?** Every person, team, and organization simultaneously operates on multiple platforms with varying expiration dates. Simultaneously addressing all the changes—both incremental and

revolutionary—shakes the employee's sense of order, competence, and motivation. Many people are paralyzed by the thought that "everything is changing." Yet, avoiding any changes at all undermines progress. Caring leaders learn to sense the momentum about when to advocate for changes of either type. They are highly attentive to cues of change burnout, particularly of the revolutionary kind. Even as they are sensitive to these cues, they also strive to build the resiliency associated with a continuous improvement mind-set. In short, they are looking for the Goldilocks Zone—not too little, not too much.

6. **Do you set differing expectations depending on the mode?** Setting expiration dates, as difficult as it might be, ultimately proves liberating. Why? Because caring leaders can shift expectations as situations vary.

    Established platforms, like an iPhone, can always be improved through tweaking to increase efficiency or adding features. The expectations for success are much higher when refining mature platforms, since progress is measured more incrementally. For instance, we expect the latest version of the iPhone to show modest improvements in features, like battery life and processing. We don't necessarily expect anything groundbreaking.

    On the flip side, building new platforms, like launching a new business or developing a novel tool, requires more exploratory innovations. We expect to see something entirely novel and, perhaps, spectacular. Therefore, we will endure the inevitable growing pains and glitches. Consider the example of Elon Musk in his quest for satellite-based internet, Starlink.

    Caring leaders toggle between these different sets of expectations even as they educate others about the process.

They encourage people during the inevitable setbacks and blind alleys everyone experiences when launching a new venture. These failures represent part of the learning needed to establish any new platform that will wow people. In contrast, tweaking the performance of existing platforms usually doesn't wow outsiders. The caring leader expects this with mature platforms and praises the tweaker's progress along the way!

7. **Do you resist the lure of the status quo?** The greatest enemy of exploring and refining is the status quo. It lures, entices, and binds many employees with promises of comfort, stability, and even riches. Widely accepted procedures, processes, and tools often have hidden and powerful allies. For example, lean protocols eliminate unnecessary or non-value-adding steps in critical processes. Employees often grumble, "We've never done it that way before" or "If it isn't broken, don't fix it." These retorts protect the status quo. To be fair, at times that may be an appropriate stance; more often, though, it hinders progress making.

   Of course, not everyone defends the status quo. Some employees possess or develop a passion for crafting new platforms and continuously improving existing ones. However, the cumulative impact of these activities can be tiring and debilitating. The verbal commitment often endures while the mental, physical, and psychological energy starts to wane.[11] Deep in their psyche, employees may say to themselves, "When will this ever end?" or "Is anything ever enough?"

   These comments reveal a fundamental misunderstanding about the nature of progress. Some people treat progress as a goal rather than a mind-set. What's the difference? A goal is something that, once it's accomplished, it can be checked off the list.[12] A mind-set, like a lifestyle, lasts forever. Caring leaders master the art of building this progress-making mind-set in all they influence because they know the outcome—amazing performance that dazzles everyone.

CONCLUSION

Leaders who advocate for both exploring and refining may feel like they are embracing contradictory and paradoxical positions. Consider F. Scott Fitzgerald's marvelous insight "The test of a first-rate intelligence is the ability to hold two opposed ideas in the mind at the same time, and still retain the ability to function."[13] In one sense, making progress through exploring AND refining represents two conflicting ideas. Advocating both exploring and refining means something more than noting "We are changing the rules of the game" in each mode. Rather, it's more like proclaiming "We are playing different games, with different rules" in each mode. That's precisely how caring leaders foster progress. In short, embracing both games requires an adroit mind and a flexible set of sensibilities. Only those leaders with a first-rate intelligence and wisdom can simultaneously win both games and make extraordinary progress.

Values are everything. If you get those right, everything else follows.

—OSCAR C. BOLDT

CHAPTER 3
THE RIGHT VALUES CULTIVATE A SPECIAL SENSE OF IDENTITY

Your core identity as a leader emerges from your values. Leaders' values govern their behavior, influence their judgment, set their standards, and guide their aspirations.[1] The values that leaders live every day serve as their organization's foundational filter for perceptions, sentiments, and decision-making. Values shape your responses to situations and tell you what to pay attention to and how to proceed.

A leader who values respecting others would observe a squabble between two colleagues with great interest. How would this leader view the situation? The primary issue would be "Who is showing the most respect when making their point?" The secondary issue would be "Which argument is the strongest?" Caring leaders use their respect lens to glean insight and perspective on the conflict but also to set their coaching agenda for their colleagues. In short, values not only enrich leaders' fundamental sense of identity; they also provide direction, insight, and perspective.

VALUES IN THREE DIMENSIONS

Most leaders talk about values. That's good news. The bad news? Many leaders do not fully understand all the dimensions of leading by values.[2] Caring leaders embrace a robust perspective on values in the following ways:

First, caring leaders think of values in three dimensions (see Figure 3.1). If you value something, then it guides your actions, attitudes, and aspirations while providing you a sense of identity. Consider a person who values physical fitness. That's her aspiration, to be physically fit. She will commit to a regular exercise plan, feel good after a workout, and be a bit depressed if forced to the sedentary sidelines when injured. The exercise plan represents the actions related to her aspiration. Feeling good or even depressed ties her attitudes directly to her physical fitness aspirations.

Ideally, every value would be lived out in all three dimensions. Of course, that does not always happen. Someone may say that they are committed to physical fitness but never have a day-to-day plan to act on those sentiments (aspiration-action gap). Caring leaders notice these gaps and act.

Second, caring leaders recognize that values are expressed in abstract, aspirational terms. Abstract concepts, like love or justice, operate in an ideal realm of our minds. The aspirational nature of values cuts both ways. On the plus side, aspirational values motivate people in profound ways that they find meaningful, often launching them on a lifelong quest to live up to the ideal.[3] To extend on our previous example, what physical fitness means to someone in their twenties might mean something quite different to that same person in their sixties. That's okay.

Figure 3.1

DIMENSIONS OF VALUES

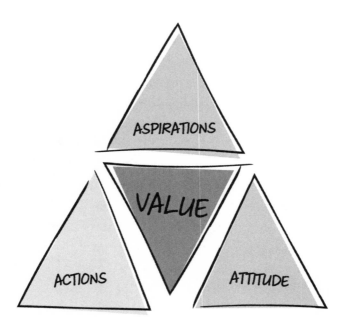

An evolving commitment makes perfect sense for this personal value. On the downside, the abstract nature of values may result in people interpreting the core idea in quite different ways. After all, what the physical fitness value means to one person often means something different to another. But that's okay. People usually tolerate some interpretative squishiness. If they don't, then the inherent ambiguity can be wrongly interpreted as hypocrisy. Caring leaders make sure that doesn't happen.

Third, caring leaders know that values may be expressed in aspirational terms, but they are lived out in daily interactions, personal habits, and a host of other acts. That means there will always be a gap between any espoused value and the practices implied by the value. Consider the Western value of equal treatment under the law. The news media pounces on virtually any incident where some public official failed to live up to this ideal. In one sense, that's okay, because it promotes fidelity to this founding principle of justice. But, in another sense, we can never expect perfect fidelity to all our values. After all, we are always encountering new situations where the value comes into play. For example, what does equal treatment imply in the social media world? Caring leaders know this gap will always exist, so they acknowledge the gap and seek to narrow it.

Unfortunately, many leaders have a one-dimensional (e.g., aspirational) sense of their values. The abstract expression of values subtly conceals the other two vital dimensions (e.g., actions and attitudes). So, it can be easy and tempting to merely espouse "value-based" leadership principles but fail to walk the talk. In contrast, caring leaders recognize that their leadership success hinges on how well they live by their espoused values. They know how to transform values into action and continually try to do so.

So far, we've only provided the framework for a rich understanding of how values should influence caring leaders. So, what exactly are the fundamental values we've observed in caring leaders?

FOUNDATIONAL VALUES OF CARING LEADERS

To paraphrase a maxim of Oscar Boldt, a business visionary who transformed the family business into one of the nation's largest and most respected construction firms, "If you get the values wrong, then everything else will be a mess!" That notion implies an obvious question: What do caring leaders value? Based on our observations and interviews, we've discovered that caring leaders consider the following values as fundamental.

Safety

Feeling safe is a state of mind where the risk of getting injured, harmed, or hurt is not a constant worry. The first and most important responsibility of a caring leader is to ensure the safety of others. People deserve to feel that their lives and physical well-being are not at undue risk. When this sense of safety is not omnipresent, other dimensions of employee engagement quickly fall apart. A sense of personal safety enables all the other values, beliefs, and practices discussed in this book. Since team members have personal concern and responsibility for their own safety, caring leaders can work with employees to build a safe workspace.

Resiliency

We think of rubber balls as being resilient because they bounce back. Caring leaders take it one step further: they think of resiliency as bouncing forward. Why? Facing adversity and setbacks requires an emotional "bouncing back," but it also means learning to adapt to shifting circumstances and changing dynamics. Bouncing forward in the face of uncertainties and disappointments allows leaders to make progress in even the most trying circumstances. In that sense, the resiliency value is baked into the first two chapters: resilient leaders are optimistic because they are open, flexible, and confident enough to seek out and solve important problems.[5] Two researchers studied resilient communities after natural disasters and discovered that:

when we found a resilient community or organization, we almost always found a very particular species of leader at or near its core. Whether old or young, male or female, these translational leaders play a critical role, frequently behind the scenes, connecting constituencies and weaving various networks, perspectives, knowledge systems, and agendas into a coherent whole.[6]

In short, valuing resiliency sets in motion many of practices outlined in Part Two of this book; without resiliency, it's hard to imagine how someone could become a caring leader in a tough world with all its crises, challenges, and disappointments.

Trust

Caring leaders value trust. They want to be viewed as trustworthy, and they strive to trust others.[7] Here are some ways caring leaders translate those sentiments into action and attitudes:

- Trusted leaders bring people together and create a sense of belonging.

- Trusted leaders are not afraid to say they were wrong.

- Trusted leaders freely apologize for inappropriateness.

- Trusted leaders are genuine and not afraid to be vulnerable.

- Trusted leaders are selfless—it's more about others than it is about them.

- Trusted leaders have the backs of their team because they genuinely care about their outcomes.

- Trusted leaders create safe and transparent environments.

- Trusted leaders are generous with praise.

- Trusted leaders do not convey a sense of greed or power.

- Trusted leaders have the propensity to see the good in others over the bad.

- Trusted leaders do not have an air of suspiciousness.
- Trusted leaders are not afraid to say, "I don't know."

You may well find other behaviors and related attitudes to fulfill your trustworthiness aspirations.

Respect

On an aspirational level, respect means "having appropriate regard for the feelings, wishes, rights and traditions of others."[8] We can show respect by being thoughtful, courteous, and polite. Acting respectfully means we are civil to others and avoid excessive criticism or displays of contempt.

Sadly, in our social media–rich world, displays of incivility and disdain for others garner headlines. The dominant attitude often seems to be that we live in an "I win, you lose" world. I win when I denigrate someone; that person loses. Often, disdainful comments represent a display of politically correct solidarity rather than some evil intent. Unfortunately, regardless of intent, such disrespectful attitudes perpetuate a win-lose worldview. Caring leaders respect others to build a win-win world, because we can accomplish so much more when we all pull together.

Sincerity

Sincere leaders are free from pretense, deceit, and hypocrisy. On the other hand, the fake-it-till-you-make-it crowd acts with pretense by putting on a show for others. They pretend to be someone they are not. Or they are deceitful and act like they know more than they really do. They may even quip that they can "100 percent guarantee what is going to happen." No one knows all the answers, and predictions about the future are always tenuous. Insincere leaders are hypocritical because they say one thing and do another; their standards are not well aligned with their behaviors.

Sometimes you can find inspiration in unexpected places. A number of years ago, one of your authors (Bob) worked with an especially insightful man, William Ramsey. He was smart, thoughtful, and sensitive. One morning, he shared one of his particularly moving and insightful pieces; this happened to be his penetrating reflections on trust.

TRUST FROM WILLIAM RAMSEY

Trust is as elemental to all relationships as is the atom to the material world. Both bear component parts of great beauty that might shield us from their true importance.

Just as trust is of several parts, it is also intertwined with honor, faith, and belonging. Each adds its own richness to life but always with the others, working together to the same goodness of purpose.

Trust is not of substance such that it may be made or possessed. It is much more of spirit, a form of energy that can be given but not taken, that can be held and cherished but never owned. It arises in response to the coming alive of its parts. Like the spirit of love and honor and faith, it may be given freely by those in whom it dwells but can never be commanded by those who desire it, no matter their power or zeal to possess it. It too swiftly dies when unrequited or deceived.

Although by itself it can never be brought into being, when all its parts are sought with equal zeal, trust grows to its fullest. As it dwells within us and is held out and offered to share and is received and brings joy, then does it open to a full flower.

In its very nature, trust lives as a part of a relationship between beings as they nurture and enjoy and share it. As with a flower, it flourishes only with tender care. It withers and dies, and, in an instant, it exists no more.

The seeds of trust find fertile ground in the comfort between beings and the safety, companionship, familiarity, and goodwill. It has no existence with stress and the taking of advantage. Trust is the confidence that one is ever safe when in the presence of the other. Trust is the assurance that, to place all one's fortunes in the care of another, all will be well in the end.

Trust is the sure belief that the other will fly to one's defense in the presence of dangers unknown and unseen. Trust arises and grows out of protection and defense by one on behalf of the other. Trust is the confidence that one's interests are always of concern to the other with never the taint of personal gain.

So often in the world as it has become, trust dies on the sterile rock of greed and power.

But with this all, if we covet and pursue trust with other beings, this all can be ours. As we offer these treasures to share and as they are received and returned, so will our relations with others grow and gain a sense of purpose.

Sincere leaders act with good faith, genuineness, and openness to others. They freely admit if they don't know the answers. Caring leaders are open to other people's ideas; after all, they may be more informed than the leader. A caring leader's genuineness often emerges when seeking input and perspective, which relates directly to the value of humility.

Humility

The word *humility* has its origins in the Latin word *humilis*, which means "low to the ground." Consider the vertical contrast to traditional views of leadership, which emphasize the "heights of command" or "views from the mountaintop." Indeed, leadership research and opinions from decades ago—and continuing to present day—highlighted that the tallest person often emerged as a leader. So what? Thinking of leaders as being "low to the ground," listening to all the footsteps rumbling as people move about, feels almost antithetical to these stereotypical images of great leaders. One word can explain the reason: *arrogance*. As the wise King Solomon admonished, "When pride comes, then comes disgrace, but with humility comes wisdom."[9] And the demand for wisdom always exceeds the supply. That's why caring leaders aspire to be humble.

How do caring leaders translate the sentiment of humility into actions and attitudes? Consider these contrasts:

- Humble leaders use *we* more often than *I*.
- Arrogant leaders use *I* more often than *we*.

- Humble leaders are selfless and put others first.
- Arrogant leaders put themselves ahead of others, which is obvious to all who observe.

- Humble leaders ask, "How can I help you?"
- Arrogant leaders tell their people what to do.

- Humble leaders give advice from their experience.
- Arrogant leaders expect others to follow their advice.

- Humble leaders say "no" at times, but they do it in a way that explains the rationale for the direction.
- Arrogant leaders say "no" without offering any sensible reason.

Thinking of humility as a stark contrast to arrogance may well be the first step toward developing a commitment to a value many high-performing people find extremely challenging.

Honesty

Caring leaders are respectfully truthful. They don't spin issues for the purpose of self-gain. They act in a way that lives up to the commitments they make. They walk the talk. Caring leaders say what is on their minds in a tactful manner, face-to-face, and, ideally, not in passing. Caring leaders never knowingly lie or misrepresent a situation.[10]

But being open and honest does not give leaders the license to say anything, no matter how it comes across.[11] Caring leaders will speak the truth but have high sensitivity for the words they choose. Honest leaders recognize boundaries; they don't break confidences or share secrets. After all, no one would accuse the director of the CIA of being dishonest because she refused to share confidential information with the press. Instead, honest leaders accept responsibility for sharing information at the right time and place, because they respect others and their professional obligations.[12] Navigating these boundaries has challenged ethicists since even before the time of Aristotle. Yet, as we shall reveal in the next section, defining the parameters of any value often proves both illuminating and motivating.

Fairness

Fair leaders treat others with common standards even as they respect others' individuality. But that does not mean leaders use a one-size-fits-all method when working with others. Fair leaders take into consideration an employee's responsibilities, career stage, and professional situation. But they do so without discrimination or favoritism. Managing this dynamic often proves challenging in practice, because employees naturally compare how they are being treated by their leaders. That's why establishing a fluid, growth-oriented relationship with others provides the foundation for fairness.

Patience

We think of patience as "the capacity to accept or tolerate delay, trouble or suffering without being angry or upset." Yet, leaders are often pushed in different directions by shareholders, government officials, and boards who often demand aggressive schedules with brisk expectations of progress making and superior results. Reconciling this tension requires finesse and understanding. After all, leaders achieve results through others, and people react at different speeds. Some invent the future; some adopt things early, others later, while a few completely resist change. Caring leaders recognize this dynamic and exercise appropriate patience to help people through changes. That's really the only way to build commitment and sustain progress.

Caring leaders respond by setting robust but realistic schedules and expectations. They adjust time frames to respond to changing conditions and levels of buy-in and adoption. This is not to say that anything goes and patience lasts forever; instead, patience, appropriately placed, will benefit leaders many times over with support and buy-in.

Caring leaders learn that patience can be expressed by a sense of calmness. Patient leaders seldom get angry, irritated, upset, or frenzied. Instead, they maintain a sense of focus with a calm demeanor. In the movie *Anger Management* (a must-watch film for caring leaders), Jack Nicholson cools the situational temperature with the lovely word *Goosfraba*. It's an expression Inuit people use to calm their children when they feel the temperature rising in the room. Saying that word, slowly, might help some leaders. For others, they might take a walk around the block or go kick a soccer ball; better to take it out on the ball instead of booting away someone else's ego.

ARE VALUES MORE LIKE A CLIFF OR A CONTINUUM?

As you ponder these values, you might be tempted to think of each on a continuum with gradients. For example, some people might suggest evaluating trust on a scale from "absolutely trusted" to "not trusted at all," and points in between. That's the spirit of a comment like "You have to earn my trust."

Upon further thought, you might question what it means if you are "almost trusted" or "sometimes trusted." In fact, people often view others in more binary, cliff-like terms: trusted or not trusted, respected or not respected, sincere or not sincere—in other words, they are or they aren't. Leaders are seen as either on top of the cliff or at the bottom. Since caring leaders aspire to be on top of each value cliff, they hold themselves to a much higher standard (See Figure 3.2).

SO WHAT?

When high-profile leaders are interviewed by the press, they often espouse the power of values. Yet reporters rarely dig deeper and ask compelling questions about those values. Caring leaders take a deeper dive by contemplating the following questions:

1. **Can you identify your core values?** If you can't articulate what you truly value, then make it priority number one. Possibly you have a set of values but have never taken the

Figure 3.2

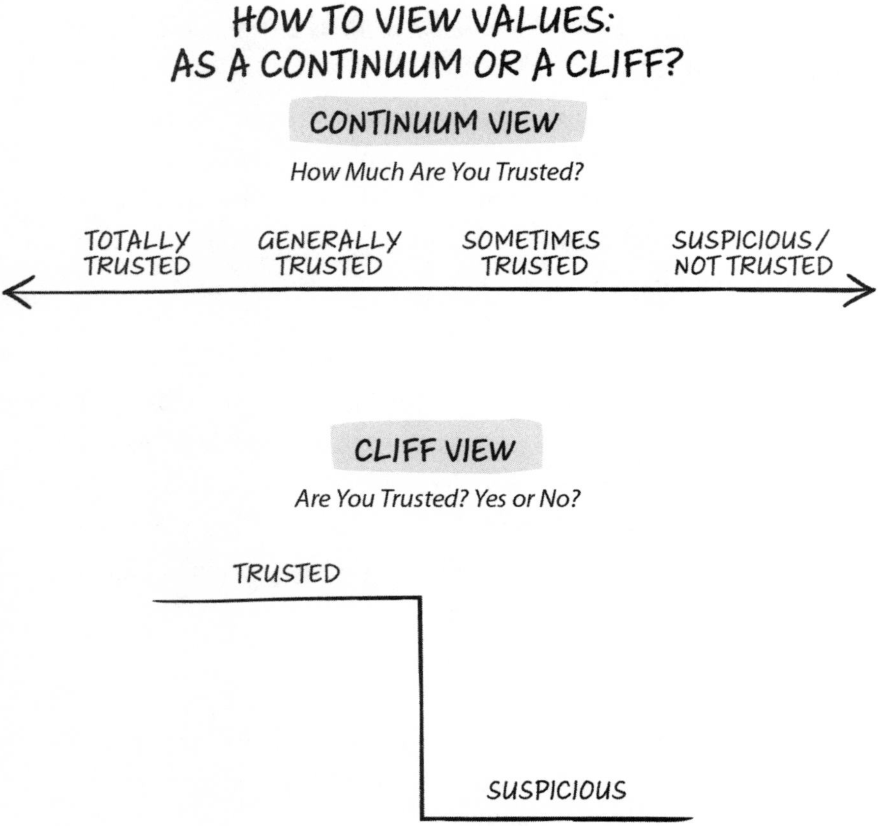

HOW TO VIEW VALUES: AS A CONTINUUM OR A CLIFF?

CONTINUUM VIEW

How Much Are You Trusted?

| TOTALLY TRUSTED | GENERALLY TRUSTED | SOMETIMES TRUSTED | SUSPICIOUS/ NOT TRUSTED |

←————————————————————————————————→

CLIFF VIEW

Are You Trusted? Yes or No?

TRUSTED

SUSPICIOUS

time to write them down. That step often proves illuminating, but be careful: selecting your values is not like ordering something from a fast-food menu. Too often, people read the list of values like those above and say, "Looks good. I'll take one of those, and that one, too." Leaders who use this approach fail to appreciate what they are incorporating into their daily diet. Fast-food values satiate in the short term but fail to nourish in the long term. The conscious act of selecting values deeply influences your aspirations, actions, and attitudes. Caring leaders approach the selection process more like selecting seeds for a garden that they will cultivate, weed, and nurture. That's the only way leaders can grow their espoused values.

2. **Can you express your core values in different modes (e.g., picture, metaphor, definition, story)?** Caring leaders articulate their values in multiple dimensions. This helps them grasp the actions and attitudes that should be associated with their aspirations. The bonus: doing so facilitates communication with others about the leader's perspective and decision-making process.

   When we work with leaders on maximizing the yield from their values, we ask them four related questions:

   - Can you define the value and the associated key terms?

   - Can you provide an image of the value?

   - Can you share a story related to the value in terms of what it means to do and what not to do?

   - Can you articulate why this value matters to you?

   Figure 3.3 provides one result of a team's ten-hour deep dive into answering these questions relating to their value of honesty. The discussion and debate revealed that not everyone understood the basic value in the same way. The disagreements and subsequent collaborative consensus on their final product bonded the group in a profound way. They now share a common language and a way to measure themselves against their aspirations.

3. **Do you understand the price of living by the value?** One senior administrator of a nonprofit organization proudly displayed his core value of collaboration on his letterhead, office posters, and even in his email tag lines. But behind his back, employees up and down the hierarchy mocked his collaboration incantations. Why? Because he never really understood the price of this value. Consider some of the costs of collaboration (see Table 3.1):

    - Admitting you don't have all the answers—yet he never uttered the words *I don't know*.

    - Allowing others to shape solutions—but he thought he had all the answers.

    - Acknowledging when your ideas are wrong—when his initiatives went south, he blamed others.

    - Taking time to bring people together to problem solve— the only time he held meetings was after he solved the problem and sought buy-in; it was faux collaboration, and everybody knew it.

    - Allocating time to discuss differing perspectives—he was too busy or it was "time to move on."

    He craved all the benefits of collaboration, like attaining strong buy-in, arriving at novel solutions, and achieving speedy implementation, but he never wanted to pay the bill.

4. **Can you identify gaps between your stated values and actual behavior?** All values are aspirational, prodding us to be

Figure 3.3

THE VALUE OF HONESTY

Honesty: Be respectfully truthful and candid within the scope of the relationship

KEY TERMS

Truthful – Not lying or misrepresenting

Candid – Forthrightly sharing concerns and disagreements

Scope of Relationship – Relational dynamics (e.g., supervisor/employee, customer/employee, etc.) moderate the degree of openness

DO THIS

- Respectfully speak the truth
- Thoughtfully listen to bad news
- Build relationships that encourage candor
- Listen to other viewpoints
- Be humble about what you know
- Quickly admit mistakes
- Acknowledge when you don't know the answer or situation
- Assume positive intent until proven otherwise

DON'T DO THIS

- Misrepresent or lie
- Forsake candor to maintain relationships or meet deadlines
- Gossip or share rumors in the name of honesty (i.e., undisciplined openness)
- Let emotions fuel candor
- Omit important or relevant information
- Fail to express empathy
- Avoid tough conversations
- Hide bad news
- Play the blame game

WHY HONESTY MATTERS

- Is a source of learning
- Promotes productive learning
- Builds character
- Supplies more clarity and focus
- Improves performance
- Enhances reputation
- Demonstrates courage and bravery
- Builds collective knowledge

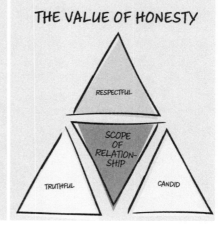

THE VALUE OF HONESTY

Table 3.1

BENEFITS AND COSTS
OF THE COLLABORATION VALUE

POTENTIAL BENEFITS

- Fosters buy-in

- Facilitates generating novel solutions

- Speeds implementation

- Builds team morale

- Enhances members' sense of accomplishment

POTENTIAL COSTS

- Admit you don't have all the answers

- Give up power to let others provide solutions

- Acknowledge when your ideas are wrong

- Take time to bring people together

- Allocate sufficient time to share differing perspectives

better versions of ourselves. Versions 2.0 and 3.0 of a particular value should be fundamentally better than version 1.0. Living out your values in the fullest represents a lifelong learning experience.

Assume early in your career (version 1.0) that you decide it's important to embrace the value of trust. That's aspirational, and you may not fully grasp what that means in practical terms. At that point, you might naively assume that everybody should trust you because you are a trustworthy person.[13] Soon, though, you learn that's not enough. As you move from version 1.0 to 2.0, you realize that you'll have to change certain behaviors, like sharing concerns more freely, that influence others' impression of your trustworthiness. A style shift in communication such as this moves you ever closer to your aspirational desire of being trustworthy. For another leader with the same ambitions, the behavioral shift might be in a totally different direction by eliminating a propensity to share gossip. In short, while caring leaders may agree on core values, they may differ on the behavioral tweaks needed to achieve worthy ambitions.

5. **Can you reconcile the inherent tensions between values?** Some values nicely complement one another—take patience and respect, for instance. In fact, one of the most powerful ways to show respect is to show patience with others. However, other laudable values, at some point, might clash.

Consider honesty and humility. Can you simultaneously be humble and honest? Assume you are the most qualified person in the room to manage a particular project. You make this evaluation based on the scope of the project and the people in attendance. Assume the most senior person in the room poses the question "Who here is most qualified for this task?" In a momentary flash, humility taps on one side of your psyche, reminding you to be deferential to others. But honesty raps on the other side of your spirit, urging you to forthrightly point attention to yourself. What to do? Caring leaders acknowledge these kinds of inevitable value clashes and artfully learn how to reconcile such dilemmas.

Conclusion

If you google Mahatma Gandhi, you would find a list of career accomplishments, topped by his successful campaign to win India's independence from British rule. You'd certainly encounter abundant praise for his nonviolent views and ambitions to improve women's rights, end the pernicious practice of untouchability, and build acceptance of a multireligious society. But discovering the source of his charisma, persistence, and ethical beliefs would be more difficult. And he might not have been able to articulate how he developed into such a compelling and iconic "great soul" (or mahatma). We may never know, but we can glean strong inklings from his thoughtful words: "Your beliefs become your thoughts. Your thoughts become your words. Your words become your actions. Your actions become your habits. Your habits become your values. Your values become your destiny." A caring leader may never achieve "great soul" status, but if you want to make a difference in this world, then committing to the right values would be a great place to start.

Tell me and I forget. Teach me and I remember. Involve me and I learn.

—BENJAMIN FRANKLIN

CHAPTER 4
LIFELONG LEARNING FOSTERS HUMBLE ADAPTABILITY

What's a dovekie supposed to do? These small seabirds launch off icebergs and ice floes, diving into the ocean depths for plankton. As the climate warms and icebergs melt, many scientists believed these ecological events could lead to the shrinkage or even demise of the flock. That has not happened. Why? Because these tiny flying black-and-white tanks soon learned to hunt in new ways.[1] Their adaptability ensured their survivability. Species that can't adapt and learn new habits will face their demise.

In the same way, leaders boost their adaptability and simultaneously their humility by committing to lifelong learning. One well-regarded researcher put it this way:

> To succeed in [a] new environment requires continual learning—how to do existing tasks better and how to do

entirely new things. If we fail to learn, we risk becoming irrelevant... But we're bad at learning. Supremely bad. In fact, we're our own worst enemies.[2]

Ask almost any leader, "Do you believe in lifelong learning?" and they resoundingly and perhaps incredulously respond, "Well, of course!" Yet, if you followed up by asking, "So, what does it mean to learn?" you might be greeted with a blank stare or an equivocal, top-of-the-mind response. Those responses indicate that most leaders have not thought deeply about their core belief in lifelong learning. Without a deeper understanding and perspective, many leaders will ultimately be stranded looking for relevance on a melting iceberg. This chapter provides the insights necessary to build a richer understanding of lifelong learning.

WHAT IS LEARNING?

If caring leaders need to develop a deep, professional commitment to lifelong learning, then they should be clear on the scope of their commitment. The simple model below provides the jumping-off point for a deeper understanding of this professional responsibility (see Figure 4.1). The model highlights three stages in the learning process:

Priming—Priming represents the initial stimulus for learning. Priming occurs when someone savors new experiences, participates in some kind of educational event, or interacts with people in different ways. These ignition points serve as the starting point of learning.

Reflecting—Reflecting refers to the lessons learned from any priming event. Every priming event encompasses an almost limitless number of cues and stimuli that might command our attention, meriting further contemplation.

Figure 4.1

THE LEARNING PROCESS

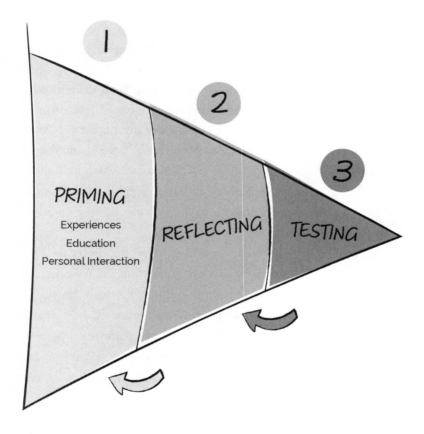

So, people make choices—some deliberate, others unconscious—about what they reflect on as well as what they ignore. For instance, a person placed in a new job will quickly attend to understanding the parameters of the new responsibilities, sometimes overlooking more subtle cues about the working environment. Likewise, during the first week of classes, students will zero in on the course requirements and may fail to appreciate novel teaching approaches.

Testing—The final step in the learning process involves testing in the most robust sense of the word. Of course, in the classroom, tests are routinely administered to see if the instruction and reflection yield the desired result. If not, then skilled teachers will encourage more reflection or perhaps a new priming event. That's the reason for the arrows looping backward in the model. Testing does not need to be formal; it could involve experimenting with a new skill in the workplace, such as improving meeting management through better agendas. Or it could involve trialing a new opinion or idea with a colleague based on recently acquired information.

Once most people learn something, they usually try to incorporate it into their daily lives or ways of thinking. Three other important implications emerge from this simple model of learning:

First, learning is not inevitable. Experience may be inevitable, but learning is not. Clearly, we all have priming experiences (stage one), but we may or may not reflect on those priming events (stage two) or even test out lessons gleaned from our

---------------------------------- **66** ----------------------------------

Teachers...lead their students to achievements so great that it surprises the achiever and creates excitement and motivation—especially the motivation for rigorous, disciplined, persistent work and practice that continued learning requires. —PETER DRUCKER

reflections (stage three). Think of a student in class who plays video games during class discussions. Without the guidance of a teacher through the reflection stage and an assessment such as a test, paper, or project, we cannot be sure learning class lessons has occurred. Likewise, a skillful leader might delegate a project to an employee as a growth opportunity, but without reflection, testing, and usually some coaching, the leader cannot be sure that the new assignment has produced the desired growth.

Second, learning occurs at different rates. Certainly, some people learn more quickly than others. And people often show a natural proclivity to learn one subject more easily than another. Think, for instance, of someone gifted at learning new languages but who struggles with math problems. And some things are just easier to learn than other things. A child who accidentally puts her hand in the campfire swiftly speeds through all three stages and concludes a new life rule: don't play with fire! Other learnings, like how to be an effective leader, require much more time, because the reflection stage involves detecting both visible and subtle patterns gathered from a wide variety of priming events. It may take time to synthesize these insights and transform them into practices that will be beneficial.

Third, learning barriers can emerge at any stage in the process. Employees who complain about "being stuck in the same old job" may well have too few priming events to spawn learning.

More frequently, learning gets short-circuited at the reflection stage. The obstacles at this stage are many and varied, but several of the most prominent (and correctable) ones are:

- **Confirming views**—Most people have a strong bias toward confirming their existing beliefs and perfecting their current skill set. Like some annoying fly at our mental picnic, we typically swat away contradictory information to our own well-established beliefs or impressions. This makes perfect sense, because it affirms our sense of worth and perspectives on life. But, on the flip side, seeking confirmation can obscure important new lessons or undermine the development of a new skill. For example, a family that never took active measures to inhibit the spread of COVID can point to selective examples of others who ignored warnings yet survived the pandemic. In short, confirming rarely equates with learning.

- **Detecting errors of omission**—Most people learn from their errors. Usually, though, those lessons emerge from a mistake of commission. A quarterback who throws an interception knows he committed an error; he'll study the film to make sure it doesn't happen again. Errors of omission are different and harder to detect; consequently, they present greater learning challenges. These kinds of errors lead to missed opportunities. For example, consider a candidate for a position who fails to get her dream job. Thinking back to the job interview, she cannot recall making a specific mistake in answering a question. But the missing piece might be that she forgot to mention a particular experience that could have made the difference. Unless she takes the time to ask, "What might I have missed or failed to mention?" she is unlikely to transform the experience into a learning event. In short, our mental autocorrect specializes in tracking errors of commission; it is less attuned to errors of omission.

- **Analyzing complex situations**—Complex events present special learning challenges because there are so many possible signs and inklings competing for our limited attention. For example, learning how to collaborate with a team presents so many possible variables to untangle that it can be difficult to discern clear lessons. A failed collaborative effort might be the result of the timing, people, situation, working environment, or even the meeting mechanics. Or it could be some combination of these variables. Learning to tease out these issues may well accelerate a person's career trajectory.

Even during the testing phase, learning barriers can pop up. Sometimes the testing goes awry because we attempt a new learning opportunity in the wrong circumstances. Testing your newly acquired barbecuing skills on your vegan friend doesn't make much sense. Likewise, checking out your new assertiveness training during an employee counseling session is equally problematic. This does not mean that the new skill lacks relevance in other situations; instead, the testing needs to be done in the right situation or you are likely to draw the wrong conclusions. We often advise leaders, "Use the right skill at the right time." This applies to virtually any leadership skill, including collaboration, negotiation, and coaching, to name a few.

SO WHAT?

Translating your lifelong learning core belief into a sustainable commitment requires deeper reflections that can be revealed by contemplating the following questions:

1. **Do you routinely chronicle your learning expedition?** Every aspiring leader should place Alfred Lansing's book Endurance: *Shackleton's Incredible Voyage* on their must-read list. This astonishing and harrowing tale about the explorer's attempt to reach the South Pole in 1914 reveals leadership lessons that we can still marvel at today. Yet, without Shackleton's daily journals, we could not fathom the depth of his leadership struggle and extraordinary rescue of his

---

66

The world is a huge place. How will you know where you fit in unless you explore beyond your comfort zone?

—ERNEST SHACKLETON

entire crew from the polar extremes. Routinely recording your leadership journey—whether on paper or audio—can be incredibly illuminating and motivating. Simply taking the time to do so on a regular basis disciplines the mind to record key lessons learned. Some of those lessons may have never moved to the testing phase; the journal provides a reminder to push through to that stage. Writing down the lessons also brings together threads of experience that can be woven into a larger quilt of your leadership style.

Stepping back and rereading your chronicle can be equally revealing, because you'll notice patterns emerging. Do you tend to learn the most from experiences, people, or reading? Bob's learning inflection points come not only from meeting new people from a wide variety of backgrounds, but also from reading a diverse selection of books to enhance his depth of knowledge (see Acknowledgments).

Flipping that lens around, do you overlook certain types of priming events? Is this oversight hindering your development in some way? Your chronicle might also reveal a tendency to stop short of the full learning process. For example, are you recording reflections (stage two) but are neglecting to test out those ideas (stage three)? Likewise, are you simply testing a lot of ideas, skills, and perceptions but not spending enough time reflecting on them? Answers to these kinds of questions take your learning to new heights and will enhance the speed and quality of future learning. And, perhaps, most importantly, it will help you, like Shackleton, endure the challenges of the day.

2. **Do you visualize learning as a staircase or more as an ascending spiral?** A staircase suggests that after we learn something, we move on to the next step until we ascend to the highest plateau. A staircase image mirrors the traditional

Figure 4.2

HOW DO YOU VISUALIZE LEARNING?

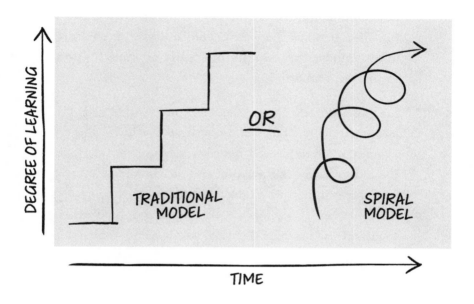

education model; pass one grade level and you move on to the next plateau (see Figure 4.2).

Graduation rightly represents a time to celebrate a major life accomplishment. But does learning stop there? We hope not. And that's why a more evocative image might be an ascending spiral. The ascendant direction of the spiral expresses a continual desire to learn, grow, and excel. This never-ending quest seldom plateaus, at least for very long. The looping backward, spiral structure signals a need to constantly reevaluate and reconsider what you've already learned. After all, circumstances change, and what works today may not work tomorrow. In short, committing to lifelong learning translates into never being satisfied with your current state of understanding and skill set. Lifelong learning requires constant nurturing, pruning, and a regular dose of insights from a variety of sources. Perhaps educational institutions should consider adding a novel memento to the graduation ceremony. In addition to the diploma, perhaps graduates could be given a young tree as a reminder that education requires continual watering, fertilizing, and pruning.

3. **Do you regularly identify lessons you've unlearned?** Great learners quickly forget less useful lessons, which helps them to refine their skills and knowledge base. Consider one of the most astonishing learning episodes in almost every person's life—the acquisition of language. By the age of six, the typical child has learned the meaning of between eight thousand and fourteen thousand words (semantics) and how to put them in proper order (syntax).[3] The priming event of parents talking to their children proves crucial in the process. Scholars are still trying to fully understand how infant brains process cuing incidents, producing an almost magical fluency in childhood.

    We do know that children often test their linguistic skills with parents and others. They make a lot of mistakes, often quite humorous ones, like confusing a red apple with a red tomato—after all, both are red, round, and similar in size.[4] Researchers find this kind of overgeneralization quite normal and easily correctable. The child's "failed test" (e.g., phase three), helps them to forget and refine their generalizations.

    Unfortunately, many leaders lose this childlike ability to quickly test and amend their knowledge or tweak their skill set. Instead, leaders get stuck in repeating patterns that don't yield optimal results. They are often pressed for time, falling into the overgeneralization trap; they may see similarities in situations where they should see differences. For example, consider a leader who repeatedly relies on email to communicate organizational changes. In some but not all cases, he meets what he considers random resistance. He fails to detect an important distinction between major and routine changes. He overgeneralizes and assumes that all organizational changes can be treated alike. The discerning leader would not confuse the apple with the tomato and lump the two together; instead, the caring leader would communicate routine changes via email but major changes in a more rich, face-to-face environment. In this sense, the leader needs to unlearn his rule of thumb and replace it with a new one based on the type of change.

4. **Do you routinely build a variety of priming events into your schedule?** Some people learn best from books, others from classes, and still others from experiences. But sometimes we fall into learning ruts with this approach; it's like the person

---- **"** ----

It is not the critic who counts; not the man who points out how the strong man stumbles, or where the doer of deeds could have done them better. The credit belongs to the man who is actually in the arena, whose face is marred by dust and sweat and blood; who strives valiantly; who errs, who comes short again and again, because there is no effort without error and shortcoming; but who does actually strive to do the deeds; who knows great enthusiasms, the great devotions; who spends himself in a worthy cause; who at the best knows in the end the triumph of high achievement, and who at the worst, if he fails, at least fails while daring greatly, so that his place shall never be with those cold and timid souls who neither know victory nor defeat.

—THEODORE ROOSEVELT

who only reads one newspaper or listens to one cable news program. Sure, they are learning new information, but their perspectives tend to be shaped by one viewpoint orchestrated by the information providers. Other news sources could suggest different viewpoints worth considering.

Multiple sources of insight enhance and enrich the depth of your understanding. For example, a book outlining a decision-making framework comes to life when you talk to or read about an "in the arena" decision maker like President Teddy Roosevelt. Observing leaders in action might raise new questions about traditional decision-making models or reveal nuances to the decision-making process that add richness to your leadership repertoire.

5. **Do you properly balance depth and breadth in your learning?** Almost everyone gravitates toward particular subject matters. Often organizational members develop a wonderfully rich expertise in particular areas such as finance, human relations, or supply chain management. They recognize nuances about the subject that few others think about. That kind of profound understanding often accelerates career paths in ways that are both lucrative and genuinely satisfying.

Successful leaders, though, need breadth, as well. Why? If your primary interest area is personality profiles, then you are likely to view all personnel challenges through that lens. That's myopic and unhealthy. In fact, some human relations problems could emerge from other factors, like organizational structure or even the HVAC system in the building. For example, few people know that 57 percent of all sick leave can be attributed to poor ventilation.[5] Developing a working knowledge in areas beyond the zones of your expertise allows you to connect with others in a more collaborative manner.

Leaders always encounter complex challenges at the crossroads of various types of expertise. Those are exactly the moments where a leader's learning breadth can make the difference between success and failure. For example, during the COVID pandemic, leaders needed to collaborate not only with public health experts, but also with specialists in finance, logistics, manufacturing, and even propaganda. A working knowledge in these areas enhanced the probabilities for success. And that starts with planning the right priming events early in your career.

6. **Do you allocate the proper amount of time to each learning stage?** Often, through force of circumstance, allocating the proper time to the three learning phases can get out of whack. For example, one busy executive of a billion-dollar firm revealed in a coaching session, "I just don't have any time to think." That was a signal that he wasn't reflecting enough on his vast array of priming experiences that filled his day. He further lamented, "The only time I can think is when I go running. Then when I get back to the office, I get caught up in the events and forget everything. Ugh!" The light bulb of insight flashed twice in that moment. First flash: the executive was indeed reflecting during his run. Second flash: he needed a way to record his reflections during his runs so he could test them out later. What to do? The executive needed to build more runs into his schedule to encourage more reflection, and he needed a mechanism to record his thoughts while he was jogging. An inexpensive pocket recorder tethered to his running vest did the trick. By acting on these simple, personal insights, he enhanced not only his learning but also his confidence while making strategic decisions.

Likewise, seasoned educators regularly encounter students who excel on exams but stumble over applying those lessons in real life. Consider students who might ace a public speaking exam but haltingly deliver their well-crafted speech. What's the core issue in this case? Away from the podium, they know what to do, but in front of the podium, they fall flat. In this instance, a written test is not the best measure of competency for this skill. This is both a priming and testing challenge for the educator. A skillful instructor learns to shift more class time to behind-the-podium practice sessions, which allows students to test their skills in a low-pressure situation. For the educator, the time allocation at the various stages proves critical for maximizing student learning.

7. **Do you regularly consult with others to evaluate your learning?** Some lessons are best learned in solitary contemplation. Others, though—particularly leadership lessons—can best be learned by talking them through with others. Often a spouse, a trusted friend, a former teacher, a work colleague, or even an informal advisory team will provide a different perspective to your private musings. They see what you may not see, nuances that you may not recognize, issues that should brought into sharper focus, and perspectives not yet entertained. That's why effective leaders often seek counsel from those they respect.

    Caring leaders often find that advisers with a wide range of expertise and passions work best. These leaders are not necessarily seeking specific advice; rather, they frequently use these forums to test out ideas before deploying or even discussing them in their organizations.

CONCLUSION

Physicians have a long road of learning: they study for years in medical school, rotate through several medical specialties, then pursue specialized residency requirements. Even during their years of practice, their careers are interspersed with continuing medical education. There's a similar course for lawyers: after they graduate from law school, they often serve as a clerk for a judge or a lawyer, followed by years of practice, interspersed with continuing education. Likewise, architects, engineers, and a host of other professionals require a strong educational background followed by years of continuing education and practice.

Why don't we strive for this same level of educational rigor for our leaders? After all, people in leadership positions, like those in other professions, require expert knowledge, specialized talents, and a deft touch. With this perspective in mind, we believe that organizations should seek to develop talented and confident leadership professionals by promoting lifelong learning.

A note of caution: as leaders develop confidence in their abilities, it might undermine their sense of humility. You might ask yourself, can leaders be both confident and humble? We think so. Lifelong learning allows the magical synthesis of these seemingly clashing leadership qualities: humility emerges from realizing there is always much more to learn; confidence emerges from a belief that you will learn the lessons necessary to tackle the challenges of the day. Some people adapt because they must; caring leaders, though, adapt out of a humility by self-reflecting, admitting their weakness, acquiring new skills, and entertaining new perspectives. That's humble, not forced, adaptation based on a commitment to lifelong learning. Perhaps that's why the dovekie birds still fly and thrive in the harshest of conditions, just as we would expect from these little black-and-white tanks in the arctic sky.

—————————————— **66** ——————————————

Never let formal education get in the way of your learning.

—MARK TWAIN

You can accomplish by kindness what you cannot accomplish by force.

—PUBLILIUS SYRUS

CHAPTER 5
LEADING WITH KINDNESS IS NOT BEING SOFT

Have you ever hung up from a phone conversation with someone you had never met and thought, "Well, that was a very pleasant person"? How could you possibly know—after all, you didn't meet face-to-face, and you may not have ever talked to the person before. Still, you came away refreshed and pleased by the interaction.

Some people just seem to have a smile in their voice. On the other hand, have you ever met someone new, or even reconnected with someone you know, and immediately concluded they are having a bad day? They were gruff, reserved, or distant. We all have, and it doesn't feel good.

Everybody enjoys working with people who are likable, friendly, and pleasant to be around. These people project a warmth that feels magnetic. There's no drama. Their attitude says everything: they seem cooperative, open, and positive about the prospects for the future.

How do these everyday experiences translate into leadership? Too often when people get into leadership positions, they don a different demeanor. All of a sudden, they feel the need to become more serious, more distant, by projecting an air of authority. Or they become so engaged in the problems of the day that their personality shifts to one of all business. To be sure, acting with deliberateness and seriousness may be necessary on occasion. However, defaulting to this style as your dominant manner can feed on itself and, before you know it, you have unwittingly adopted a business-only personality. Caring leaders don't let this happen; instead, they almost naturally exude kindness. That's not an accident or a mere quirk of personality; rather, it emerges from a core belief in kindness, grounded in three comingled commitments.

KINDNESS AS SENTIMENT

Core sentiments emerge from a vibrant union between your viewpoints and attitudes. For many people, patriotism represents a fundamental sentiment. Patriots exude pride in their country because they believe in what their country stands for (their viewpoint) and are motivated, enthused, and passionate about what that means to them (their attitude).

Likewise, caring leaders adopt the viewpoint that treating others with kindness translates into an attitude of respect for others. They find joy working with others in a tolerant, friendly, and open manner.

While essential for a caring leader, these core sentiments are not enough. A person can be a patriot but never act on those sentiments, much like a Minnesota Vikings "closet loyalist" fan might do who lives in Green Bay, Wisconsin. She may never let her neighbors know about her true loyalties. Caring leaders, though, take the next step of translating sentiments into actions; they proudly don their purple jerseys on game day in Green Bay.

KINDNESS AS BEHAVIORS

Kind leaders act in accord with their sentiments. It's not so much about putting smiley faces on every situation but more about their daily interactions with people. Kind leaders project warmth by paying attention and showing interest in others. When greeting people, they go beyond the obligatory "How's it going?" Caring leaders inquire about important life events others just experienced or an issue they're grappling with by paying attention to people's tone and cadence, looking for unspoken cues about their disposition. Kindness in action means talking and listening to others, not about yourself. In short, be more interested in others than yourself.

Seemingly small behaviors can make big impressions. Caring leaders make eye contact, avoid fidgeting with their phones, and minimize distractions. Expressing gratitude in the form of a thank-you and a handwritten note can demonstrate kindness that many people rarely experience. Think of these small acts as regular deposits in a caring account that will yield compound interest for years.

There are plenty of kind people who cannot be leaders. And there are plenty of leaders who are not particularly kind. Is it possible to be kind AND a leader? We believe so. And, in fact, kindness makes you a better leader.

KINDNESS AS LEADERSHIP

The sentiments and practices of kindness make people better leaders. Kind leaders personify a positive, can-do attitude while setting expectations at levels that challenge, but do not overwhelm, people. Big Hairy Audacious Goals (BHAGs) have their place, but constantly pushing people to excel to the highest levels can be tiring, stressful, and damaging to mental health.

No one would question Simone Biles's commitment to excellence; after all, she has won a treasure chest full of Olympic medals in gymnastics. Yet, she stepped away from several events at the Tokyo Olympics to "prioritize her mental health."[1] This courageous act speaks volumes about a leader's responsibility to help others strike the right mental balance.

Kind leaders are inviting, encouraging, and inquisitive about others. You often hear them ask, "Do you have any questions?" or "What are you concerned about today?" They actively listen by asking for clarifications and allowing people to safely say what's on their minds.

Consider an illuminating finding from our research on working climate. We've surveyed thousands of employees, often asking, "What was the best thing that happened to you at work in the past month? Over 50 percent of respondents recalled a simple expression of kindness or positive feedback (see Table 5.1). On the other hand, in response to "If you could change one thing about the workplace, what would it be?" less than 5 percent of employees mentioned the day-to-day acts of kindness and pats on the back. We've concluded that many people genuinely value these almost-invisible acts of respect, but they may be either too polite or too embarrassed to mention them. Caring leaders recognize this hidden dynamic and do something about it. When deserved, caring leaders are gracious in giving credit to others rather than taking the glory themselves.

Kind leaders exude calmness and never allow their tempers to outpace their good judgment. That's not to say that caring leaders don't get upset; sometimes it's necessary to show your emotions, but in a measured way. Some caring leaders need to retreat to a quiet place, away from the public, and blow off steam rather than take it out on others. You don't want to be viewed as a hothead or someone easily frustrated or flustered. Likewise, you don't want to be viewed as too relaxed and easygoing, because people might surmise you lack sensitivity to others' issues and concerns.

Table 5.1

WHAT WAS THE BEST THING THAT HAPPENED TO YOU AT WORK THE PAST MONTH?

- My supervisor told me they got unrequested, good feedback on my performance.
- Culture moments being shared have had a positive effect on the team.
- Completing several challenging projects.
- Being recognized for hard work.
- Gathering workers together and going on an outing outside of work to help morale and increase camaraderie.
- Seeing so many lessons learned to date be applied to the newest project; I am so optimistic! This is a great team to begin with and I am watching it get better all of the time.
- I was told me being on this project has improved performance.
- Realized true benefit to the project through innovation.
- Watching work be executed for shutdowns go better than expected due to the amount of planning and thought being done on the front end.
- The challenges of the project have been very rewarding to me.
- Seeing the rewards of the group making a positive impact.
- There are many good things that happen daily. I work with a good group of people.
- During a recent team meeting, our discipline was able to work through several issues fairly quickly. Because everyone understood the constraints and what the end goal was, we were able to work together to find solutions quickly.
- Watching a family take a walk with their sick child and stopping by the construction gate to watch the tower crane make some picks, the smiles were priceless.
- Large decisions being made more expediently.
- Gained more responsibility and trust throughout my team.
- A performance review…I was encouraged to grow and thrive in everything I do.
- Given the opportunity to receive additional skills training.
- Our team has met our workforce goals in the last month and has received praise from our client success.
- Watching our team problem solve collaboratively to find solutions quickly.
- Identifying problems and finding solutions and developing best practices going forward.
- Continuously meeting up w/ colleagues and being given the opportunity to continue learning and growing.
- Learned new things and working a little better as part of a team.
- Recognized for contributions and returning to the office to see the team.
- Problem solving issues on hot items and collaborating with my team.
- Given the opportunity to take a different role on another project.
- I was able to watch our team be agile enough to shift on the fly to meet the ever-changing client expectations.
- I had a good review with my supervisor, was recognized for my hard work and he gave me good feedback on areas I can improve.
- Starting some new systems up, seeing the fruits of our labor coming true is rewarding.
- I was given a raise and told I was a valuable member of the team.

Kind leaders clearly communicate what's on their minds but with empathy for others. The former CEO of PepsiCo Indra Nooyi may have best captured how successful leaders integrate their leadership responsibilities with the spirit and practice of kindness. In an interview, she talked about the power of "assuming positive intent" on the part of others.[2] Translation: engage in conversations and discussions with the assumption that everyone at the table has positive motives for advancing certain positions—even when they disagree. For instance, an angry or confused person might blurt out an offensive remark that actually masks an important idea or sentiment. By assuming positive intent, you would be more likely to unmask the substance of the matter and cultivate a positive working relationship.

That's how caring leaders can be gracious. They demonstrate respect by assuming positive intent and rarely questioning people's motives (after all, questioning someone's motives is a zero-sum, no-win game; we can never know a person's motives and there's no way to prove it one way or the other). But they take it one step further—they help others shoulder their pressures by building a sense of confidence—not fear—in their ability to work through tough, stressful circumstances.

CHALLENGES

Leading with kindness can be challenging for any number of reasons. Three issues emerge as the tougher ones that caring leaders master:

Sentiment-behavior gap

Assume you are presenting a seminar for one hundred randomly selected people in leadership positions. You begin the discussion on kindness with three questions:

- *How many of you would consider yourself a kind person?*

- *How many of you routinely practice kindness in your leadership position?*

- *How many of you think that others would describe you as being kind?*

In most cases, almost every hand would go up in response to the first question. Upward of 90 percent of the hands would remain up for question two. The mood in the room would shift dramatically when you ask the third question, as many hands sheepishly return to nervous laps.

It's an amusing and revealing little exercise where most people quickly recognize the seductive lure of self-deception. That's important. After all, one of our favorite Nobel Prize–winning physicists, Richard Feynman, was fond of saying, "The first principle is that you must not fool yourself...and you are the easiest person to fool." Those folks who would lower their hands between the first two questions instantly recognize the gap between their sentiments and their behaviors. They are not fooled into believing their kindness sentiments can always be transformed into acts of kindness. By recognizing the potential for self-deception, they are well positioned to narrow the gap through experiments, self-exploration, and "doing to learn." In fact, research has revealed that successful employees do this early in their careers.[3]

Most people in the room will immediately understand the gap between self-perceptions and others' perceptions. If the first principle is about fooling yourself, then we would like to add a second, related principle: "You must not fool yourself into thinking that others will view you based on your self-perceptions... and, in the moment, that's easy to do."

This unsavory slice of the large self-deception pie becomes easy to understand with a diagram. If leaders only pay attention to the sentiments or individual acts of kindness (note where the arrows are pointing in Figure 5.1), then they are failing to heed Feynman's principle one and your authors' principle two. It's easy to do.

Figure 5.1

LEADER PERCEPTIONS: GAPS BETWEEN SENTIMENTS AND BEHAVIORS

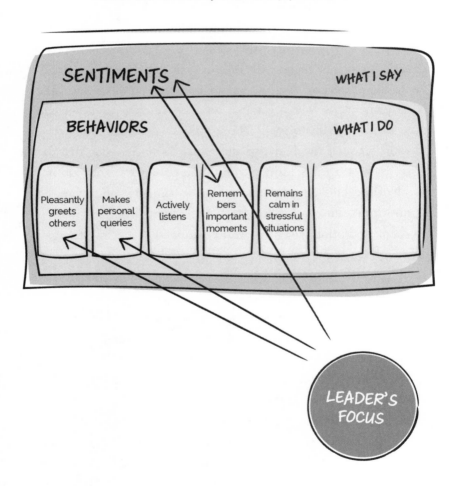

The problem is that other people pay attention to the blank boxes in the diagram (note where the arrows are pointing in Figure 5.2). They see a pattern that screams, "The leader doesn't walk the talk" (e.g., gap between sentiment and behavior—see line one) or "The leader doesn't care about me" (e.g., noticing only the empty spaces in the diagram).

Figure 5.2

EMPLOYEE PERCEPTIONS: GAPS BETWEEN SENTIMENTS AND BEHAVIORS

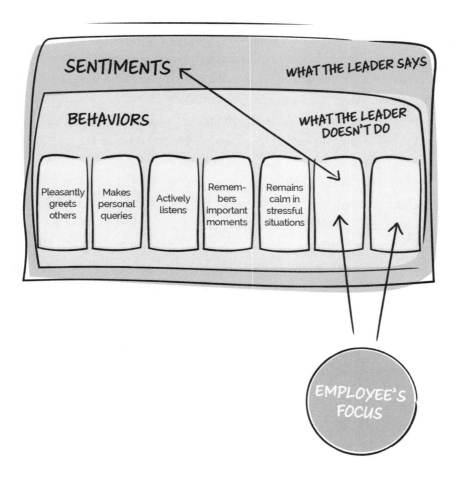

Rectifying these challenges can be as straightforward as:

- Realizing there will always be gaps between sentiment and daily practices

- Acknowledging the gaps to others

- Seeking to narrow those gaps

In fact, in Part Two of the book, we devote a number of pages to practices based on this strategy.

Softness Misperception

Leaders who are kind often face nearly imperceptible rumblings about their leadership abilities. Frequently, the issue revolves around the leader being perceived as too soft, too forgiving, too indecisive. Bluntly stated, can a person be kind and a good leader?

Let's go the history books for an answer. Consider President Dwight D. Eisenhower's career: he was born into poverty to pacifists but went on to graduate from West Point. He eventually became the supreme Allied commander in Europe during World War II and a two-term US president. He was known for his disarming smile, affability, and genteel manner. His wife, Mamie, said, "Ike has the most engaging smile of anybody I ever met."[4] In fact, one newspaper reporter said, "I think his grin saved Ike a lot of trouble." The smile, friendliness, and patience signaled caring kindness to others. One iconic picture shows Ike smiling and joking with paratroopers before they launched the D-day invasion. He knew, of course, that many of them would never return home.

In 1967 Ike was visited by a former general, Harold K. Johnson. During their conversation, the general misquoted a famous maxim about war. After Johnson left, one of Ike's presidential speechwriters (who was in the room at the time) asked Ike about the quote. The speechwriter must have been astounded when Eisenhower precisely corrected every error in the general's statement. The speechwriter asked why Ike didn't correct the general on the spot—after all, as president, he outranked him! Ike's reply provides a revealing perspective on caring leadership: "I got where I did by knowing how to hide my ego and hide my intelligence. I know the actual quote, but why should I embarrass him?"[5]

Such acts of kindness opened Ike to charges of weakness and a lack of decisiveness. During the war many of his top generals grumbled. According to some, Ike didn't do things leaders were expected to do, like "make the tough calls," "challenge others," "rally the troops in hard times," and "envision the future." Is that fair? You be the judge:

- Make the tough calls: General Eisenhower launched the D-day invasion—the largest, most risky invasion of military history—despite dire warnings about dreadful weather conditions.

- Challenge others: General Eisenhower sidelined one of his best generals, George Patton, after a much-publicized incident involving a soldier suffering from what today would be considered post-traumatic stress.

- Rally the troops: The supreme Allied commander not only encouraged soldiers as they marched off to battle; he also forged enduring alliances with commanders who had huge egos and conflicting styles and operated under extraordinary pressures.

- Envision the future: Everyone who drives on the US interstate highway system owes a debt of gratitude to President Eisenhower. He not only imagined a better transportation system but set the wheels in motion to make it happen.

Eisenhower, no doubt, knew he was often misperceived by others as being "too soft," but he bore that burden for the greater good. And the world should be thankful for such kind, caring, and effective leadership in the toughest of times.

Emotional Camouflage

Some leaders believe they should camouflage their emotions and maintain a facade similar to a good poker player. On occasion, concealing reactions and hiding sentiments might make some sense; after all, Ike was a pretty good poker player! In the long run, though, the odds are stacked against this type of unemotive demeanor. Why? Suppressing these totally human feelings under a facade makes leaders appear artificial and phony. After all, they experience emotional highs and lows and have moments of joy, fear, anger, sadness, disappointment, and elation. Emotional intelligence is not about suppressing emotions but identifying, channeling, and even challenging them.[6]

At some point, leaders who camouflage their exasperations will likely be unable to conceal their feelings any longer and explode with a rat-tat-tat of verbal abuse. It saps psychic energy to suppress feelings over the long run. On the other hand, leaders who camouflage their joy deprive the group of an energizing, motivational opportunity. Caring leaders seize these moments to bask in notable achievements that will propel the team to the next level. Yet, they do so while recognizing the challenges that remain.

In essence, kind leaders don't try to suppress or camouflage their emotions as much as they transcend them, channeling them in a more useful manner. Caring leaders avoid overly optimistic or pessimistic predictions with a transcendent, calm view of situations. They do not overreact or underreact to events. In short, they train emotions to be subordinate to their thoughts and focus on encouraging others.

Toxic Positivity

The flip side of emotional camouflage is what one high-tech worker insightfully called "toxic positivity." He lamented:

> I tell my superiors about the challenges we are facing and plead for resources and help, but it's always greeted with,

"You are an amazing asset to us. You'll figure it out." For a while that works, but then you realize it's just token happy talk. They put rainbows on storms before the thunderclouds subside and call it a good day. That's toxic positivity, and that's why I'm leaving. Then they will be forced to understand the challenges our team faces.

What he describes could best be characterized as faux kindness—saying all the right, soothing words but not acting with understanding. There's nothing kind about ignoring legitimate employee concerns. It's not respectful. It's not caring. And, over time, it becomes toxic.

SO WHAT?

By pondering the following questions, you can transform your conviction about the power of kindness into action that will provide the foundation for all the practices in Part Two of the book.

1. **Are you committed to beyond-the-situation kindness?** Social psychologists tell us that one of the least appreciated aspects of human behavior is how many of our actions, speech, and responses are driven by situational cues. Most people are kind and gracious at weddings and funerals. After all, that's what is expected. Those very same people, though, may be tyrants at work. Even the vilest dictators can point to moments of kindness. Joseph Stalin starved millions of people to death, yet this tyrannical poet "could glow with a soft, capacious smile...could be utterly solicitous and charming."[7] Jeffrey Epstein, who sexually assaulted underaged girls, charmed many and even gave unsolicited gifts to the police department.[8]

    Here's the real test, though: Can you be kind when conflicts emerge, tensions mount, or stress multiplies? Those are the moments people will remember and which will define you as a kind leader.

Both your authors have had the unfortunate task of relieving people from their positions because of performance issues, even after many coaching attempts. You need to be firm, but you can be kind by not embarrassing them, allowing them to leave with a modicum of respect, and avoiding badmouthing them afterward. In the moment, that person may not feel like you are kind, but years later, they may well realize it. More importantly, you are signaling to your team how to handle tough situations with dignity, respect, and a commitment to excellence.

2.   **Are you willing to take the hit of being considered too soft?** Kind leaders, like Ike, take reputational hits for being too soft. In response, some leaders counterpunch against such charges with spontaneous acts of harshness.

Consider the following scenario one leader faced: Working with his team on a tough issue, the team leader sought his team members' opinions to better understand the core dilemmas. Many on the team became very frustrated with this process; in fact, one team member got so frustrated with the perceived lack of decisiveness (e.g., softness charge) that he blurted out, "You're the most senior person in the room; just stop dillydallying around and make the damn decision." That's an aggressive, bold statement that people rarely voice. In this case, the leader shot back, "OK, we'll go with plan EZ. Now you can all go, too—the meeting is over." The stunned employees quickly herded to the exits. The one team member who had candidly shared his frustrations lingered and tried to explain. The leader barked, "I made the decision, now go. I don't need to hear from you again on this issue."

In this nearly hostile swing between softness and harshness, these defining moments revealed that this leader could not tolerate a misperception of softness. To be sure, none of these employees will ever think of the boss as soft again. But at what price? They will certainly not think of him as kind again, either. Additionally, they will never again risk total candor out of fear of being verbally chastened out of the room. The dynamics changed forever, regardless of other acts of kindness.

If the leader had responded differently in the moment, he could have set in motion inspirational and innovative dynamics that would have propelled the team. Remarks like "I know this can be a challenging and circuitous process, but I don't want any of us to make hasty decisions that emerge out of our frustrations" demonstrate kindness by legitimizing frustrations, even as they suggest a guiding principle about good decision-making. Caring leaders think of the "too harsh" or "too soft" debate as secondary; instead, they focus on being calm and balanced regardless of the situation (see Figure 5.3).

3. **Can you corral your emotions and practice kindness even when you might be angry or just plain tired?** Nobody would accuse any navy SEAL of being soft. These warriors are the toughest of the tough, the elite of the elite. Yet, nearing graduation from their grueling training, these elite warriors are implored to show their appreciation to all the people who supported them. One of their graduation speakers, the legendary SEAL Dick Couch, drilled down even further into this sentiment. He challenged every one of them with these words:

    > Administrative personnel, armory technicians, and supply experts … deserve our respect and appreciation. So at least once a day, I want you to compliment

Figure 5.3

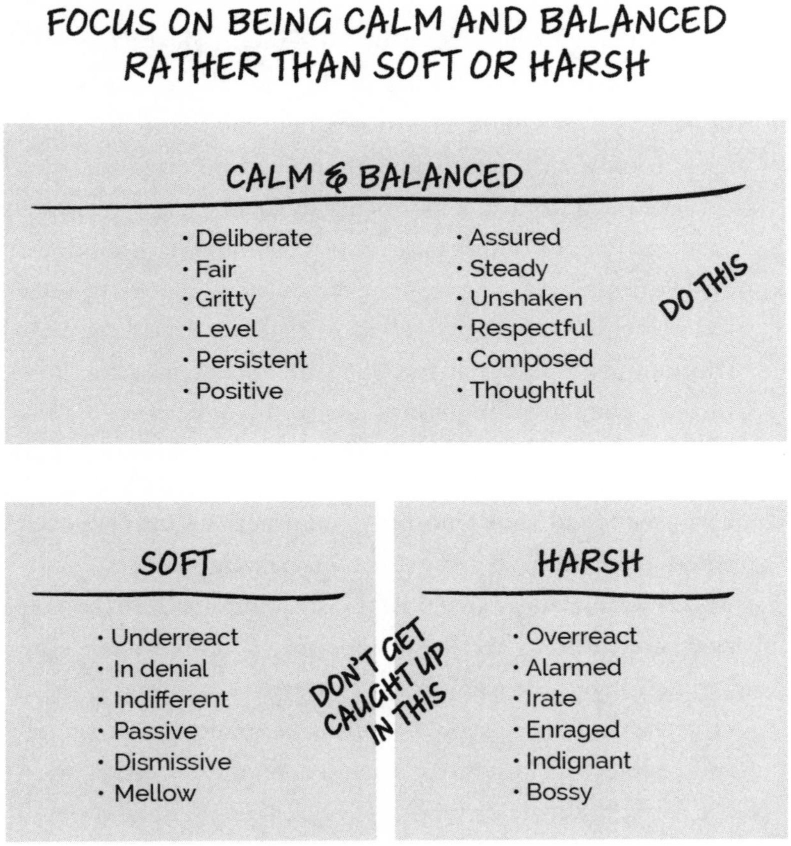

FOCUS ON BEING CALM AND BALANCED RATHER THAN SOFT OR HARSH

CALM & BALANCED

- Deliberate
- Fair
- Gritty
- Level
- Persistent
- Positive
- Assured
- Steady
- Unshaken
- Respectful
- Composed
- Thoughtful

DO THIS

SOFT

- Underreact
- In denial
- Indifferent
- Passive
- Dismissive
- Mellow

DON'T GET CAUGHT UP IN THIS

HARSH

- Overreact
- Alarmed
- Irate
- Enraged
- Indignant
- Bossy

one of them or give them a good word. They do so much for us and seldom get credit for it.[9]

That's the spirit and practice of kindness from the toughest of the tough.

Most leaders will never endure the emotional and physical exhaustion of an elite warrior. Yet, SEALs are expected to show kindness to the support staff, regardless of their weariness—every day. When you feel good, it's easy to be the best, most kind version of you. But when you don't feel good or are exhausted, it's far more difficult. But if you build kind habits into your daily routine, then you'll act like a SEAL, "instinctively, when there is no time to think."[10]

4. **Are you always learning about new ways to show kindness?** One of the subtle self-deceptions we all naturally fall victim to is assuming that acts that we deem as kind will be viewed as kind by others. Caring leaders avoid this trap by always searching for new ways to show kindness to others. In their inspiring book, *The 5 Languages of Appreciation in the Workplace*, Gary Chapman and Paul White describe five fundamental arenas (i.e., languages) where leaders can show appreciation: words, time, acts of service, gifts, and touch. Their research shows that "what makes one person feel appreciated does not necessarily make another person feel appreciated."[11]

    Embracing this idea may be the best way to close the inevitable gaps between the sentiments of kindness and daily practices. Sometimes leaders discover the last missing piece to the kindness puzzle by observing how caring leaders deal with people. Studying how these role models greet others, ask questions, refute poor arguments, arrange meeting rooms, select different communication tools, and perform a host of other daily practices often proves revealing.

On occasion, you might have to ask further questions to understand the situational circumstances the caring leader uses to adjust his or her style. An intern shadowed one of your authors (Phil) to learn how to respectfully facilitate group collaboration. After watching one rather taxing session, the intern asked, "I know you knew that person X was going in an unproductive direction. Why didn't you just correct person X in the moment, like you do with me in the classroom?" Fantastic question! The answer:

> Because our relationship has developed to the point that I can be direct with you. Everybody is different, and I adjust my style accordingly. I knew person X's heart was in the right place and that I could use a series of questions to nudge her in the right direction. I didn't want to burst her bubble in the moment. However, in other cases, with different people motivated by different passions, I may decide to be more direct.

Such explanations may be the only way to learn about some of the subtle ways to practice kindness.

5. **Can you assume positive intent even when you are dubious?**
    Effective senior leaders usually possess finely tuned antennae that quickly recognize suspect data, dubious analysis, cliché-riddled reasoning, and charlatans posing as experts.[12] In fact, honing good BS-detection skills may well be an essential skill for all leaders.[13]

    So, how should caring leaders reconcile these laudatory critical thinking skills with kindness? Or, more specifically, how do you assume positive intent when you detect something dubious or suspicious? We've coached many bright and insightful leaders through this exact dilemma by working through incidents such as the following:

- A usually reliable employee fails to deliver on a project deadline. What do you assume?

  - Option A: the employee is slacking and needs to be reminded of the importance of deadlines.

  - Option B: the employee has run into some unusual circumstance; I need to understand the situation more fully.

- A colleague starts nitpicking a presentation you are preparing to deliver to a client. What do you assume?

  - Option A: The colleague is trying to irritate me or trying to demonstrate superiority.

  - Option B: The colleague is trying to improve the presentation for an important client, as it would benefit the entire organization.

- A vendor presents a proposal that misses the mark. It appears to be boilerplate and not tuned to your organization's needs. What do you assume?

  - Option A: The vendor is not very smart or didn't do the right homework.

  - Option B: The vendor was misinformed about the nature of the proposal. Asking the right questions might reveal the vendor's suitability for the project.

In each case, option B reflects the "assume positive intent" principle. It doesn't mean that option A is off the table; option B merely demonstrates respect by giving people the benefit of the doubt, at least until proven otherwise.

After reviewing numerous incidents and possible options, aspiring leaders often suddenly realize that they don't need to turn off their naturally insightful minds in these situations. They do, however, need to channel their impressions and allow their natural curiosity and other skills to take center stage. Soon, these leaders realize that kindness and thoughtful skepticism cannot only coexist but can actually enrich one another.

CONCLUSION

David Sarasohn, a longtime columnist for *The Oregonian*, penned a wonderful piece, titled "How Kindness Appreciates— How a Gracious Act Can Resonate for a Lifetime." After reporting on many of his daily experiences, he wrote,

> There's a reason we remember great kindnesses. It's not that people are keeping accounts and preparing to repay them. In a transactional world, luminous kindness is a combination of the act and the time, and that produces something beyond evaluation. Trying to repay it is like calculating the price of Versailles as an Airbnb.
>
> The inability to figure out an exchange rate, a way to have the same impact on a giver's life that he had on yours, has spurred the concept of paying it forward. If you can't repay the person who lives permanently in your appreciation, you can at least adjust your balance sheet with the universe—and maybe plant yourself enduringly in someone else's memory.[14]

Leaders are constantly looking for powerful ways to engage people and shepherd them in a positive direction. For many years, the question of "How do I motivate and engage people?" has generated leadership practices such as management by objectives and expectation setting. For sure, these are useful tools to help create positive momentum.[15] Yet, practicing kindness on a daily basis may be more powerful than any tool a leadership guru might ever dream up. It is not commonly recognized as an influential leadership trait, but genuine kindness will motivate extraordinary visceral responses that will have lasting impact on people. Unseen nuclear forces bind particles together in nearly imperceptible ways; likewise, the nearly invisible force of kindness can powerfully and magically bring people together.

_____ **"** _____

Kindness is the language which the deaf can hear and the blind can see. —MARK TWAIN

PART 2

THE PRACTICES OF CARING LEADERS

Championing caring leadership beliefs is one matter; channeling those beliefs to accomplish the amazing is another matter altogether. Part Two knits together the core beliefs of caring leaders and transforms them into a series of actionable practices. Often the challenge is how to translate sincerely held commitments into everyday visible and subtle practices. This section directly addresses that challenge.

We make a living by what we get, but we make a life by what we give.

—WINSTON CHURCHILL

CHAPTER 6
CARING LEADERS PRIMARILY COACH, NOT COMMAND

Should leaders be more like a commander or a coach?

The word *commander* refers to someone of authority or rank. Commanders issue directives, write orders, and demand swift follow-through. A US president acts as the commander-in-chief of the military; the president's missions must be executed by the armed services, regardless of the military leadership's personal politics.

The verb *coach* means "to train, teach, or instruct." The head coach of an athletic team is someone who has the primary responsibility for teaching her team.

In a book about caring leadership, the answer to the commander-versus-coach question appears hardly worth mentioning. It's obvious, right? Coaching wins hands down. But we disagree. Why? First, many people in leadership positions carry titles that underscore their commander role (e.g., chief executive, commander, commodore, captain, command sergeant, chief medical officer). Second, in the stereotypical military tradition of years ago, successful leaders were expected to issue crisply written directives and firmly barked orders to win the battle of the day. Third, some leadership challenges can only be resolved with commander-like decrees. Consider, for example, an emergency room physician making life-and-death decisions as a trauma patient gasps for breath or a battlefield general thwarting a vicious counterattack.

In short, we don't want to summarily dismiss the commander-or-coach question without exploring the nuances it implies. One illuminating way to answer the question is to examine the dilemma through the lens of the five beliefs reviewed in Part One:

- **Embracing uncertainty accelerates growth.** Commanding people feel compelled to do something that removes uncertainty from the situation, as in "Do this; don't do this." However, barking orders rarely promotes growth or encourages people to look at other, uncertain possibilities. In contrast, a coach would calmly instruct and guide people to explore unique opportunities with a statement such as, "What if we tried this?"

- **Progress emerges through exploring and refining.** Commanding and coaching can both spawn progress. However, coaching is more likely to inspire people to spontaneously tweak and leap to new platforms on a consistent basis.

- **The right values cultivate a special sense of identity.** Commanders espouse values and expect obedience; it's an external kind of motivation. Commanding erects a structure of rewards and punishments designed to gain adherence to often poorly understood values. In contrast, coaches teach the values and cultivate internal commitments that will unpredictably, but consistently, guide people's perspectives and decision-making. Coaching builds a sense of "This is who I am" and "This is what I stand for."

- **Lifelong learning fosters humility.** The biographies of extremely successful military commanders, such as Alexander the Great, Ulysses S. Grant, and George Patton, prove instructive.[1] These leaders learned powerful, life-changing lessons, often early in their lives, that fueled their feats of glory. When they stumbled it was often because they misapplied a singular, profound lesson—they overgeneralized and failed to remain humble about their knowledge. That's exactly what happened to General Douglas MacArthur. He was highly successful in certain environments; he proved almost dangerously reckless in others.[2] Conversely, successful coaches must learn to respectfully adapt to every situation and every person they lead.

- **Acting with kindness is not being soft.** Commanding is certainly antisoft. Coaching, if done well, should be also. Kindness, though, emerges directly from a coaching mentality rather than a commanding one.

The brief analysis above suggests that a coaching mind-set snugly syncs up with the core beliefs of caring leaders reviewed in Part One. The commander-versus-coach issue suggests more nuanced questions, such as: How frequently do caring leaders command and how frequently do they coach? What's the proper mix? Do some circumstances demand more of one than the other?

Simply put, most of the time, caring leaders adopt a coaching mentality first and only command in the few circumstances requiring it. By the nature of their role, caring leaders often possess hierarchical authority, but they keep that authority in the background. One of the secrets to former German chancellor Angela Merkel's longevity was that she "repeatedly demonstrated how much a leader can get done quietly, without boasting of her achievements."[3]

Unfortunately, the celebrity CEOs who are showcased in the media often lean toward a commanding style of leadership by emphasizing tough decision-making practices or a founder's singular, profound vision. The vital role of coaching often goes unmentioned; it's not easily understood, reported, or appreciated. And it's certainly not as dramatic as a commander growling, "You're fired." This chapter tries to rectify the imbalance by focusing attention on the both the visible and subtle practices of superior coaches.

COACHING PRINCIPLES

Three basic principles guide great coaches:

- **Ninety-five percent of team members come to work every day desiring to do good work and contribute.** Their relationships with their peers and supervisor, as well as their feeling of belonging, greatly influence their desire to transform their noble intentions into doing something beneficial. Caring leaders release these latent sentiments in others.

- **Only 5 percent (or less) come to work every day and don't care if they do a good job.** Caring leaders need to make hard decisions and deal with this 5 percent appropriately. Caring leaders don't give up on people until they give up on themselves and on their own self-development. Good coaches discern these signs. They give those employees one more chance, and if that kind gesture fails, the leader relieves the employees of their position. That's the tough side of caring leadership.

- **Caring leaders understand team members' motivations, desires, and challenges.** Great coaches spawn revealing conversations designed to discover firsthand knowledge of people's beliefs, aspirations, and frustrations. Coaches then channel this special knowledge as they guide them through their career and skill development.

THE PRACTICE OF COACHING

Coaching starts with the basic question "How can I help you?" This broad-brush query uncovers the challenges people face, the stresses they feel, and the barriers they perceive. Note that the question avoids presupposing any particular concern or issue. The coach takes in all the verbal and nonverbal cues, much like Sherlock Holmes searching for some hidden or undetected pattern. At times people don't even know how to articulate the kind of help they really need; they may not have the experience or the background to see a clear path to progress.

Asking the question "How can I help you?" does not mean that leaders should do the team member's work, nor does it mean that the leader steps in and fill the gaps of underperformance. What it does mean is that leaders need to excel at actively listening for subtle cues and are skilled at asking nonconfrontational but revealing questions. Delivering on this responsibility as a coach requires mastering a set of coaching practices, some of which are visible and some of which are quite subtle (see Figure 6.1).

VISIBLE PRACTICES FOR COACHING

The visible practices are the ones that people anticipate, see, and clearly remember. This section enumerates those practices, describes the rationale, and provides some pointers on how to successfully apply the practice.

Figure 6.1

GREAT COACHING EQUATION

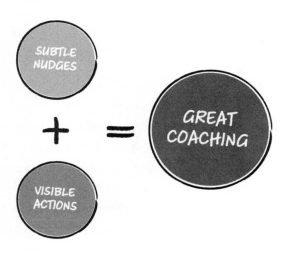

1. **Establish the right coaching rhythm and environment.**
    Coaching represents an investment in another person. So, if
    you ask questions like, "How often should the caring leader
    coach a person?" it's like asking about how often you should
    invest in the stock market. The best advice is to make regu-
    lar contributions on an ongoing basis. One lump sum every
    year, like one big performance review, is not a smart alterna-
    tive. Rather, more routine, smaller investments of time are
    more likely to yield long-term results. Beyond that general
    advice, the specifics depend on the individual and the cir-
    cumstances. For one person, a weekly conversation may be
    needed; for others, monthly conversations may be sufficient.

Importantly, these conversations need to be reliably scheduled and conducted at a frequency that the two parties agree is appropriate. It is much more important to have reliable, high-quality discussions, less frequently, than to commit to something you can't maintain.

2. **Share feedback about patterns you've observed.** Caring leaders excel at observing people's behaviors and detecting underlying patterns that contribute to team members' effectiveness or ineffectiveness. For example, caring leaders detect revealing signs about team dynamics and sensitively listen to team chatter with their mind tuned to questions such as:

   - How are team members working together?
   - Are the team dynamics positive or negative?
   - Are people encountering barriers that hinder progress?

   These are often delicate matters to address. Caring leaders avoid simply sharing a litany of all the things a member is doing wrong. Instead, they might start the coaching session with a statement such as "This is what I am observing; do you see this, too? Or do you see it differently?" Suggestions, encouragement, and potential corrective measures could be entertained at that point. This should not be a one-way counseling session; instead, a conversational spirit should prevail with an objective of cocreating an agreement about a path forward. The primary reason for initiating this kind of discussion is that unraveling patterns is a complicated issue and requires insight from multiple perspectives. Most team members have a thirst for feedback along the way, particularly about team-based behavior. Caring leaders don't avoid these delicate situations; instead, they recognize these as real-time learning opportunities that often represent career inflection points.

3. **Seize spontaneous opportunities to thank, applaud, and praise (TAP).** Sincere compliments and thank-yous for well-completed work are small acts that build a rich relational foundation that will reap long-term benefits. We think of these day-to-day, ten-second moments as small but regular investments in a person's coaching portfolio. And they act like compound interest, accumulating goodwill that extends throughout the team members' career. It's one of the great mysteries of leading that small TAPs can have such a great influence. But as Albert Einstein once said, "Compound interest is the eighth wonder of the world. He who understands it, earns it; he who doesn't, pays it." In sum, TAPs pay off long term.

4. **Be wary of substituting high-tech solutions for thoughtful performance reviews.** Performance reviews represent one of the central tools of great coaches (as long as they are not the ONLY coaching venue). Team members expect these sessions to be motivational and developmental. Ideally people look forward to these reviews as an opportunity to grow.

   Yet, in all too many cases, the three words that come to mind when thinking of performance reviews are *dreadful*, *obligatory*, and *demoralizing*. In many cases, team members hate to receive them, and leaders fear to deliver them—or worse, leaders avoid them altogether. Any discomfort can quickly tumble into distress when dealing with underperformance. Leaders may subconsciously conclude, "I don't like to do it, but I have to," while team members may grumble under their breath, "I don't want to hear it—especially from him." From this vantage point, how can you possibly achieve a positive outcome? This is the exact recipe for a demoralizing dialogue.

What's the remedy? Since many leaders dread conducting performance reviews, the HR and IT professions have jumped to the rescue. If you google "performance reviews," you will quickly find top job-performance software:

- **Culture Amp**—The complete performance solution, including performance reviews, goal tracking, continuous development, and 360 reviews.

- **Performance Pro**—Performance management software that uncomplicates the execution of your current, and future, performance management strategies.

- **ClearCompany**—A simplified, automated workflow to easily set up and analyze performance reviews.

- **Review Snap**—Performance reviews in a snap—easy, fast, and time-saving.

Reviews of these systems are stellar (four and five stars):

- "Technology couldn't be simpler."

- "You even get automated reminders to do your reviews."

- "It even organizes notes, so you don't have to scramble at the last minute."

- "It has an intuitive interface which means minimal training is required."

- "It also offers coaching tips (subtext—is this some kind of AI that does the leader's thinking for them?)."

Who is reviewing these platforms and providing this commentary? There are three possibilities:

Group 1: The leaders who are desperate to get this painstaking job over with

Group 2: The HR team who can now keep everything organized and on track

Group 3: The people receiving this impersonal job-performance feedback

In all likelihood, every positive review came from groups one and two. Team members who crave more thoughtful, face-to-face discussion (i.e., group three) would be sadly disappointed with this tech-heavy approach. They are unlikely to give the system any stars except imaginary ones, as they are knocked out of the technology boxing ring.

In short, technology can be a great friend but can become a foe when used in place of personal touch. These tools may undermine and even sabotage relationships between a leader and a team member. Caring leadership is all about having high-quality discussions with people. Most team members yearn for face-to-face, one-on-one private conversations, with no interruptions or diversions, which focus on their needs and concerns. These technology platforms can be very helpful with documentation, but they can't replace a leader's thoughtful attention.

5. **Document performance and careers.** We have developed a format to document performance discussions and career discussions (see Appendix 1). These revealing questions focus conversations by turning the spotlight on both strengths and areas of improvement to optimize team member performance. Note the lack of numerical ratings. We are not big fans of numerical ratings, because they often direct too much attention to the number rather than to the desired outcomes.

SUBTLE PRACTICES FOR COACHING

Two researchers insightfully noted the power of subtle leadership practices: "Much of our behavior is nonconscious, habitual, and driven by cues in our environment or the way in which choices are presented."[4] People rarely notice the subtle practices of caring leaders because they work best in tandem with the more visible ones. This section profiles those practices, describes the rationale, and provides some pointers on how to successfully implement each practice.

1. **Inspire others by incorporating your reasons for wanting to be a leader into your interactions.** Coaches zealously believe in people. Caring leaders yearn to help others achieve their potential and fulfill their aspirations.

    The famous conductor Leonard Bernstein may have captured this sentiment best in his book *Findings*. The famous passage "This I Believe" underscores how leadership takes patience, persistence, and an understanding that people change at different rates. The joy of seeing others succeed and grow is the ultimate leadership high.

    In your discussions, assure people that your goal is to help them realize their dreams, spur their continuous growth, and fulfill their potential. This is particularly important when sharing how to address problems and correct mistakes. Ironically, enabling others to realize their dreams has a curious, almost mysterious way of transforming and ultimately fulfilling your ambitions, as well.

2. **Think incrementally about people's careers.** One of your authors (Bob) was greatly influenced by the insightful advice of a job recruiter who helped Bob through an early career job loss due to downsizing. The recruiter stressed,

    > As you look for your next job, force yourself to think beyond this next job in increments of five, ten, fifteen, twenty, and twenty-five years. Think of

yourself as having an out-of-body experience, walking down an imaginary career path, through the forest of opportunities, and looking back over each five-year interval. Ask yourself, "What will make you the happiest at each step along the way, as well as at the end of your career? How will you feel the most fulfilled for having invested a lifetime getting there?" Think about the underlying reasons for the things that make you the most fulfilled: Wealth? Position? Influence? Respect? Helping people? Also reflect on what kind of jobs you find the most—and the least—fulfilling.

These questions focused Bob's career visions and enhanced his ability to evaluate opportunities.

Likewise, we can build on these thoughts to help caring leaders coach team members through their career path. Specifically, caring leaders can take the following actions:

- Highlight how one position builds on the next as their team members' experience and knowledge increase.

- Help their team members sell to their strengths to get the next position, while encouraging them to improve on their weaknesses. By doing so, they will be in a more competitive position as career opportunities emerge.

- Advise team members on how to gauge their fit with the job structure of their organization and the challenges it faces. It's possible that their passions may not fit with the organizational needs.

- Urge team members to document their plans. By having something physical to refer to—on paper—it will be easier for them to develop a decision road map and a plan to systematically evaluate their progress.

- Encourage team members to routinely update and revisit their plan (e.g., monthly or quarterly usually works best).

3. **Clarify career aspirations of team members.** Most team members desire to know what the future holds for them and where opportunities exist. Caring leaders help their team ponder the possibilities so they're in a better position to make decisions. Team members may see a myriad of job titles in front of them; walk them through the forest by imagining the scenery at various levels and intervals. You want them to take a drone's-eye view of the forest of career possibilities. Why? You are encouraging the person to move from their day-to-day experiences to a big-picture view.

   Use their criteria to focus on positions and challenges they will deem fulfilling. And suggest that they include family or partner issues in this discussion. By asking the right questions, a leader will help strip away emotions to help them make wiser, more objective decisions.

   Consider these as a starting point:

   - Whose career do you admire? What do you admire about them?

   - If you were a career or lifestyle coach, how would advise someone like yourself?

   - If you had to draw a diagram of your career trajectory, what would it look like?

   In short, assisting others to see what they cannot see for themselves may be one of the most important coaching tasks of any leader.

   After codeveloping this picture of career opportunities, become a matchmaker. Caring leaders consider how the dreams and aspirations of people can be matched with organizational needs. Caring leaders often reach beyond their own areas of responsibility to create potential matches in other parts of an organization. At times, the best match might cause you to lose good people under your direct supervision. The upside? The organization and the individual benefit greatly. At other times, you might lose a team member to opportunities outside the organization. But no worries—caring leaders seek to help others realize their dreams. That's why they deservedly acquire reputations as career matchmakers.

4. **Develop a dynamic coaching menu of discussion items.** Leading with care means taking the time to develop a thoughtful yet flexible coaching agenda for each person under your direct guidance. For instance, a caring leader might seek to enhance someone's time-management skills or improve their abilities to collaborate. Approach these discussions with your own menu of topics to discuss, but encourage team members to have their own lists, as well. Discussions about current work assignments and their related challenges could also be part of this menu.

    To set a developmental tone, consider starting the session with some nondirective questions, such as:

    • How are you doing?

    • What are your challenges? What are your pain points?

    • How can I help you remove barriers?

    As a coach, you need to learn to listen for the stated issues, the unstated problems, as well as the difficult to articulate concerns. A senior partner at the consulting firm Korn Ferry, Alida Al-Saadi, offers this advice:

    > Everybody has concerns, quandaries, and ambitions. Ask thoughtful questions, listen freely, and be

"THIS I BELIEVE," FROM *FINDINGS*

LEONARD BERNSTEIN

I believe in people.

I believe man's noblest endowment is his capacity to change.

Armed with reason, he can see two sides and choose.

He might be wrong. I believe in man's right to be wrong. Out of this right the future is built.

I believe in the potential of people.

We must believe strongly, more strongly than before, in one another.

In our ability to grow and change.

In our ability to communicate.

We must not enslave ourselves to how things once were.

We must believe in the attainability of good.

We must believe in people.

curious. The more invisible you can be as a coach, the more you create an environment that allows you to become aware of patterns, perceptions, paradigms, and assumptions that are driving actions, and ultimately, results.[5]

As you can see in the sample conversation (Table 6.1), skilled coaches avoid taking words strictly at face value. This does not mean the person intends to deceive; perhaps they lack awareness or have a blind spot. When expert coaches hear a comment like, "No problem," they see it as a potential sign that some issues merit further exploration.

Carefully craft any messages that might be viewed as critical or a personal attack. Assume someone had deficient organizational skills that hinder team performance. The caring leader would avoid saying, "You're poor at organizing." Instead, the caring leader might start a series of inquiries designed to address the issue, such as, "Do you think your organizing skills are at their optimal level?" "What would be the impact on your team if organization was improved?" "How do you think we could improve them?" "What can I do to help?" Consistently framing your feedback in this manner builds a continuous improvement mind-set that motivates people to excel. Tone matters, as well. We're all aware of how someone's style of communicating, regardless of the content delivered, can have a dramatic effect.

The expert coach gently prods the engaging conversation toward action plans that can be reviewed in subsequent coaching meetings. These coaching sessions are akin to continuous cycles of improvement (see Figure 6.2). Lean practitioners call this the Plan-Do-Check-Act (PDCA) cycle for continuous improvement and problem-solving.[6]

Table 6.1

NOVICE VS. SKILLED COACHING

NOVICE COACH

Coach: *What problems are you having on the job?*

Team Member: Nothing, really. All is going well. Well … (interrupted by coach)

Coach: *Great. Are you sure?*

Team Member: Everything is great. Love what I'm doing. No problems at all.

Coach: *Super. I was just checking in*

SKILLED COACH

Coach: *What problems are you having on the job?*

Team Member: Nothing really. All is going well.

Coach: *Great. I see…*

Team Member: Everything is great. Love what I'm doing. No problems at all.

Coach: *Well, do you think you're sufficiently challenged?*

Team Member: What do you mean? I'm really good at what I'm doing.

Coach: *Fair enough. But I'm curious, do you feel like you're growing and achieving your potential?*

Team Member: Well, that's a slightly different question. I could use some new challenges.

Coach: *Hmmm… tell me more about what you had in mind…*

ANALYSIS

Notice that the coach takes the team member's first statement at face value. The coach almost half-heartedly asks for detail, but nothing surfaces.

Notice that the coach does not take the team member's first statement at face value. The coach treats it as a potential red flag and directly probes about growth and challenges. Then, the coach uses more nondirective queries to elicit further information and continue the dialogue.

Figure 6.2

PLAN-DO-CHECK-ACT OVER TIME

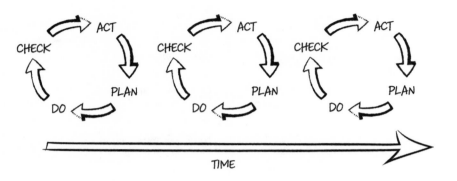

5. **Craft and assign meaningful job titles.** While some people feel that job titles don't matter, we take a different stance: we believe that titles are important because they foster a strong sense of personal satisfaction and identity. Team members should take pride in their role and the implicit responsibilities of the title. When caring leaders approach title creation, title selection, and title granting from this angle, they subtly inspire engagement.

    Typically, you begin with a framework of standard titles, but don't let that standard list hold you back. Before his untimely death, the founder and CEO of Zappos, Tony Hsieh, made it a practice to develop wacky but evocative and engaging job titles. He invented the title, zookeeper for his new director of Zappos University, where the company trained associates on their cultural values.[7] You may not have "zookeeper" in your repertoire of job titles, but you can break established norms to boost engagement and pride in positions.

Caring leaders think about the job title from the standpoint of others, by considering questions such as, "How does the title make people feel about their responsibilities?" "How does it compare to their peers' titles?" "What will it signal to those on the outside? Family? Friends?" Caring leaders are sensitive to these dynamics and relationships, so they appropriately describe levels of responsibility, without causing job-to-job inequality. Likewise, for those team members in positions that have a more public face, care must be given to craft titles that position them respectably in their markets and with their professional peers. The benefit: it serves to enhance their effectiveness. Caring leaders consider these dynamics in their decision-making.

6. **Strategically shift between directive and nondirective queries to guide coaching sessions in a meaningful direction.** The subtle art of questioning may well be the top secret tool of inspiring coaches. There are two basic types of queries: directive and nondirective (see Table 6.2). These are the fork and spoon of the coaching conversation, serving up different dimensions of an illuminating feast of possibilities.

   Coaches use directive queries, like the fork, to dig into specific areas of concern. These include follow-up questions, such as, "Did you ever think about…" "How have others reacted to…" or "Can you give me an example?" Directive inquiries seek to elicit more specific information or hint at different perspectives.

   Expert coaches use nondirective questions, like the spoon, to scoop up hidden issues that might not surface with more directive queries. Nondirective questioners assume the team member's perspective should drive the conversation as the coach nudges the discussion forward in a productive direction. Neutral phrases like "I see…" or "Hmm…" might

Table 6.2

DIRECTIVE VS. NONDIRECTIVE QUERIES

	NONDIRECTIVE	DIRECTIVE
Purpose	Encourage team members to continue talking and revealing their thoughts	Allow the coach to ask for clarification or provide further direction
Rationale	The coach encourages team members to plot their own path forward or continue talking to reveal underlying issues	The coach wants to offer perspective or seek more specific information
Examples	• "I see …" • "Tell me more" • "Could you elaborate?" • "Would you like to add something else?"	• "Have you thought about …?" • "Could you give me an example?" • "I'm not understanding. It appears that two issues conflict. Can you clarify?"

be all it takes. Comments like, "Tell me more..." "Could you elaborate?" or "I don't think I understand; can you explain further?" also fall in the nondirective category. All these expressions are designed to keep the team member talking as the coach scans for relevant and actionable notions. By asking these types of questions, other issues may emerge that the questioner never even though about.

What's the proper mix of directive and nondirective queries? How does a coach know when to shift between them? Getting the mix right requires experience, but here are some general guidelines:

- Avoid always using the "fork," or directive questions. This might suggest that you are too focused on your own coaching agenda.

- Avoid always using the "spoon," or nondirective queries. This might imply that you are letting the team solve their own problems and not offering other perspectives that should be part of the calculation.

- Calibrate the mix based on the team member's preferences and stage of development. Some people take pride in solving their own problems and mapping out their own journey. In this case, more subtle, nondirective nudges would tend to work best, punctuated with a few timely, directive inquiries such as, "Did ever think about..." Other people, particularly those in the early stage of their career, need more direction to enhance their perspective. In those cases, flip the toggle switch toward the directive questions.

THE TOUGH SIDE OF COACHING

As you read this chapter, you might be sensing that these practices represent a "soft" approach to dealing with performance. It's fair to say this coaching style embodies respect, compassion, and understanding of team members' circumstances. It requires patience to allow people the opportunity to show what they can do and how they will improve.

Staying true to the ideals of respect and employee growth does not equate with tolerating sustained poor performance or breaches of integrity. So, the question becomes, when is it time to part company? Here are three specific conditions:

- If a team member does not embrace and live the values—A breach of the organizational values not only undermines the team member's career, it also imperils the organization. Tolerating these breaches signals acceptance that cannot be allowed.

- If after patient, continuous coaching, the team member is unable to step up.

- If you observe that the team member has simply given up on any attempt to improve.

- If the leader consistently works harder at achieving improvement than the team member.

Sometimes caring leaders conclude that moving a member to a different assignment will give more opportunities for improvement. In some cases, we endorse that approach. But be cautious: we don't want to move an inevitable problem somewhere else or delay a hard decision.

Remember: high performers carefully scrutinize the decisions you make about performance. Members will never really appreciate the depth of circumstances surrounding another team member's performance. And they shouldn't; after all, those circumstances are private matters. But they will notice and be impacted by poor performers, and most often they will react in a less patient way than the leader does. Hanging on too long to poor performers erodes morale. The caring leader communicates clearly about the framework for employee decisions regarding values and performance while giving people every chance to succeed.

Caring leaders too often reflect on employment decisions with comments such as, "I waited too long," or "I tried too hard." That's a natural reaction of being a caring leader. In your authors' careers, we have saved more people than we've lost, and we are proud of that record. The ones we lost are more because they failed themselves or they didn't live appropriate values. The leader's litmus test? Can you look in the mirror every day and say, "I did the best I could"? Or, as the former German chancellor Angela Merkel replied when asked about how she wanted history to remember her, "She tried."[8]

CONCLUSION

Nelson Mandela once remarked, "There is no passion to be found playing small, in settling for life that is less than the one you are capable of living." Caring leaders echo these sentiments, infusing others with this passion through skillful coaching. This spirit requires practice, practice, and more practice. At first, this may be an uncomfortable exercise, but sweet satisfaction magically materializes as you mature into proficiency. It boils down to having high-quality, one-on-one discussions with people. For caring leaders, the enjoyment comes from helping others live the lives they are capable of living.

End of Chapter 6

COACHING SELF-ASSESSMENT

These questions are designed to provide developmental insights to enhance your effectiveness. Rate yourself, choosing either Improvement Needed, Solid, or Excels.

SELF-REFLECTION QUESTIONS

	Improvement Needed	Solid	Excels
1. I work with team members to develop actionable plans as a result of my coaching.	○	○	○
2. I help my team members think about their career aspirations 5, 10, 15, and 20 years out.	○	○	○
3. I routinely show appreciation and give praise for the work people do.	○	○	○
4. I am careful and sensitive in awarding people the job titles they hold.	○	○	○
5. I meet with team members at the appropriate frequency to coach and mentor.	○	○	○
6. I conduct routine performance reviews; I prepare them on my own, using technology tools only as an assist and not relying on them to do the job for me.	○	○	○
7. I take the time to understand career path opportunities available to people in my organization and use that knowledge in my career-building discussions.	○	○	○
8. In my planning, I think about the balance between the resource needs of the organization and the career aspirations of my team members.	○	○	○

The most beautiful fate, the most wonderful good fortune, is to be paid for doing that which you passionately love to do.

—ABRAHAM MASLOW

CHAPTER 7
CARING LEADERS INSPIRE PASSIONATE, HIGH-PERFORMING CLIMATES

Managers, leaders, educators, and coaches often surround themselves with the latest leadership books and articles. Leadership and management fads come and go. At one time, scientific management, which focused on improving efficiency, was the rage. Over the years, this movement was replaced by participative management, which shifted focus to employee input, motivations, and needs. Then the thinking swung back to issues of efficiency and quality with the quality movement, which emphasized elimination of waste and error. All these historical movements have served a useful purpose by focusing leaders on key issues of the day while adding to our understanding of great leadership practices.[1]

Most scholars and thought leaders distinguish between management and leadership. We agree. However, we've seen how movements like scientific management and all the others tend to greatly influence a leader's style and decisions. Yet, we can learn a great deal by comparing one movement to another. One of the historic lessons is that many popular and highly touted leadership approaches emphasize one leadership dimension at the expense of another dimension. Thought leaders and practitioners soon recognize the issue and related concerns. Then the correction turns to another movement, usually in the counterdirection.

Consider this relatively recent example: the drive toward data-driven management exploded with technology-enabled "big data" analysis. This approach yielded sophisticated tracking of performance by the numbers and key performance indicators (KPIs). Yet, a recent *Harvard Business Review* article entitled "Stop Overengineering People Management" challenged this approach. The author argued that this kind of "optimization" disempowers employees because the systems and processes undermine a leader's connection with people, snuffing out the spirit that will cause people to be the best they can be.[2]

At the core of the historical swings is how to properly balance a leader's performance expectations and employee aspirations. Simultaneously engaging on both dimensions dodges the whipsaw-like swings between programs emphasizing performance management and those promoting team engagement.

THE PASSIONATE PERFORMANCE DEVELOPMENT GRID

The Passionate Performance Development Grid (PPDG) suggests a way that caring leaders can develop a high-performing, passionate working climate. The core assumption is that developing an inspiring working climate often requires adjustments by both leaders and team members. Caring leaders aim to match their leadership approach with team members' need for direction.

The horizontal axis of the grid describes the employee's need for guidance and direction on a continuum from high to low (see Figure 7.1).

Figure 7.1

PASSIONATE PERFORMANCE DEVELOPMENT GRID

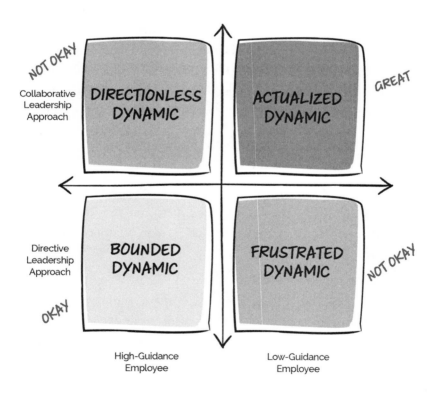

- **High-guidance employees** rely on clear, direct, unequivocal, and explicit expectations that are often tied to tangible rewards like pay or promotion. Sometimes the implicit bargain takes the form of "If you perform at this level or do this task, then you'll receive this particular reward" (cash, incentive pay, etc.).

- **Low-guidance employees** need little direction or oversight. These team members' professional experiences and expertise may well provide all the guidance necessary. Often these team members derive their motivation from the intrinsic nature of what they do because it's meaningful to them. They still want to know the expectations, but they are willing to go beyond to satisfy their own inner instincts or values. The operative principle for low-guidance employees is "Give me the general direction and the freedom to do things I find personally or professionally motivating, and I might surprise you with the results, ideas, and innovations."

The vertical axis designates the leader's style on a continuum from directive to collaborative:

- **Directive leaders** proclaim explicit directives with well-defined expectations, deadlines, and results. There is little room for deviance or skillful equivocation about expected outcomes.

- **Collaborative leaders** share expectations but dialogue with employees to further shape them while providing a mutually agreed-upon framework for the employee. In some instances, collaborative leaders provide minimal direction, which at times leads to challenges. In short, the collaborative leader trusts the employee to deliver results and perhaps dazzle with some unexpected innovation.

The Passionate Performance Development Grid combines both dimensions, which, in turn, suggests four basic leader-employee dynamics:

- **Bounded dynamic** (directive leadership with high guidance employee)—The leader clearly outlines expectations, accountabilities, and deliverables. The employee understands them and seeks to meet them because they are often tied to some external incentives, like pay. This represents a match between the leadership approach and employee need. It may well represent a place to start with new employees or a seasoned employee given a new assignment. The key word in the previous sentence is "start," because it represents the bounded nature of expected results. It is not ideal as a sustainable dynamic. Instead, over time, caring leaders avoid restricting team members to the boundaries of explicit expectations.

- **Directionless dynamic** (collaborative leadership with high-guidance employee)—Employees who need more explicit directives often find the collaborative style challenging because they seek more guidance to perform tasks. Frankly, you couldn't concoct a better recipe for disaster in the workplace, because both the leader and the employee will be disappointed in the outcomes. However, in some cases employees take advantage of a leader with a collaborative style who is basically hands-off. In this case, the employee might be quite happy, but the team or organization suffers from lack of direction.

- **Frustrated dynamic** (directive leadership with low-guidance employee)—Employees who need little guidance but receive too much direction will often become frustrated with what they perceive as artificial constraints. Many will feel stifled and disengaged and may seek other employment.

- **Actualized dynamic** (collaborative leadership with low-guidance employee)—This represents a match between the employee's sentiments and the leader's approach. Collaboration works well with low-guidance employees, because they are always looking to go beyond expectations and wow everyone.[3] These employees, like NBA star Stephen Curry, thrive on self-motivation. As the NBA's best shooter, Curry still wasn't satisfied, so he started practicing with a downsized basketball hoop in a quest to hit "swishes within swishes."[4] We designate this as the optimal zone, because it's the sweet spot where employees maximize their engagement and performance.[5] It's exactly the spot where caring leaders want their entire team to operate.

We've labeled this quadrant "actualized" as a nod to Maslow's notion that most people seek to be self-actualized and to achieve their highest potential. Caring leaders create the conditions for people to go beyond the boundaries of explicit expectations to innovate beyond the preconceptions of either the leader or employee. This approach allows employees to discover their true potential as they make progress by exploring and refining.

So, the obvious question emerges: How do caring leaders craft organizational environments with actualizing dynamics? Once again, it comes down to the skillful use of subtle and visible practices.

SUBTLE PRACTICES FOR HIGH PERFORMANCE

Subtle—and often "invisible"—practices are those that, at times, the leader engages in before any interactions with team members.

1. **Determine if your team members require more or less guidance.** Caring leaders ask their team members questions such

as these to determine how much assistance and direction they need:

- What are your thoughts about this assignment?

- What ideas come to mind about how to proceed?

- How much background do you need to get started?

- What kinds of skills and expertise would someone need to properly execute this assignment?

- How will you judge your effectiveness at the end of the assignment?

By listening to the answers to these questions, caring leaders extract insights about the amount of guidance team members need. The questions also assist leaders in calibrating the level of detail, structure, and assistance employees need to successfully carry out assignments.

Ideally, for employees with minimal guidance needs, leaders would suggest general frameworks and provide minimal direction. They would occasionally check in but generally get out of their way, which allows these employees to thrive. In contrast, for employees who need more guidance, leaders would provide more structure, specific task outlines, and coaching to keep people on track.

2. **Pinpoint the quadrant where key employees are positioned on the Passionate Performance Development Grid.** Assess where you lie on the grid regarding your own leadership style with each team member. The best practice is to write the names of key employees in the appropriate quadrant.

Properly locating team members positions on the PPDG involves answering two questions:

- Is the team member in need of more explicit direction or less specific direction? That will determine the location on the horizontal axis.

- In your leadership role with that person, is your style more directive or collaborative? That will determine the location on the vertical axis.

By placing the names on PPDG, you can start to envision a path forward.

3. **Develop a plan to properly position your employees on the Passionate Performance Development Grid.** Caring leaders recognize the dysfunctionality of operating in the directionless and frustrated zones, and the less-than-optimal position of operating in the bounded zone. So, how do caring leaders attain the goal of moving team members to the actualized zone? Caring leaders flexibly choose their approach along the axis of development, depending on the circumstances (see Figure 7.2). They adjust their position depending on the needs of individual people and issues involved. Sometimes caring leaders are directive; at other times they move to the optimal collaborative style. The leader's first move depends on the starting point (A, B, D, or F).

Frustrated dynamic: Recall that employees in this zone require less direction, but they receive too much guidance from more directive leaders. They feel overmanaged. The leader will need to become less directive and more collaborative, moving from point F (frustrated zone) to point A (actualized zone).

Directionless dynamic: Team members in this zone require more structured tasks and expectations, yet they are working with a leader with a collaborative approach. The team members do not respond well to collaboration, because they may not know how to collaborate or are new to the position. The caring leader may be uncomfortable or lack the

Figure 7.2

AXIS OF DEVELOPMENT

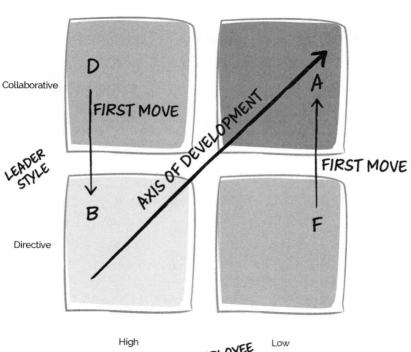

skill to specify explicit direction and guidance for the team member. After all, these leaders have laudable motivations in fostering collaborative relationships. In this case, collaboration is the right skill, but it's the wrong time to use it. The objective remains the same—moving the employee to the actualized zone—but it requires a more indirect path.

In the directionless zone, the leader should provide more direction to satisfy the needs of the employee, moving to the bounded quadrant. After a period of time, the leader then coaches the employee about how to function with less direction, building on the employee's successes from projects or volunteer work where the employee was more self-directed. The leader would then establish a more collaborative working environment. In other words, the moves would be from point D (directionless zone) to point B (bounded zone) to point A (actualized zone).

You might ask, "Why should leaders use a two-step approach rather than directly coaching the employee to the actualized zone?" In our experience, employees have a tough time making that jump, and they need to build their confidence with more direction first. This confidence acts as a springboard to move the employee to the actualized zone.

Bounded dynamic: Employees in this zone require guidance and are working with a leader who has a more directive style. Leaders provide direction and detail to satisfy the employee's appetite for guidance. This approach works, but it's not optimal. So, the leader coaches the employee about how to function with less direction, building on successes from the employee's past experiences. This allows the leader to establish a more collaborative, less structured working environment, moving from point B (bounded zone) to point A (actualized zone).

Actualized zone: In this zone, caring leaders use a more collaborative, bottom-up style with these employees who are internally motivated to continuously improve. Almost magically, ideas and results appear as leaders and employees self-actualize, unleashing their true synergistic potential.

4. **Recognize that an employee's motivation remains relatively stable but may shift for particular tasks.** In general, some employees tend to want less guidance and seek to tackle most issues on their own. They prefer to learn how to master the task through experience or self-selected educational opportunities. Likewise, other people tend to want more guidance and explicit direction on most issues. They prefer more explicit directions with specific training guidelines about how to perform a task. The key word in the sentences above is "most." Why? Because low-guidance employees, from time to time, desire explicit directions on a new task or a particular kind of task. Likewise, high-guidance employees may have areas where they are motivated by their own exploratory tendencies; consequently, they don't want to be told what to do in these situations. Caring leaders sense these dynamics and adjust their style accordingly.

5. **Give people some latitude or "running-around room."** Plans are important, schedules are important, and goals are important. Leaders are faced with achieving outcomes and results. Yet, team members work at different paces and learn at different speeds. Some are methodical; others work in bursts of energy. Consequently, most employees crave the latitude to structure their work to fit their personal style and abilities. Caring leaders

❝

Let yourself be silently drawn by the strange pull of what you really love. It will not lead you astray. —RUMI

recognize this desire and allow as much flexibility as possible while still keeping efforts focused on the necessary results.[6] Giving people running-around room allows them to show what they are capable of doing, which generates pride and confidence in their accomplishments.

VISIBLE PRACTICES FOR HIGH PERFORMANCE

The subtle practices above set the stage for these more visible practices.

1. **Use engaging language.** As we've pointed out many times, words matter.[7] This is especially true as leaders talk about performance issues. So much of the advice today focuses on words such as *locking in expectations* and *holding people accountable*. In the media, when something goes wrong, almost the first words spoken involve holding someone accountable. Fair enough. Certainly, people who fail to meet their responsibilities or engage in malicious acts need to be held to account. However, these tough performance cases rarely emerge from a lack of good intentions. More often, it's a convergence of poor leadership and poor coaching.

   To get to the next level of performance, words need to engage the spirit of people (see Table 7.1). We've discovered that the words *setting expectations* and *holding people accountable* may unintentionally project a sense of detachment rather than involvement. The words in Column One tend to externalize accountabilities and allow little room for adjustment. On the other hand, the suggested language increases the odds of engaging and motivating employees, particularly for internally motivated employees. Why? Because the messaging suggests a sense of flexibility to shape contributions.

Table 7.1

ENGAGING LANGUAGE CHOICES

AVOID THESE WORDS	INSTEAD, USE THESE
• Here are my precise expectations.	• Let's jointly agree on the desired outcomes.
• I'm going to hold you accountable for these deliverables.	• How can we build reasonable check-points into the process?
• Use these specific steps to get results.	• Consider this frame-work as you move forward with the initiative.

2. **Partner with your team to untangle complexities and discover the most value-adding initiatives.** Complexity increases exponentially as leaders experience new demands from all directions. Sometimes people find the burden overwhelming. Leaders soon learn the most fundamental leadership law of all: the universe of potential initiatives far exceeds the number of tasks or projects you're able to manage and advance. Caring leaders work with people to collectively untangle these complexities with an eye on the core challenges that must be mastered. This helps team members stay focused on the mission.

    With this approach, the leader avoids dictating priorities. Instead, caring leaders partner with team members on a select few high-value issues or initiatives. By collectively deciding what matters and what doesn't matter, caring leaders build an architecture of accomplishment for employees and the organization. Cooperatively piecing together various initiatives and responsibilities ensures that the most value-adding initiatives and tasks are accomplished.

3. **Allow as much customization of the work environment as is feasible.** Rigid, standardized workplaces, where every workstation, office, and uniform look the same, may be necessary in certain cases but are not optimal in most cases. Allowing employees to personalize their environment signals that leaders want them to own the space and optimize it for their personal productivity. And this goes beyond just posting personal pictures in a workspace; in the post-COVID world, allowing workers more flexibility in scheduling remote versus in-office work may be the most viable option. After all, McKinsey's research shows that 20 to 25 percent of the workforce can efficiently and effectively work from home three to five days a week. In fact, over 50 percent of office workers say they'd leave their present position for a job offering more flexibility.[8] The former CEO of PepsiCo Indra Nooyi notes in her autobiography:

> Early in my career, my lack of work flexibility—and the feeling that I could never simply schedule my time in a way that made sense for me—were among the most stressful aspects of my life.[9]

No wonder she supports work flexibility as the norm.

In recent years, pro sports teams have loosened uniformity requirements on player jerseys. Of course, for obvious reasons, sports franchises can't allow players to pick their uniform colors or logos. But allowing them to select from a menu of approved social messages to display on their jerseys may well help many players feel more actualized.

By moving from the most physical of careers to the most cerebral, we can see other examples of this strategy. Consider chess grandmasters who often must sit for upward of six hours a day. To them, the most important customized accommodation comes in the form of selecting the perfect chair. Standard-issue, library-like chairs won't do for these cerebral warriors. They want the edge on their opponents. Some prefer rolling chairs, some rigid-back supporting chairs, and others more comfy seats. It turns out that there is no such thing as the perfect chair for all grandmasters.[10] If they are to achieve their highest potential, allowing this kind of flexibility makes perfect sense. So, caring leaders treat their employees like grandmasters.

4. **Praise and reward unanticipated accomplishments and innovations.** In the short term, praising an employee for meeting stated expectations makes sense. But, in the long term, it creates a bounded performance dynamic, because employees will not seek to exceed expectations and innovate beyond clearly articulated guidelines. That's why caring leaders primarily praise and reward employees for unanticipated accomplishments and innovations. They look for spontaneous opportunities to reward unexpected excellence. It could be something as simple as saying, "I never thought about approaching this problem in this manner. Thank you. Let me take you for a coffee to celebrate." Or it could be an on-the-spot monetary bonus outside the normal compensation-incentive cycle. By rewarding accomplishments like this, caring leaders not only recognize employees, they also reinforce the actualized working dynamic.

5. **Develop meeting protocols that continually remind employees about the value of accomplishments in the actualized zone.** One executive decided that he was unintentionally

signaling to his employees a more rigid, "meet the stated expectation" type of mind-set. He wanted an actualized working dynamic, so he tried a subtle but noticeable shift in his key meetings.

For every meeting, he built in time on the agenda for what he called the "FCT" discussion items (See Figure 7.3). He wanted each team member to have the opportunity to share something they: a) Flagged for improvement, b) Celebrated for accomplishing, and c) Tried for the first time.

He realized that prior to this new protocol, most meetings focused on reporting results and flagged concerns. By adding "celebrated it," he legitimized soft bragging that motivated his high-performing teams. (Note that the "flagged it" piece keeps humility on the table.) By adding "tried it," he encouraged innovative, out-of-the-formal-expectation-box thinking.

Figure 7.3

ACTUALIZED ZONE MEETING PROTOCOL TOPICS

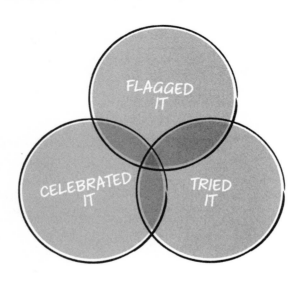

THE TOUGH SIDE OF THE PPDG

Leaders strive to build collaborative relationships with employees. They hope that all members of their team embrace the joys of working in the actualized zone and surprise everyone with results and innovations. But that's not real life.

So, here's the really tough question for caring leaders: Should they tolerate people who continually need specific performance objectives and directions? In some cases, and for some jobs, it might be acceptable; in other cases, it might not be. As Steve Jobs famously said, "It doesn't make sense to hire smart people and tell them what to do; we hire smart people so they can tell us what to do." So, what happens if you hired someone in a senior position requiring this Steve Jobs kind of ethos, but the person frequently seeks more explicit guidance and direction? Sadly, both of your authors have been in positions where we have reluctantly concluded that we needed to part ways or move them to another position. That's the tough side of the Passionate Performance Development Grid.

CONCLUSION

How well a team or organization performs depends on the match between the leader's approach and team members' fundamental need for direction.[11] Mismatches between a leader's style (directive or collaborative) and team member needs for guidance (low or high) usually produce disappointing results.[12] If the leader's approach and employees' need for guidance sync in the bounded zone, then the team or organization could very well deliver good results. Yet, if they sync in the actualized zone, then the team will deliver sustainable, long-term, high-level performance.[13] And perhaps, more importantly, this is the zone where everyone—leader and team members—excels to their potential.

End of Chapter 7

HIGH PERFORMANCE SELF-ASSESSMENT

These questions are designed to provide developmental insights to enhance your effectiveness. Rate yourself, choosing either Improvement Needed, Solid, or Excels.

SELF-REFLECTION QUESTIONS

	IMPROVEMENT NEEDED	SOLID	EXCELS
1. I quickly determine if I'm working with someone who needs more or less guidance.	○	○	○
2. I can locate all my key employees on the PPDG.	○	○	○
3. I can easily switch from a directive to collaborative approach as needed.	○	○	○
4. I give people as much running room as possible.	○	○	○
5. I tend to use engaging language.	○	○	○
6. I encourage people to personalize their work environment as much as possible.	○	○	○
7. I focus my praise on unanticipated accomplishments and innovations.	○	○	○
8. I've adjusted my meeting protocols to celebrate team member accomplishments.	○	○	○
9. I can cut my losses with employees when necessary.	○	○	○
10. On a daily basis, I seek to develop a passionate, high-performing work climate.	○	○	○

The art of communication is the language of leadership.

—JAMES HUMES

CHAPTER 8
CARING LEADERS ROBUSTLY COMMUNICATE ABOUT THE THINGS THAT MATTER

Leaders can communicate about almost anything, but they cannot communicate about everything. Of course, some naive leaders try to communicate about everything. Some even espouse a seemingly provocative mantra—"Communicate, communicate, communicate!" Regardless of a leader's laudable intentions, the results are predictable: employees feel directionless, important changes go unsupported, organizational values become meaningless, and a sense of malaise prevails. Fortunately, there is an alternative approach for leaders, outlined next, which yields much more positive reactions.

ROBUST COMMUNICATION FRAMEWORK

Caring leaders recognize that they need to make wise communication choices and not fall into the "communicate, communicate, communicate" trap. They don't try to communicate about everything. Instead, they focus on robustly communicating about the things that matter. This strategic practice obliges caring leaders to answer three difficult and related questions:

- What are the things that matter?
- How do I robustly communicate?
- How do I know when I've successfully communicated?

Figure 8.1 outlines the dimensions of the answers to these questions.

Figure 8.1

ROBUST COMMUNICATION FRAMEWORK

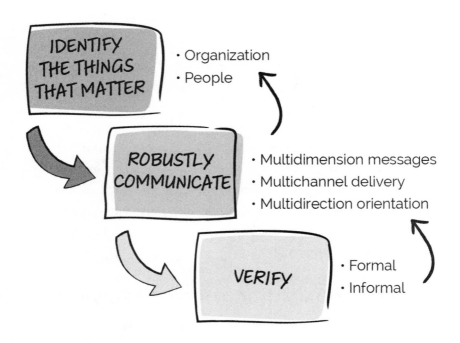

The Things That Matter

Since almost anything might matter, it's important to know how to winnow down the limitless possibilities. Caring leaders grapple with the "things that matter" question by thinking about two big buckets of potential issues: a) things that matter to the team or organization, and b) things that to matter to the individuals on the team or in the organization.

Bucket one issues would involve those necessary for the growth, improvement, and survival of the team or organization. If there was some universal definitive list of these issues that applied across all organizations, then we would happily share it. Unfortunately, no such credible list actually exists. The reason? Organizations and teams face a myriad of different issues. What a tech company needs to thrive in a fast-paced, changing world differs from what a university finds necessary to survive.

So, how might caring leaders discover the things that matter to their organizations? Some organizations go through elaborate strategic planning processes to answer this question. Fair enough. But strategic planning does not need to be an onerous task, because the fundamental questions are rather straightforward:

- What short-term pressures and opportunities do we face?

- What long-term pressures and opportunities do we face?

- What should be our priorities moving forward?

The same basic questions apply for teams within any organization. Note that the questions directly address several critical issues we discussed in the first section of the book. Bucket one, "things that matter," is about defining progress while embracing uncertainty. For example, cultural values provide guidance during times of uncertainty and new initiatives outline how the organization will make progress. Without that perspective, leaders get caught up communicating about everything. The bottom line: caring leaders answer bucket-one issues by pondering the future of their team or organization. While we cannot provide a definitive list of potential issues in the first bucket, we can suggest some potential issues gleaned from our research that might spur your thinking (see Table 8.1).

Table 8.1

THINGS THAT MIGHT MATTER

THINGS THAT MIGHT MATTER TO THE ORGANIZATION (BUCKET 1)	THINGS THAT MIGHT MATTER TO EMPLOYEES (BUCKET 2)
· Cultural values	· Major changes
· New initiatives	· Recognition
· Performance on benchmarks	· Appreciation
· Talent retention	· Career development
· Job satisfaction	· Job flexibility
· Competitor positioning	· Job security
· Future direction	· Compensation
· Product/service quality	· Personnel changes
	· Fit with the organization's future direction

Bucket-two issues often represent a more difficult challenge. To understand what truly matters to employees, leaders must overcome several obstacles.

First, while some people can candidly and directly identify what matters to them, others find it difficult. It's not that they are inarticulate, it's that they may be too close to the situation or use overly abstract language in describing what matters to them. For example, when employees say, "We need more communication," they often put leaders in a bind, because it's difficult to discern their underlying sentiments. We've discovered this may actually mean, "show me more respect," "listen to my input," or "provide more definitive direction." Caring leaders adeptly discern these underlying sentiments through proper questioning and listening.

Second, employees may self-censor because of a working climate riddled with political correctness that stifles discordant views. These employees often fear social pressures to conform with prevailing political sentiments or vocal opinion leaders' views on any number of issues. Caring leaders are particularly attuned to these issues. They recognize that failing to detect salient, shared sentiments—even by a minority of employees— enhances the likelihood of absenteeism and turnover, while fostering lower levels of engagement.

Third, discerning underlying patterns from various sources of employee sentiments may befuddle even the supplest of minds. Consider a leader who was preparing to deliver an important State of the Company year-end review. On her desk are: 1) the results from the company's latest engagement surveys from various departments, 2) a year-end report on employees who voluntarily left the company, and 3) several studies from high-profile consulting firms about nationwide trends on employee satisfaction. How does she integrate all this information into three or four themes that will resonate with most employees? And it's not just about what matters now; it's also about what will matter in the future. Such are the challenges of what to put into bucket two.

Robustly Communicate

Caring leaders recognize that the things that matter should be vigorously communicated. So, how exactly do you do that? This does not mean getting a bigger megaphone to shout louder than everybody else. Instead, there's a better, more enduring, and more profound way by using three basic tools: multidimension messaging, multichannel delivery, and multidirection orientation.

Multidimension Messaging

This messaging means that leaders fully communicate about the things that matter from different angles to enrich understanding and support. For example, leaders explaining a major organizational change (bucket one) would want to discuss the shift by addressing all the questions in Table 8.2. Too often leaders highlight the most significant features of the change while only broadcasting on the WIFO (What's in It For the Organization) wavelength. This leaves out several other questions and is likely to result in less employee support. For instance, if leaders in this situation fail to broadcast on the WIFM (What's in It For Me) frequency, employees will speculate on what it means for them, and rumors will swirl. In fact, our research reveals that when leaders communicate on major organizational changes and their messages contain all seven dimensions, they can nearly double the amount of support and buy-in, even if the change does not directly benefit employees.[1] While these questions may not apply to all issues, they provide a starting point to think about the necessary message dimensions.

Multichannel Delivery

Multichannel delivery occurs when leaders use a combination of communication tools and vehicles. For example, using an email

Table 8.2

DECISION DOWNLOADING QUESTIONS

- How was the decision made?

- What is the decision?

- Why was the decision made?

- What alternatives were rejected?

- How does the decision sync with the organization's mission, vision, and values?

- How does the decision affect the organization? (WIFO - What's In it for the Organization?)

- How does the decision affect employees? (WIFM - What's in it for Me?)

and a single team meeting to communicate can reinforce core messaging for less controversial things that matter. That's the bare minimum, though. Other, more complex, and controversial TTMs (Things That Matter) will require a colorful palette of tools including social media posts, websites, presentations, town hall–style meetings, emails, and home mailings.

Using multiple tools or channels works for several reasons.[2] First, certain tools tend to emphasize specific aspects of the message. A leader's tweet, for example, reminds people about an important issue, while the formal presentation about the same issue can fill in the details around the TTM. Second, some people are more attuned to different channels than others. Some people prefer oral presentations and never even read written documents, while others are precisely the opposite. Third, the redundancy between the channels reinforces the importance of the messages and dramatically demonstrates these issues really are the things that matter.

Multidirection Orientation

This orientation refers to the leader's desire to engage in two-way dialogue and conversations about the things that matter. One-way communication from leader to follower about things that matter rarely resonates for very long. Caring leaders might kick-start the communication cycle with an opening speech, a presentation of some type, or a written announcement (one way). To be clear, there is always a place for one-way communication via a speech or a written announcement. But caring leaders never stop there, because they want others to be part of the ongoing dialogue.

Why? Because two-way dialogue can quickly clarify misunderstandings or quell unsettled feelings. For example, in the post-COVID world, many employees are seeking jobs with greater flexibility, such as work-from-home options. Two-way communication through one-on-one interviews or Q&A sessions in meetings might reveal unexpected issues. For example, does the lack of physical employee presence in the workplace subtly undermine their career prospects? In fact, some research indicates that many supervisors equate high visibility with high performance. The visibility metric won't work very well for those working from home. Two-way communication provides leaders and employees an opportunity to address this often-hidden issue. In addition, two-way discussions tend to enhance support, if for no other reason than people feel that someone respects their opinions.

Verify

Checking all the robust communication boxes is not necessarily the recipe for success. After all, talented chefs may carefully measure out all the ingredients and faithfully follow the recipe, but they still do a taste test before serving. In the same way, caring leaders verify that the ingredients in their robust communications produce the desired outcome. They do so because they know that often the message sent does not equal message received—even robustly communicated ones.

Multidimension messaging, multichannel delivery, and a multidirection orientation significantly boost the odds of success. But a disconnect might occur for any number of reasons, such as:

Trust deficit—When trust wanes, the likelihood of communication success quickly fades. The credibility assigned to the source of any message influences the degree of receptivity. If your trusted physician recommends an over-the-counter drug for treating an illness, then you'll probably take it; if your friendly mechanic down the street makes exactly the same recommendation, you are less likely to do so. One person we trust with our health, another with our car. So, credibility and trust are intimately linked to particular areas of expertise. Caring leaders need to verify that they are considered trustworthy communicators.

Intervening events and opinion leaders—Gifted communicators are often surprised by how their message becomes garbled over time.[3] An intervening event or new opinion leader might emerge that shifts understanding or changes opinions. For example, after new employees are onboarded, they will be exposed to other, seasoned organizational opinion leaders who may undermine the training about core organizational values. Therefore, caring leaders check to see if their messaging endures over time or if employees might need a booster shot.

Preconceptions—Sometimes a leader's messages rub up against someone's firmly held beliefs. If someone has a strongly held religious belief against certain types of medical care, then it doesn't really matter how skillfully leaders communicate. Those preexisting, entrenched views tend to be quite resistant to change. Caring leaders want to discover if they are inadvertently bumping into some deeply entrenched dogmas.

Regardless of why the communication process might go awry, caring leaders make sure to verify the degree of success. They may need to enrich trust, enlist the help of opinion leaders, or confront misinformation. And they may even determine that preexisting dogmas stand in the way.

Caring leaders guide their thinking about communication by using a tool such as the robust communication framework. Of course, correctly thinking about the communication process cannot guarantee excellent results. That requires using some of the following visible and subtle practices.

VISIBLE PRACTICES FOR ROBUST COMMUNICATION

How leaders communicate may be their most visible leadership activity. So, they devote time to fine-tuning and perfecting their skills and practices, such as the following:

1. **Identify your single most important message and spotlight it in at least two modes (e.g.,** oral, written, image, video, graphic). Leaders should ask themselves a simple question—"What is the one headline I want my audience to

walk away with?" This headline will be considered your core message about the most important thing that matters. Then think of two compelling ways to illustrate your headline. For instance, during the height of the COVID pandemic, one executive of a grocery chain highlighted the message "six feet apart but closer than ever" both in written and graphic communications. This message cleverly blended bucket one and two issues by headlining two essential messages related to employees' and customers' physical and mental health.

The redundancy between the modes builds robustness into communications in a number of ways. First, redundancy reinforces the importance of the issue, increasing the likelihood of captivating listeners or readers. Second, redundancy increases the odds that people will pay attention to your key message. Different people have different ways they like to learn; some prefer oral, others visual, and still others written. If you use different modes, then you will increase the likelihood of tapping into almost everyone's preferred learning model. Third, redundancy helps leaders crystallize, enrich, and tweak their most important messages. The very process of trying to signal a similar message in different modes prods leaders to think about their messaging from different points of view.

Consider a leader who wanted to highlight that her company was experiencing an unacceptable number of customer complaints (i.e., core message: complaints are too high). In a group meeting, she first reviewed the statistics about the rise in consumer complaints using a bar chart. Second, she showed a video of a consumer complaining to an employee about poor service. Then she empathized with the employee, who had nothing to do with the service disruption but who had to field the complaint. She used the bar chart and the video (i.e., two modes) to set in motion several policy changes designed to address this problem.

2. **Enhance your public speaking skills by focusing your planning on core messages.** Leaders need to be able to speak in front of small and large groups. They use the spoken word to share messages, their plans, and their visions. You can find any number of good books and personal coaches on the subject.[4] Many people who struggle in this role focus their energy on delivery skills. But leaders don't need to be eloquent speech makers, they just need to be comfortable in this role. The nature of the content is far more important. That should be the leader's primary concern, and it reemphasizes step one in the robust communication framework—find out what matters. After all, President Ronald Reagan was often labeled the "great communicator," but his attention was more directed at the messaging than the delivery, as he noted in his farewell address[5]:

> And in all that time (my Presidency) I won a nickname—"The Great Communicator." But I never thought it was my style or the words I used as a great communicator that made a difference—it was the content. I wasn't a great communicator, but I communicated great things, and they didn't spring full bloom from my brow, they came from the heart of a great nation—from our experience, our wisdom, and our belief in the principles that have guided us for two centuries.[6]

3. **Improve your writing style by consulting others.** Leaders also need good writing skills that clearly articulate direction, inspire others, and outline the contours of their thinking on the things that matter. They should master a simple and un-

derstandable writing style that most people can easily relate to. Fortunately, leaders can enlist the help of others in this process by asking for their advice. Sometimes, just asking another person to review a document or memo before publication can save leaders a lot a grief. Other people often pick up subtle miscues in tone or ideas that need clarification.

Caring leaders master written communication because they realize that some people respond better to the written word than the spoken word. A written follow-up to a great presentation should be a part of any robust communication plan.

4. **Become a great storyteller.** People remember and relate to stories in ways that statistics or great arguments will never rival. Humans seem to be hardwired to respond both emotionally and rationally to a good story.[7] That's why caring leaders master this art.

Robert McKee, the best-selling author of the book *Story: Substance, Structure, Style, and the Principles of Screenwriting* suggests starting your storytelling thought process by asking three important questions:

- What's the inciting incident? (i.e., what event provoked the conflict, dilemma, or crisis?)
- What's the crisis?
- What's the resolution?

Answers to these questions provide the structure for the story. Leaders are not trying to create a compelling Netflix detective series, but they should use those three questions to begin crafting simple, relatable stories about things that matter. In fact, Peggy Noonan used a similar approach when writing many of Reagan's speeches.[8] See the sidebar for one of your authors' (Bob) story about how his experience with

McKee reshaped the branding for the company Bob led, supercharging its growth.

Here's a specific challenge to consider: Could you craft a three-sentence story that answers McKee's three questions? Forcing yourself to do so goes a long way toward headlining your core message and mastering this ancient art.

5. **Update people frequently.** No one expects the local weather person to be 100 percent accurate, but most people still pay attention, particularly when storms loom. Why? Because meteorologists are constantly shaping and reshaping expectations based on the latest information. That's exactly what caring leaders do as clouds of uncertainty approach. They de-emphasize precise predictions while emphasizing probable outcomes. This kind of information sharing cultivates adaptable thinking in others by encouraging them to consider different scenarios and plans of action; they might just pop their rain jacket in the car in the event that the 30 percent chance of rain materializes.

   Highlighting what you know and what you don't know builds your personal credibility and promotes attentiveness to future updates. Underscoring both sides of the known-unknown ledger highlights your realistic and sober view of the situation while preserving future flexibility. Leaders who adopt this approach orient their teams' energies, which allows them to pivot as circumstances change rather than quibbling about precise predictions. Just as we discussed in Section One of the book, frequent updates help others make progress amid uncertainty.

6. **Develop and use tools to seek feedback.** Leaders will need tools to figure out their level of communication success and identify any barriers to understanding. Thoughtful leaders have at their disposal two major types of tools to verify:

HOW ROBERT MCKEE EDUCATES

Before my first meeting with Robert McKee, I knew he was an Emmy Award–winning playwright and best-selling author of the book *Story: Substance, Structure, Style, and the Principles of Screenwriting*.[9] I was impressed that the director of *The Hobbit* and the *Lord of the Rings* trilogy, Peter Jackson, called him the "guru of gurus." I felt well prepared for a discussion about how to better sell our company. In fact, I was quite proud of my colorful deck of PowerPoint slides, and I wanted to show him how we present our company to prospective customers. He thoughtfully made marks here and there in the deck of slides and remained respectful throughout my presentation. Yet, I felt him growing more agitated and frustrated as I worked my way through the deck. I was becoming increasingly anxious and, frankly, a little frightened. At the end, he calmly closed the deck, looked at me with his penetrating blue eyes and said, "Bob—this is all BS! It's all rhetoric! Would you please set this aside and tell me a story?" So, I did. In a flash, my PhD in storytelling commenced!

- Informal tools allow leaders to make reasonable inferences about their success level. For instance, leaders who routinely advocate the importance of some core values might observe the spontaneous behaviors of key employees. Are they living by the values? Are they routinely invoking the values during key decision-making processes?

- Formal tools like surveys or focus groups can be used to measure communication effectiveness.[10] Even a basic, numerically rated question such as "I'm satisfied with communication from the leadership team" (scaling from strongly agree to strongly disagree) or an open question such as "How would you improve leadership communication?" can prove illuminating.

SUBTLE PRACTICES FOR ROBUST COMMUNICATION

Most leadership handbooks place a heavy emphasis on the visible part of the communication process. That's okay, but subtle practices, such as the following suggestions, often prove even more significant.

1. **Elevate other leadership voices.** Caring leaders recognize that a team of like-minded people almost always trumps the single-hero leadership model. Utilizing the expertise of influential people to advocate core messaging sends powerful signals. The voices of other opinion leaders amplify the core messaging through their personal networks of influence.

    Enlisting the support and voices of others requires a sensitivity to team member passions. For example, many employees might be quietly clamoring for more work flexibility (a bucket-two issue). Simultaneously, the organization could be facing a typical post-COVID issue of how to retain quality employees (a bucket-one issue). Mixing these two things-that-matter buckets makes perfect sense. Enlisting key opinion leaders' support for work flexibility should, in turn, help with the retention issue. Savvy leaders recognize these unique opportunities and build synergistic support.

2. **Maximize disclosure and minimize delay.** It's easy to talk about good news, but when there's bad news, the natural human reaction might be to hide it, sugarcoat it, or spin it to make it more palatable. Sugarcoating, like candy, satisfies for the short term, but then the doubts creep in, which leads to an inevitable crash in trust. In contrast, leaders who share the bad news as quickly as possible will be applauded for their open and transparent approach.

    Sharing any news, but particularly bad news, often creates a sense of uncertainty. People want a sense of control at these times. Some leaders, often unwittingly, imply that the future is completely chaotic, random, and cannot be influenced. Cultivating debilitating uncertainty breeds hopelessness in people and deprives leaders of opportunities to influence events that they can manage. Demonstrating what people can do now provides a degree of personal confidence—they don't feel as much like a victim. Publicizing highly visible, active measures that the organization is currently taking provides a sense of stability.

    While leaders cannot promise specific outcomes during unsettling times—even though many people crave them—they need to offer hope through resiliency: "Our people are the most resilient, innovative people in the world." Suggesting steps or phases for working through the uncertainty provides the necessary sense of forward movement. By repetitively and redundantly sharing your why and how messages, you build stability that helps your team face the potential chaos spawned by the uncertainty.

Whether the news is good or bad, report it in an honest, balanced, and unemotional way. Express your opinions and preferences as you help people fully comprehend the situation but avoid a sales-pitch demeanor. Leaders can acknowledge an alternative way of thinking about the issue while suggesting their preferred way of moving forward. Still, you want to leave some room for people to draw their own conclusions. In our experience, people usually end up supporting the path forward that the leader is recommending.

3. **Seek feedback and acknowledge contrary views.** Feedback helps leaders understand what matters to employees. Through feedback, leaders can also gauge support for initiatives and verify that core messages have been received. The insight and information gleaned from robust feedback helps leaders further shape proposals and develop new perspectives. Acknowledging and discussing dissenting views improves buy-in and allows leaders to clarify the inevitable misperceptions that permeate any organization. Providing everyone a voice and the opportunity to influence others enhances respect for leaders. Why? It demonstrates a desire to continuously learn from others and improve the organization. Even if a disagreement emerges, most people will respect the differences and move on. The feeling of being heard goes a long way toward cultivating mutual understanding, if not necessarily agreement.

    During times of uncertainty, people have a lot of questions. In fact, many questions emerge from anxiety rather than from some fundamental concern. Holding in-person sessions during times of major changes provides the leader a rich opportunity to attentively listen and patiently respond to those questions. It dampens anxieties while framing people's concerns as challenges to be resolved. And, writing down the questions on a whiteboard de-personalizes and de-emotionalizes the issues and encourages mutual problem-solving. Cultivating this open atmosphere of inquiry and resolution may be one of the most important skills of caring leaders.

4. **Gently steer discussions and deliberations.** Caring leaders have a knack for sparking the right kind of discussions about the things that matter. They invite commentary, foster participation, and make it comfortable and safe to contribute. Spirited discussions, not presentations, dominate decision-making processes. If formal presentations are necessary, the purpose should be to catalyze discussion and feedback. Caring leaders sense the direction of these discussions and use their intuition to ask unifying questions, such as, "It seems like all of this is leading to..." These suggestive questions gently nudge everyone toward common thinking.

   Every leader knows about the "meeting after the meeting," where team members hash out what really happened during the meeting. Often consensus or conflict emerges outside the formal meetings. Caring leaders influence these conversations in a number of ways. One way they do so is to ensure that their core messages are consistently and repetitively delivered, organizing them in ways that help the audience understand how everything fits together. As issues emerge in secondary conversations and private deliberations, caring leaders respond to those concerns by synthesizing the sentiments into their subsequent communications.

5. **Ponder the role of social media in your leadership position.** Some leaders routinely use social media, particularly Twitter, while others avoid it altogether. Caring leaders prudently contemplate the role and cost/benefit of social media. The comedian Dave Chappelle has been pilloried on social

media for some of his routines. His response to the woke mobsters is illuminating: "A lot of people got mad at me and dragged me on Twitter. I don't give a f*** because Twitter's not a real place."[11]

His pushback highlights an underlying social dynamic of these platforms, namely that some people use the platform to virtue signal and express outrage. This is not a "real place" (even though it might feel real), because there are few personal risks or costs of joining a Twitter mob. Jonathan Rauch of the Brookings Institution put it this way: social media "metrics and algorithms and optimization tools [are] sensitive to popularity but indifferent to truth."[12] Chappelle's experiences and the Brookings Institution's analysis should prompt leaders to carefully contemplate how they intend to use social media.

Your authors are not anti–social media; after all, one of us wrote a book about social media strategy.[13] Rather, we are encouraging leaders to carefully weigh the costs and potential benefits. And, if you do decide that a social media presence makes sense, then carefully outline your expectations and set content guidelines.

6. Listen in both active and passive modes. A leader's speech might well make national headlines, but you are unlikely to see any mention of a leader's stellar listening skills. This oddly understandable imbalance between speaking and listening skills permeates most of the leadership buzz. It's odd, because great communication is as much about listening as it is about speaking. It's understandable, though, because speeches are highly visible and good listening is far more subtle. Caring leaders rectify the one-sidedness of the communication equation and seek to become exceptional listeners.

They learn to master two types of listening: active and passive.

- **Active listening** occurs when leaders make a deliberate effort to ask questions and take careful note of the responses. Employee surveys, as mentioned above, can be particularly helpful in finding out what things matter (stage one of the robust communication framework) or in verifying the success of communication efforts (stage three). Using open-ended questions such as "What three words best capture the current mood in the department?" can be revealing about underlying sentiments. Similar open-ended queries can be used in one-on-one coaching sessions (e.g., "What issues keep you up at night?").

- **Passive listening** allows the other person to speak without interruption. This is hard to do because of the natural temptation to respond by either debating or "helping." Regardless of motive, leaders need to know when to stop talking and just listen. Debate has its place, but it can be stifling when people struggle to articulate feelings, impressions, or new ideas. As Stephen Covey noted long ago, "Most people don't listen with the intent to understand, they listen with the intent to reply."[14] So, when the speaking stops, most people gear up to express their opinion or rebuttal. Doing so usually shuts down further dialogue and dampens understanding.

Even if you can resist the urge to debate, another noble temptation often emerges—the desire to help others. Madelyn Burley-Allen, in her book *Listening, the Forgotten Skill*, put it this way:

> When I ask you to listen to me and you start giving me advice, you have not done what I asked.

> When I ask you to listen to me and you begin to tell me "why" I shouldn't feel that way, you are trampling on my feelings.

When I ask you to listen to me and you feel you have to do something to solve my problems, you have failed me, strange as that may seem.[15]

"Listening to help" may well marginalize other people's anxieties, concerns, and impressions. Oddly, listening to help may not be terribly supportive. Instead, caring leaders want to hear about these uncensored sentiments because they value what matters to others. And sometimes the best way to show you care is to simply listen and say nothing.

TOUGH CHALLENGES OF ROBUST COMMUNICATION

Communication challenges permeate organizations. The three-step framework fortifies leaders to excel despite these inherent complications. Instead of seeking to suppress pushback, the robust communication framework fuels understanding, ownership, and buy-in. Still, the issue of pushback looms in the background; that's why we devote the next chapter to mastering this particular communication dynamic.

CONCLUSION

Musically inclined leaders would be well served by including Kelly Clarkson's "Hear Me," Buddy Holly's "Listen to Me," or Trisha Yearwood's "That Ain't the Way I Heard It" in their playlists. Tracks like these remind listeners across musical genres about the delicate daily challenges of effective communication. Caring leaders use the three-step framework to position themselves to not just "communicate, communicate, communicate" about everything, but to genuinely, thoughtfully, and profoundly communicate about the things that really matter.

End of Chapter 8

ROBUST COMMUNICATION SELF-ASSESSMENT

These questions are designed to provide developmental insights to enhance your effectiveness. Rate yourself, choosing either Improvement Needed, Solid, or Excels.

SELF-REFLECTION QUESTIONS

	IMPROVEMENT NEEDED	SOLID	EXCELS
1. In public presentations, I focus on my core message.	○	○	○
2. I routinely ask others to review my important written communications.	○	○	○
3. I take personal responsibility for communicating proactively to my leadership circle.	○	○	○
4. I follow the golden rule of maximum disclosure with minimum delay in my communications approach.	○	○	○
5. I represent facts and circumstances honestly and without spin.	○	○	○
6. I appropriately use active and passive listening skills.	○	○	○
7. I seek feedback and proactively harvest opposing points of view.	○	○	○
8. I am a good storyteller.	○	○	○
9. In group settings, I nudge conversations in a productive direction.	○	○	○

*The aim of argument, or of a discussion,
should not be victory but progress.*

—KARL POPPER

CHAPTER 9

CARING LEADERS TRANSFORM PUSHBACK INTO PROGRESS

When the US Federal Communications Commission was considering changes in internet regulations, they solicited input from citizens.[1] They received over twenty-two million comments; that should be good news. In theory, soliciting feedback before launching any initiative could accomplish a number of things, such as: a) aborting an ill-conceived plan, b) thwarting unanticipated consequences, b) unearthing useful tweaks to a policy, and d) ultimately building collective support during implementation.

But, in practice, soliciting and managing pushback proves far more challenging. In this case, investigations revealed that over eighteen million of the comments were fraudulently generated by lobbying firms paid to represent one side or the other in the ongoing debate. In essence, legitimate voices were drowned out by the illegitimate ones.

This extreme example of pushback gone awry can be instructive, because it raises fundamental questions any caring leader contemplates:

- How do I know if the pushback is genuine?
- What can I do to incentivize people to offer useful feedback and pushback?
- How can I transform pushback into progress?

Before we attempt to answer these questions, we first need some clarity on the meaning of pushback.

WHAT IS PUSHBACK?

Airline passengers grow accustomed to hearing the pilot announce, "We are waiting for our pushback from the gate." In this case, *pushback* represents "forcing or moving an object backward." Lexicographers tell us that the word is also used to describe people who "voice concerns" or offer "resistance or opposition" to policies or initiatives. Caring leaders think of pushback in both senses of the word. Yes, pushback represents "concerns, resistance, or opposition." Yet, pushback might be necessary to get an initiative "out of the gate" and to "take flight." And sometimes pushback undermines progress making. In short, caring leaders think of pushback on a continuum from constructive concern sharing to destructive resistance.

Caring leaders cultivate an environment of constructive pushback designed to help everyone continuously learn while demonstrating the power of resiliency, humility, and honesty (see Chapter Three).

A variety of intertwined issues make this a challenging task. Employees have a range of pushback options, some leading in a constructive direction (e.g., listen and adjust, seek compromise, collaborate on a path forward); others in a destructive direction (e.g., feigning collaboration, resisting behind the scenes).

Caring leaders use a variety of visible and subtle strategies to encourage others to voice their pushback in a more positive direction (see Figure 9.1). Yet before we delve into the strategies, we need to understand the complex dynamics of candidly speaking up to any leader.

Figure 9.1

EMPLOYEE PUSHBACK OPTIONS

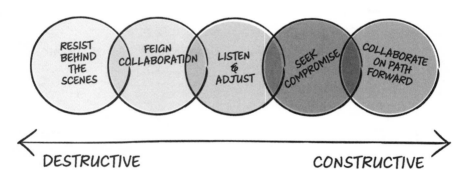

DESTRUCTIVE   CONSTRUCTIVE

PUSHBACK DYNAMICS GRID

Before employees speak up honestly and candidly, they typically make an unspoken analysis of the costs and benefits of doing so. Their calculations are based on four intertwined questions:

1. How strongly do I feel about the issue under discussion?

2. What are the likely outcomes of voicing my opinion or sharing my perspective?

3. How strongly do I believe my superior(s) feels about the issue?

4. How will my superior respond to pushback?

The strength of team members' opinions influences their willingness to share their views (question one). At the very least, the intensity of their opinion modifies how vociferously they advocate for a position. The mental calculus rarely stops there, though. Most people also implicitly calculate the consequences of voicing their concerns or input (question two). Some people self-censor because they sense the futility of sharing their perspectives. Others self-censor out of fear.[2] For example, many people avoid politically sensitive topics for fear of being canceled. So, political correctness prevails.

On the flip slide, most employees also calculate their pushback response by also reflecting on how their leaders feel about the issue (question three). The related issue of how superiors will likely respond to the pushback (question four) also enters into most employees' mental calculus. The answers to these related questions influence employees' willingness to share perspectives and how vocally they express them. We're all familiar with the proverbial yes men, who mirror everything their leaders propose—regardless of value. Thankfully, most people avoid thoughtlessly acquiescing, like bobble heads of affirmation. Still, many people adjust their approach depending on the strength of the leader's position on the issues and the likely consequences of adding their voice to the dialogue.

Pairing the two perspectives implied by these four questions places in sharp focus the pushback dynamics inherent in any discussion between parties with differing organizational positions. Power differentials influence all communications in one way or another, but particularly when discussing contentious issues or potentially prickly ones.

The Pushback Dynamics Grid highlights the pivotal underlying forces that pervade interactions between employees (questions one and two) and a person in a leadership position (questions three and four). The vertical axis represents the intensity of a leader's view regarding the issue (strong to weak). The horizontal axis represents the intensity of an employee's view on the issue (strong to weak). The resulting Pushback Dynamics Grid underscores four unique communication circumstances (see Figure 9.2):

Figure 9.2

PUSHBACK DYNAMICS GRID

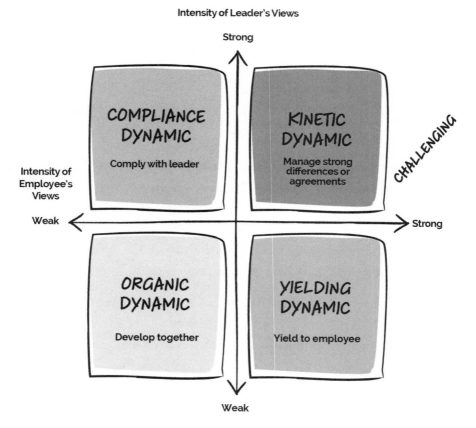

Kinetic dynamic: This is the quadrant where both parties have strong views on the issue. One possibility is that they both agree on the issue. A more contentious situation occurs when both parties have differing views on the issue. Either way, high kinetic energy of the leader and employee either pushes the initiative forward with great verve or provokes a spirited debate. Managed properly, it can spark creative collaboration or, at least, compromise. Managed improperly, it can ignite smoldering resentments that might roar out of control.

Yielding dynamic: The employee has strong opinions about the issue, but the person in the power position does not. The situational dynamics often result in yielding to the employee sentiments.

Compliance dynamic: The person in the position of authority has strong opinions about the issue, but the employee does not. The situational dynamics often result in compliance with the leader's wishes. Of course, employees can push back in unproductive ways, such as expressing opposition behind the scenes.

Organic dynamic: Neither the person in leadership nor the employee feels strongly about the issue. This situation might occur during the initial phases of decision-making, when the stakes are low for all parties. As people wrestle with the issue, the back-and-forth can be the optimal environment for collaborative solutions.

Each situation yields different expectations and tensions (see Table 9.1). For example, open dialogue with a lot of give-and-take might work well in the organic zone. Yet open dialogue may be much tougher in the kinetic zone. Participants may self-censor to a greater degree because they fear reactions from others who are in a power position. Or tensions may escalate because people can be more vociferous and easily offended when they have entrenched positions.[3]

Table 9.1

COSTS AND BENEFITS OF PUSHBACK

	EXPLANATION	POTENTIAL UPSIDE *Team may...*	POTENTIAL DOWNSIDE *Team may...*
Kinetic Dynamic	Both parties have strong preferences	• Discover novel solutions • Develop deeper understanding	• Self-censor • Offer faux support • Resist in inappropriate ways
Yielding Dynamic	Leader has weak preferences, but the employee has strong preferences	• Make quicker decisions • Empower employees • Drive decision making down the hierarchy	• Fail to look at different perspectives • Offer faux buy-in • Show tepid support
Compliance Dynamic	Employee has weak preferences, but the leader has strong preferences	• Make quicker decisions	• Fail to look at different perspectives • Offer faux buy-in • Foster fragile commitment
Organic Dynamic	Neither party has strong preferences	• Cultivate novel insights • Allow consensus to emerge • Resist poor decision-making processes	• Minimize the level of discussion • Lower the priority of the issue • Miss opportunities

Bottom line: how an employee views the situation (i.e., which quadrant on the grid) has a powerful influence on perceptions of the risks and rewards of open and candid communication. This, in turn, shapes employee a) perceptions of their leaders' motivations for discussing the pushback and b) projections about the likely outcomes of a conversation. Caring leaders orchestrate these dynamics in a progress-making direction by using the subtle and visible strategies discussed below.

SUBTLE PRACTICES FOR TRANSFORMING PUSHBACK INTO PROGRESS

Orchestra conductors shape their audience's musical experiences with their whirling batons, but they also use less visible cues, through facial expressions and body movements that many audience members never see. These subtle practices connect conductors to their orchestras in powerful ways that often go unappreciated. Likewise, skilled leaders use a variety of subtle strategies to connect with employees to create exceptional results.

1. **Sense employee perceptions of the pushback dynamics associated with specific issues.** In his intriguingly titled book *How to Read Water: Clues and Patterns from Puddles to the Sea*, Tristan Gooley, a celebrated navigator and explorer, wrote, "The study of water signs does not lend itself perfectly to an impatient checkbox approach."[4] Likewise, sensing where people or teams fall on the Pushback Dynamics Grid cannot be relegated to a series of discrete, visible signs. Rather, caring leaders discern how people might be viewing the power dynamic patterns, just as pioneers read animal patterns in their search to locate fresh water sources.

   Leaders, of course, usually know how strongly they feel about the issue at hand. That calculation seemingly takes care of one dimension of the grid. But it really doesn't. Why not? It's the employee's perception of the leader's opinion that really counts. For example, employees might wrongly assume that the leader has a particularly strong opinion on an issue and decide not to share their own counterviews because they consider it a futile gesture. That's where sensing the underlying currents of sentiment can prove as revealing as detecting signs of an impending thunderstorm.

Sensing these dynamics requires observation, insight, and testing. Insights emerge from the experience and knowledge of people in the room. Caring leaders learn to discern, for example, whether a question rippling through a discussion signals a pebble tossed into the conversational waters or a permanent obstacle. Sometimes the only way to discern the answer is to test it out with a pointed question designed to determine underlying sentiments (e.g., "This is what I'm sensing; is that correct or incorrect?").

2. **Be wary of too much silence.** The brilliant, taciturn philosopher Ludwig Wittgenstein remarked in his famous *Tractatus*, "The limits of my language mean the limits of my world." This much-debated axiom suggests that those who self-censor and remain silent are limiting their world and, frankly, the worldviews of others whom they might influence. Viable options may never be contemplated by the person or the team that remains silent on key issues of potential disagreement.

   Consider a dean at a Midwestern university who held regular monthly meetings with his twenty department heads. He believed these meetings were enormously effective because "everyone had a chance to voice their concerns." He failed to detect that three people—one of whom was his wife—dominated the discussion. He also failed to detect a bright-red flag: that silence by the others in the room was a sign that the compliance dynamic was in play and useful input was not being sought.

Although the pushback was not voiced in the meeting, it did occur. And it was destructive in nature because it was voiced behind the scenes and accompanied by feigned collaboration (see Figure 9.1). As one professor privately noted, "The dean was too unskilled to know how to solve certain problems and too arrogant to honestly ask for help." Perhaps her assessment was overly harsh. Or maybe the dean never noticed the silent red flags and didn't know how to solicit more constructive pushback to build consensus. Regardless, the lesson is simple: often, silence is golden, but sometimes it's poison.

3. **Provide different venues to share pushback and feedback.** Some people are reluctant to verbalize insights or concerns in open meetings. They may well prefer to express their thoughts in writing or in a private conversation with the leader. Introverts, for example, prefer to thoroughly think through their remarks before responding. An environment dominated by extroverts can be isolating for those who have introvert tendencies. Caring leaders recognize this possibility and create multiple pathways to share constructive pushback during their decision-making process, rollout of new initiatives, and a host of other activities.

    One team's typical approach to problem-solving was to verbally share concerns in meetings. An executive on the team noticed that certain members remained silent. At that point, he encouraged everyone to write down their concerns and forward them to him after the meeting. The executive then used that input to craft an agenda for a follow-up, face-to-face meeting when the team discussed the broader array of issues that surfaced. This simple, subtle gesture ensured that the voices of both introverts and extroverts were heard.

4. **Write down concerns on paper or a whiteboard.** Writing down pushback almost magically creates an organic, collaborative dynamic, even when the issues are highly contentious. Why? A written record signals a willingness to entertain the idea and moves the inherent power dynamics to the background. A written concern, no matter how crazy or poorly expressed, legitimizes employee input while de-emotionalizing and depersonalizing the issue. This, in turn, allows the pushback to be dispassionately analyzed and resolved.

5. **Shift communication strategies as dictated by the conversational flow.** A caring leader's approach should shift depending on the nature of the employee pushback. For example, if an employee offers an objection to a proposal that has been thoroughly debated and resolved, then the leader might opt to inquire and persuade further. On the other hand, if that same employee offers a new perspective on another issue, then the leader might seek to collaborate on this new proposal.

   Some people might perceive these shifts in strategy as wishy-washy leadership, because they seek a one-size-fits-all approach to managing feedback. At the core of the misperception is that employees lack a clear understanding of the rules of the pushback conversation. They may feel trapped in a conversational cul-de-sac that stalls progress. Few organizations have thoughtfully reviewed the rules of engagement, such as:

   Rule 1: As issues emerge, allow people to shift opinion, without loss of face.

   Rule 2: Seek to understand viewpoints you don't agree with.

   Rule 3: Depersonalize issues or perspectives (e.g., say "Plan A," not "Chuck's plan")

These rules preserve the fluid and dynamic nature of pushback conversations, thereby ensuring that all ideas, initiatives, and perspectives can be thoroughly and rigorously scrutinized.

VISIBLE PRACTICES FOR TRANSFORMING PUSHBACK INTO PROGRESS

Coupling the subtle strategies with more visible ones enhances the probability that progress-making initiatives will lift off while the ones not fit for flight are grounded.

1. **Encourage respectful pushback even to your own arguments.** This encourages open debate and flexible, collaborative decision-making. It signals that the best idea wins, not the idea associated with the highest-ranked individual. Simple statements can be enormously liberating to others in the room. Consider comments such as, "Tell me where this idea might be wrong" or "I'm not sure I thought through all the angles on this issue. Does anyone want to provide a different perspective?" Remarks like these free up the team to think critically about all the ideas and perspectives on the table.[5] Perhaps more importantly, it signals the power of humility, tolerance, and embracing uncertainty, as we discussed in Part One of the book.[6] In short, to update a popular political slogan, leaders need to learn that to collaborate better, they must often "back down better."

2. **Clarify the possible outcomes of any input or pushback discussion.** Employees use a variety of cues, situational assessments, and past experiences to calculate the likely outcome of any discussion. These personal and usually private calculations influence employees' willingness

Avoid having your ego so close to your position that when your position falls, your ego goes with it. —COLIN POWELL

to speak up or shut up. If, for example, a supervisor mar-ginalizes every counterargument the employee offers, then the employee may well conclude that all such dis-cussions represent a fait accompli or done deal. Even if employees trust that leaders are sincerely seeking input, a pattern of thwarted past attempts at tweaking a proposal might be enough to dissuade them from offering candid feedback. In essence, they deem that any proposal, ini-tiative, or decision advocated by the leader will simply move ahead as planned regardless of pushback, much like a government mandate.

Clarifying and legitimizing a range of possible out-comes sets the proper employee expectations (see Figure 9.3). The proposal may well move ahead as planned, with a few tweaks. At the other end of the continuum, the right kind of pushback might result in abandoning the idea altogether. In between these extremes are delaying implementation, mod-ifying the proposal, and rethinking the decision. Ideally, the entire range of options would be considered as reasonable and viable outcomes of any feedback discussion.

3. **Plainly state your motivations.** Unwarranted assumptions about the leader's intent for soliciting feedback may under-mine any genuine goodwill.[7] For example, one frustrated senior-level employee confessed, "Why would the most se-nior executive in the room solicit feedback about issues he feels so strongly about? Why wouldn't he simply exercise his legitimate authority?" Employees with these kinds of legit-imate questions might believe leaders are merely feigning collaboration or trying to temper resistance.

    After all, few people couple their feedback requests with a revelation about their underlying motives. That is, you are un-likely to hear, "I'm soliciting your feedback so I can debate you and tell you that you are wrong" (temper resistance) or "I'm

Figure 9.3

RANGE OF PUSHBACK OUTCOMES

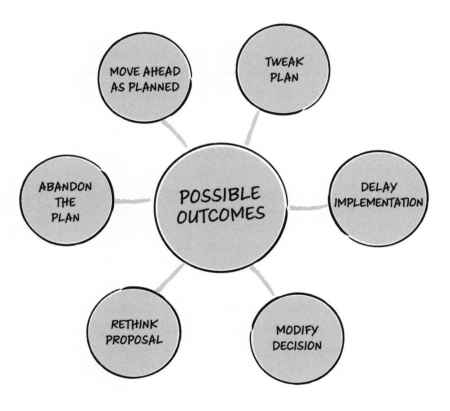

soliciting your feedback to make you feel better, but nothing you say is going to change my opinion" (feign collaboration). When anyone solicits feedback, the other person's response is moderated by the perceived—but not necessarily actual— reasons for the query. Caring leaders address this underlying and often unstated question by proactively and forthrightly spotlighting their rationale for seeking feedback.

An employee cannot reasonably expect a leader to change opinions, seek a compromise, or even collaborate on every decision. However, employees could reasonably expect that anyone soliciting feedback has honest motives. Specifically, both parties enter into the dialogue with the entire range of options on the table (e.g., "move ahead as planned" to "abandon the idea"), even if they hold strong opinions about the issue (see Figure 9.3).

Employee expectations should be based on the likely motives of the person requesting feedback, not on the likely outcomes of the discussion. Fair-minded leaders avoid soliciting input for manipulative purposes. For example, they would not pretend to collaborate or use feedback to identify "troublemakers." These gray-zone motives undermine candor and honesty throughout the organization.

4. **Clearly signal when a decision has been made, will be made, or will be reevaluated.** Theoretically, pushback and feedback discussions could go on endlessly, like some ever-evolving philosophical debate about the meaning of life. Of course, at some point everyone realizes that we will never have answers to all of life's big questions. The clock ticks. We have to make choices, because no choice may be the worse choice.

———————————— **"** ————————————

You can't always be pushing people away. Someday nobody (will) come back. —JACQUELINE WOODSON

Endless debate can paralyze people and their organizations. Deciding on that point—where more discussion is counterproductive—is a matter of judgment, based primarily on indications that all relevant issues have been discussed. Redundant arguments with nuanced changes in language often signal it's time to move on. So, caring leaders clearly signal when that point has been reached with a statement like, "Unless someone has another issue that brings us closer to resolution, let's move forward with this decision." Statements like this communicate that all viewpoints have been duly considered and further discussion may not be productive. In short, effective leaders marinate new ideas in respectful debate until they have reached the right saturation point to implement.

5. **Thank everybody for providing input, even if it wasn't fully accepted.** One core challenge of managing the pushback conversation is that employees who end up losing the debate may feel that the motives for seeking their feedback lie at the dubious end of the continuum. While that may not be fair, it is a potentially unconscious calculation. That's why all parties in a pushback conversation about contentious issues should expect—and be satisfied with—a result like, "We understand each other's concerns, but we agree to disagree."

TOUGH PUSHBACK CHALLENGES

The most challenging time for caring leaders occurs in the kinetic zone. Even after using all the strategies previously discussed, the tensions may be great and emotions raw. Reassure those involved that your motives for seeking feedback are genuine (e.g., inquire and persuade, listen and learn, seek compromise, or collaborate on new path). Acknowledge that the process of transforming pushback into progress is always messy but is worth the angst, energy, and effort.

Caring leaders assume a big-picture perspective on all push-back—winning or losing on a particular issue is secondary to making sure the best ideas prevail. Ultimately, caring leaders act as a catalyst for good decision-making.

CONCLUSION

Kate Johnson, former president of Microsoft US, was once asked about the single best piece of advice she had ever received. Her reply was revealing, as she shared a humorous but inspirational Brené Brown quip:

> "Don't try to win over the haters, you're not a jackass whisperer." While it's important to listen to all feedback signals and keep an open mind, we can't waste time and energy on converting those who are defined by negative energy.[8]

She put her finger on the core dilemma of listening to pushback. On the one hand, you don't want to waste time on vociferous complainers; on the other hand, you want to find the nuggets of insight that move the organization forward. That's exactly what caring leaders do.

End of Chapter 9

TRANSFORMING PUSHBACK SELF-ASSESSMENT

These questions are designed to provide developmental insights to enhance your effectiveness. Rate yourself, choosing either Improvement Needed, Solid, or Excels.

SELF-REFLECTION QUESTIONS

	IMPROVEMENT NEEDED	SOLID	EXCELS
1. I recognize how power dynamics may shift levels of candor.	○	○	○
2. I actively seek out pushback.	○	○	○
3. I clarify my motivations for seeking feedback on initiatives.	○	○	○
4. I can shift my communication approach as new issues emerge in discussions.	○	○	○
5. I try to depersonalize issues under discussion.	○	○	○
6. I provide different venues for people to share feedback.	○	○	○
7. I'm comfortable with the best idea winning, even if it's not mine.	○	○	○

Relationships are like sand held in your hand. Held loosely, with an open hand, the sand remains where it is. The minute you close your hand and squeeze tightly, the sand trickles through your fingers. You may hold on to some of it, but most will be spilled. Relationships are like that. Held loosely, with respect and freedom for the other person, it is likely to remain intact. But held too tightly, too possessively, the relationship slips away and is lost.

—KALEEL JAMISON

CHAPTER 10
CARING LEADERS BUILD DYNAMIC RELATIONSHIPS

Webster defines relationships as "the way in which two or more people are connected, associated or involved." Note two key concepts of this definition: 1) the way, and 2) connection, association, or involvement. The implications of those two concepts boggle the mind. For instance, think of the many ways people can connect, ranging from the fleeting to the enduring. The types of connections, associations, or involvements vary to such a degree that it would be hard to enumerate them all. To be sure, we have handy labels for the most enduring types: customers, employees, peers, stakeholders, media elites, to name a few. The bottom line: How should caring leaders manage this daunting and ambiguous challenge? That's the issue this chapter addresses.

A PERSPECTIVE ON RELATIONSHIPS

Caring leaders think about relationships in phases: 1) nurturing, 2) building, and 3) maintaining. Each phase represents a different art form, requiring related but differing talents:

> **Nurturing phase**—With almost eight billion people in the world, the odds are pretty good everyone will establish relationships with people outside their immediate family unit. Caring leaders, though, don't leave relationship formation to mere chance. They actively seek out people who could use their help, advance their organizations, broaden their perspective, or facilitate innovative thinking.

Figure 10.1

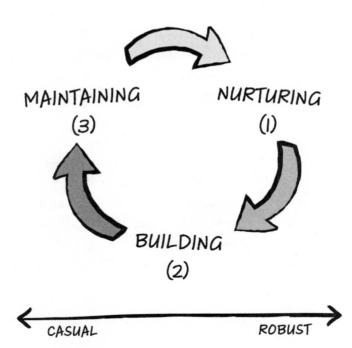

RELATIONSHIP CYCLE

MAINTAINING (3)

NURTURING (1)

BUILDING (2)

CASUAL   ROBUST

Caring leaders think of relationships on a continuum ranging from casual to robust. Casual relationships tend to involve few or infrequent interactions, and those interactions often occur in lean channels, such as social media. Robust relationships tend to be highly interactive, with frequent communication through a variety of channels ranging from text to face-to-face discussions.

Caring leaders nurture both types of relationships. Some may prove fleeting; some may become deep and enduring, while others may reemerge at a deeper level at a later point. Regardless of the relational intensity, caring leaders continue to nurture mutually beneficial relationships across the spectrum.

Building phase—Regardless of strength, all enduring relationships entail a building phase. Shared experiences tend to build robust relationships. Competing together on teams, collaborating on a project, or even comparing notes on a challenge might build the foundation of more enduring, rich relationships. More casual relationships can be built through regular, widely disseminated communications. For example, cable news commentators or national newspaper editorialists build sustainable, casual relationships with large audiences through the regular and consistent delivery of ideas, thoughts, and perspective.

Both types of relationships can prove beneficial. Casual relationships help caring leaders maintain their commitment to lifelong learning with a continual exposure to new ideas. More robust relationships provide opportunities for caring leaders to give back through coaching and empowerment.

Maintaining phase—Both casual and robust relationships need to be maintained with an investment of time and intellectual resources. To be sure, the degree of investment varies a great deal from person to person and situation to situation. Casual relationships developed on social media, for instance, can be preserved with regular updates and short, personalized responses.

Oddly, though, stronger relationships can endure more lapses because of the power of deeply shared experiences. Think, for example, of wartime buddies who shared life-and-death experiences. Long silences due to family situations, punctuated by a yearly gathering, might be enough to maintain an enduring relationship. Nevertheless, this is not ideal; maintaining robust relationships usually requires more frequent investments.

This relationship framework suggests several important principles that we implied in the values and learning chapters (Chapters Three and Four):

First, caring leaders' relationships are guided by core values. Everyone in a leader's circle yearns for quality relationships. What are high-quality leader relationships and how do you go about developing and nurturing them? In one word: trust. In times of disagreements and conflict, trust, coupled with respect, honesty, transparency, empathy, and listening, will get you through. These form the heart of high-quality relationships, regardless of strength. The values we discussed in an earlier chapter come together here, in a unique way, and form the heart of relationships among people (see Figure 10.2).

Second, caring leaders need to excel at three phases. Some people naturally excel at one phase or the other. For some people, networking at large events resembles a super bowl of excitement, entertainment, and possibilities. For other people, though, these same events feel like the terror of facing a bunch of 350-pound linemen sprinting toward them at full speed. We've seen leaders display similar, if perhaps less extreme, clashing reactions to the building and maintaining phases. For instance, one leader

Figure 10.2

VALUE-DRIVEN RELATIONSHIPS

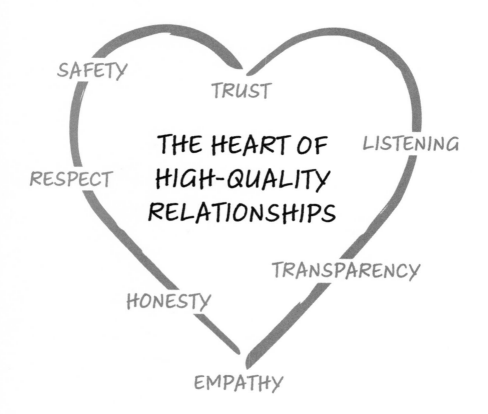

enjoyed networking events and building key relationships but felt overwhelmed by maintaining all the relationships; there never seemed to be enough time to do so.

Yet, caring leaders learn to adroitly manage all three phases. They may well have natural artistic talents in one phase but deficiencies in others. In that case, they seek to enrich their technique, even if it might mean "painting by the numbers" for a time. As a result, they grow their aptitudes across the entire relationship cycle and the spectrum of relationship intensity.

Third, caring leaders establish the right balance between casual and robust relationships. Pop star Justin Bieber, with millions of Twitter followers, would be at one end of the continuum. He maintains a lot of casual relationships. On the other hand, someone who stays in touch with immediate family members frequently through Facebook and phone calls would be at the other end of the continuum.

In the 1990s, British anthropologist Robin Dunbar discovered that the average person has the capacity to maintain meaningful relationships with only 150 people.[1] He further explained this by saying that 150 was "the number of people you would not feel embarrassed about joining uninvited for a drink if you happened to bump into them in a bar."[2] More recently, a Facebook study zeroed in on a similar number of people that typical users maintain robust, personal relationships with over its platform.

Let's assume that 150 is the approximate number of robust relationships leaders can build and maintain. Even though these relationships take more of the leader's energy and time, that does NOT mean the leader should neglect developing and maintaining casual relationships. A routine tweet about an issue or thought might be all that is needed for casual relationships. Clearly, developing and maintaining informal relationships takes less psychic energy, but they are still important; after all, there is innovative power and potential insights that can only be gleaned from a wide array of people with differing perspectives. And it's possible that someone at the informal end of the spectrum could potentially move into the inner, 150-people circle.

Fourth, caring leaders maintain the right balance between the phases throughout their careers. As we noted above, many people let their natural proclivities drive the people investments toward one phase or the other. One person might be so naturally skilled at nurturing relationships (phase one), that he keeps adding to an already-bulging contact list, to the exclusion of building stronger relationships (phase two). Another person might avoid seeking out new relationships (phase one) because she is satisfied with the status quo.

These natural tendencies can creep up on leaders over time. For instance, researchers have consistently shown that as we age, we tend to prune our relationship tree. That is, we tend to narrow down the number of relationships we build and maintain, even to the extent of failing to entertain new possible relationships. These inclinations are understandable but not optimal for caring leaders. Why? Overly emphasizing one phase or the other starts to limit personal and professional growth. Letting that happen subtly undermines beliefs about embracing uncertainty and continuous learning.

Fifth, caring leaders respect the unique dynamics of different types of relationships. Leaders engage in all kinds of relationships—with team members, customers, employees, colleagues, coworkers, peers, consultants, stakeholders, and community members. Terabytes of words, images, and models have been devoted to almost every one of these relationships.

Yet, you may have noticed that up to this point, we have only discussed relationships in general and not by type. We believe that all relationships, regardless of type, need to be grounded in caring leadership principles and practices—and that these principles and practices can be applied to virtually any kind of relationship.

That said, we understand that leaders need to respect the unique dynamics of different relationships; customers are different than team members. You might spend more time collaborating with one person, coaching with another. Yet regardless of the relational label we attach to another person, at the core, we are dealing with human beings. As we often say, "Customers (or students) are people, too!"

VISIBLE PRACTICES FOR BUILDING DYNAMIC RELATIONSHIPS

Caring leaders translate the five principles above into action and results. How? They incorporate the following relevant, visible practices into their professional routines:

1. **Maintain and routinely evaluate your relationship network.** Maintaining an organized list of names, titles, and contact information provides the starting point for a robust relational network. Categorizing your contacts by organization, project, geography, and date of initial meeting can provide insights for future opportunities and professional growth. You might discover hidden connections that could unlock special opportunities. Or, as you're looking at dates, you might notice patterns to gauge how well you are balancing the three relational phases (i.e., nurture, build, maintain).

   Regardless of the form of the database—be it file folders, spreadsheets, or technology-based relationship-management software—the records of contacts can be a source of guidance, inspiration, and recollection. The form is not nearly as important as the function and the dogged maintenance and utilization.

2. **Maximize interactive moments.** Caring leaders do practical, everyday things to nurture relationships. In fact,

they do what some might consider unexpected in today's technology-driven world: they still routinely write personal letters and note cards, promptly return phone calls, and respond to emails. And, as a University of Portsmouth study revealed, by answering a phone call with a smile, the receiver can actually "hear" a smile in the tone of voice.[3] In short, they orchestrate all their daily interactions from the electronic to the personal to convey a consistently welcoming tone. During normal times, a health spa used to greet each guest with a welcoming hug. When they remained open during COVID, the virus made that gesture impossible. So instead, to convey warmth and a welcoming environment, they taught their staff how to do "eye hugs."[4] This novel, small gesture symbolized the supportive climate of the staff despite the pandemic limitations on contact.

3. **Schedule times to nurture both the casual and robust relationships.** Caring leaders take responsibility to initiate routine contact. Robust relationships flourish with regular face-to-face encounters like we described in the coaching chapter.

   More casual relationships require regular grooming and upkeep, as well. For example, effective social media managers recognize the power and utility of creating a regular posting schedule. The calendar creates the discipline to maintain their large and casual network of relationships. Caring leaders may not post as frequently as a social media manager, but they often put reminders in their schedules to send out mass emails or tweets. For instance, one university chancellor scheduled biweekly, thirty-minute coffee breaks via Microsoft Teams to share news and answer questions from hundreds of faculty and staff members scattered across five campuses.

4. **Use lean channels for routine matters, rich channels for nonroutine issues.** Caring leaders may use emails, texting, and social media, but they recognize that these are lean media, which strip away certain valuable nuances. In fact, remote workers often cannot state specifically what they miss by not being physically in the office. Research shows that 41 percent of remote/hybrid workers report that they struggle with feeling a lack of camaraderie with their coworkers.[5] No doubt these feelings emerge from their overreliance on lean media to communicate about issues that would be better suited to face-to-face communication.

    Leaders who care recognize these under-the-radar communication dynamics. So, they expand their tool kit into broader and richer media. For more robust relationships, the personal touch trumps technology every time. And, as a general rule, they avoid emails or text messages to deal with potentially emotional or conflict-laden situations.[6] In those situations, it's best to use far richer channels, like the face-to-face or even the phone. Why? Those channels provide you more clues about how to interpret moods and read the situation. As a result, you'll be able to respond to concerns before they fester. Caring leaders wield these differing tools like a skilled craftsman, seeking just the right tool for the situation at hand.

5. **Seek out areas of mutual benefit and shared interests.** Robust, high-quality relationships have a great chance of enduring, because the benefits flow to both parties. Ditto for more informal relationships. Caring leaders discover how the parties can help one another. Uncovering overlapping benefits facilitates the mutual sharing of new ideas, beneficial information, and intriguing insights. The result? A more supportive and caring relationship.

SUBTLE PRACTICES FOR BUILDING DYNAMIC RELATIONSHIPS

Adding the right subtle practices to your more observable practices supercharges your relationship-building skills in all three phases. Consider adding the following:

1. **Challenge yourself to move out of your comfort zone.** Caring leaders take personal responsibility for developing relationships. They put themselves out there by courageously and proactively seeking out opportunities. Maybe it's the small talk that's required at social gatherings that many people find to be polite conversation about "nothing at all"; a *Seinfeld*-type innocuous dialogue. It may feel phony and unimportant, but those feelings may dissipate if you shift your mind-set to think of small talk as an exploratory laboratory with the aim of serendipitously discovering points of commonality and mutual interest.

    It's likely you'll stumble into awkward encounters at face-to-face events. But, over time, you'll learn to skillfully address these situations. One of your authors shares his experiences of how he learned to work a room in the sidebar—how to walk into a room full of strangers, introduce yourself, and carry on conversations. Regardless of how you put yourself out there, you'll probably need to engage in some positive self-talk to quell your uncertainty-induced concerns.[7] When you couple that psychologically healthy activity with practice and some of the other tips discussed below, you should soon master this often-uncomfortable activity.

    Other than face-to-face encounters, you can challenge yourself to develop a presence on social media platforms. To be sure, you'll have some gaffes and rejections. Every social media personality knows about the trolls that purposely

"WORKING THE ROOM" CASE STUDY: THE COURAGE TO MEET PEOPLE

A number of years ago, one of your authors (Bob) worked with a man who helped him recruit great people. John Bach owned an executive search business in Milwaukee, a market that Bob was interested in developing for his business. John introduced Bob to many business executives and leaders in the Milwaukee market, including him in many meet-and-greet occasions.

At dinners at prominent country clubs, John asked Bob to watch the goings-on closely. One by one, members would get up from their table, walk around the room, and talk to others whom they obviously knew—business associates, colleagues in the community, and friends at the club. After watching the activity for a while, John turned to Bob and said, "Now it's your turn." Bob stared at him with an "Are you serious?" look, and John responded, "I'm absolutely serious." To say Bob was stunned and a bit squeamish was an understatement. After all, these people were complete strangers. John continued, "Go ahead—that's how it happens around here. If you want to meet important people, now is the time."

So, Bob mustered up the courage, put a smile on his face, and started to meander around the room. He introduced himself at Table #1 and started a little chat. As he walked to Table #2, he thought to himself, *that wasn't so bad*. He introduced himself to four tables that night and met some very welcoming people. And Bob continued to make more personal connections in future visits to the club. In fact, some of those meetings turned into important business contacts.

sow discord or inflame networks. That's the price of putting yourself out there on the internet. Yet, over time, caring leaders learn to respond with facts and humor. Or they simply block or ban them.

2. **Explore others' interests, activities, and personal history.** Being visually attentive to common interests may well kick off deeper conversations about any variety of topics. A picture in a person's office might spark a conversation or a connection point. Before attending a networking event, consider preparing some questions designed to seek connection points. Even starting with prosaic questions about a local sports team can spin into some more meaningful conversation points as you pick up on other cues. Getting to know people personally by learning about their interests, their hobbies, and their families will be a springboard for conversation and will help you develop a personal, authentic, and respectful connection.

3. **Stay informed about national and local events.** You can use this knowledge to generate and sustain conversations. Of course, many people learn to tread lightly around political discussions, because passions may well run high. With casual relationships, this may be the safest course. Social media, for instance, is notorious for exposing unbridled passions. Caring leaders usually avoid these potentially dangerous minefields in the interests of building relationships on other issues. One university administrator with fund-raising responsibilities failed to heed this advice and stumbled in his efforts to raise much-needed capital. His routinely acrimonious, inflammatory, and highly partisan tweets were well-known in the community. Potential donors hesitated to support the institution because of this undercurrent of

disrespect for differing views. Sadly, he never knew that his communications to his casual relationship network undermined success.

Still, major political events—regardless of your personal opinion—provide a natural point of commonality, if not necessarily agreement. Skillfully using equivocation or humor regarding a recent political event may be the starting point of a productive relationship. If emotions run too high, then steering the conversation in another direction may well demonstrate respect and build a firmer foundation for future communication.

4. **Listen more, talk less.** Caring leaders are empathetic listeners. They discern how people are feeling and understand their fundamental concerns and how they reach conclusions. That means picking up signals about when to pause the conversation or detecting when to pursue a new line of thinking. A timely question might be the only way to carry the conversation forward to deeper engagement levels. Let others talk through an issue, even if it lacks clarity—the insights can be sharpened later. By doing so, you are deepening the relationship as the person senses that someone has taken the time to be attentive. The civil rights activist and poet Maya Angelou summarized this issue best: "I've learned that people will forget what you said, people will forget what you did, but people will never forget how you made them feel."[8]

For example, one team leader starts every meeting by going around the room, asking everyone to identify a personal and/or professional win since the last meeting. This allows everyone to sense the mood in the room and learn what each person values. Injecting insights from this simple exercise into a challenging discussion later in the meeting not only shows that people have been listening to the wins that were shared; it may also help break the tension in the room, resolve the issue, and build stronger relationships.

Even in more lean communication channels, like social media, listening should be priority one. Look for underlying trends and sentiments in posts and responses. Insights gleaned from your social listening can help you better tailor messaging that enhances relationships.

5. **Strive to underpromise, overdeliver and meet implicit expectations.** One of the quickest ways to undermine relationships is to fail to deliver on expectations. Some expectations are clearly stated, such as "I'll get back to you tomorrow." Leaders who fail to deliver on that expectation will dent relational trust. This happens even if there might be a legitimate reason for not following through, such as "I have nothing new to report." Even in that situation, a caring leader will report the no-news information in the interest of maintaining a good working relationship.

   To take the "underpromise, overdeliver" maxim to the next level, caring leaders look at unstated promises, as well. Some expectations are implicit and are more difficult to meet. For example, most people have an unspoken expectation about being courteous. What that means on the East Coast of the United States might be quite different than on the West Coast. In this case, the promise, or the expectations, were not explicit. This poses a challenge for people, because they need to learn about unstated expectations that are situationally or relationally driven. In short, caring leaders learn to deliver on both stated and unstated promises.

THE TOUGH SIDE OF RELATIONSHIPS

Even with the best of efforts, all meaningful relationships endure tough patches. They happen for any number of reasons—

misunderstandings, misperceptions, disagreements, and perceptions of breach of trust. How you respond will determine if the relationship can recover and grow from the incident. The caring leader assumes personal responsibility for initiating corrective actions. This might involve proposing further discussions to explore different perceptions or even apologizing for misunderstandings. If a breach of trust occurs, then caring leaders accept their part of the responsibility and codevelop a path forward.

CONCLUSION

Developing fulfilling relationships takes patience and persistence; it yields personal growth that cannot be duplicated in any other way. You can't demand one, legislate one, or contract one. Relationships develop over time, by building trust, a brick at a time, one discussion after another, and one shared experience after another. Each brick supports the trust building blocks underneath. And like the mason's mortar, the values of trust, respect, listening, honesty, empathy, and transparency bind relationships together.

—————————————— **"** ——————————————

... [I]f the relationship can't survive the long term, why on earth would it be worth my time and energy for the short term?   —NICHOLAS SPARKS

End of Chapter 10

BUILDING DYNAMIC RELATIONSHIPS SELF-ASSESSMENT

These questions are designed to provide developmental insights to enhance your effectiveness. Rate yourself, choosing either Improvement Needed, Solid, or Excels.

SELF-REFLECTION QUESTIONS

	IMPROVEMENT NEEDED	SOLID	EXCELS
1. I routinely update and evaluate my professional networks.	◯	◯	◯
2. I put myself in situations to meet new people.	◯	◯	◯
3. I maintain a routine schedule to nurture my key relationships.	◯	◯	◯
4. I'm comfortable talking about a wide range of topics.	◯	◯	◯
5. Other people would say that I'm a good listener.	◯	◯	◯
6. I recognize situations or topics that demand richer communication channels.	◯	◯	◯
7. I'm good at identifying areas of shared values and benefits.	◯	◯	◯
8. I maintain the right mix of robust and casual relationships.	◯	◯	◯
9. I properly balance the demands of nurturing, building, and maintaining relationships.	◯	◯	◯
10. I know when it's time to terminate certain relationships.	◯	◯	◯

*It's amazing what you can accomplish
when you don't care who gets the credit.*

—HARRY TRUMAN

CHAPTER 11
CARING LEADERS COLLABORATE BEFORE THEY NEGOTIATE

How would you react to the following situation? You traveled to a major US city with your partner. You were enjoying a beautiful evening on the top floor of a lovely hotel, taking in the breathtaking view of the waters beyond. As you waited for your cocktails, your attention was diverted to three people energetically chatting in the next alcove. The configuration of the windows perfectly amplified their every word, like you were sitting next to a loudspeaker piping in their voices. All three were business school professors from prominent universities on the East and West Coasts. Their spirited conversation revolved around their opinions about the most popular and profitable business school courses. It was unanimous—they quickly concluded that negotiation courses were in the highest demand. They hastened to add that courses that focused on hardball negotiations—"I win, you lose"—were the most popular. The bonus? They could charge more for these courses, so they were more profitable. They laughed it all off and then drew lots for who would pay the bill.

Would you be surprised? Would you be impressed or depressed?

One of your authors, Bob, found himself in exactly this situation. And he walked away from this lovely evening profoundly depressed. Why? Clearly, negotiation is essential in business. We negotiate contracts, we negotiate disputes, and we negotiate pricing. Leaders often negotiate with employees about salaries, career plans, and responsibilities. But caring leaders rarely think of negotiation as their first step and certainly not the most fulfilling part of business. That's what Bob found disheartening. What about the thrill of successful collaboration? Why weren't elite MBAs excited about that?

COLLABORATION VERSUS NEGOTIATION

Collaboration and negotiation can coexist. In fact, results improve if leaders start business discussions with a spirit and intention to collaborate and then follow up with structuring a business deal through respectful negotiations.

Yet, the spirit of collaboration clashes with negotiation. Collaboration focuses on promoting shared interests, while negotiation describes a process that resolves issues between parties that both find acceptable. Our modern use of the term *collaborate* originated from the Latin idea of "working together." Intriguingly, the original Latin term for negotiate literally means "deny leisure," which doesn't sound nearly as invigorating and fun as "working together." A quick scan of synonyms for both words suggests why collaboration should be more enjoyable and invigorating than negotiation (see Table 11.1). Great collaborations result in optimizing, while good negotiations often end with compromise.

Table 11.1

COLLABORATION VS. NEGOTIATION

COLLABORATION SYNONYMS	NEGOTIATION SYNONYMS
· Connection · Cooperation · Oneness · Unity	· Arbitration · Mediation · Transaction · Bargain

Reflecting on the dynamics behind these two concepts proves revealing. The environment where connection and cooperation thrive is far different than the environment where arbitration, mediation, and bargaining occur. Caring leaders are masters at creating environments where connection, cooperation, oneness, and unity can thrive.

Negotiation involves holding your cards close to the chest, giving a little to get a little, and going back and forth in a guarded fashion until you reach an agreement. A negotiator's verbal tone and body language imply confrontation, not collaboration. Often people come away from these experiences feeling weary and depleted. Some pundits even argue a sign of success is when a negotiator concludes proceedings feeling drained, tired, and abused.

In contrast, caring leaders take the responsibility to bring people together, oftentimes with different points of view, to a position everyone can support. As people collaborate, it's important for participants to see some of their contributions (e.g., ideas or energy) in the collaborative outcome. If you approach these types of discussions using "I win/you lose" logic, you may win in the short term but not have buy-in for long-term sustainability. Instead, caring leaders ensure that unique perspectives emerge by creating an environment where 1) team members learn from one another, 2) differing points of view are valued, and 3) unique perspectives magically materialize.

Participants in collaborative conversations have responsibilities, too. They must respectfully communicate with one another, sharing their views while inquiring about other people's views, as well. Being open and honest, though, doesn't grant people a license to say anything they want. Once the insensitive words come out of someone's mouth, no amount of apology will erase what the person felt in the moment. This is not a matter of being politically correct; it's just being sensitive and civil, even when disagreeing.

One cautionary note: most people prefer to collaborate rather than negotiate, except maybe those three elite business school professors discussed previously. Yet, expressing a preference differs from possessing the ability to translate a preference into reality. In fact, cultivating a collaborative culture requires a special mind-set, which we discuss next.

CULTIVATING A COLLABORATIVE CULTURE

Caring leaders know that they can't bark a drill sergeant's "Collaborate now!" command. Rather, cultivating collaboration requires a mind-set similar to a master gardener committed to blending the right soils, planting the right seeds, and nourishing growth. In essence, caring leaders master three interrelated issues (see Figure 11.1).

Figure 11.1

BUILDING BLOCKS FOR A COLLABORATIVE CULTURE

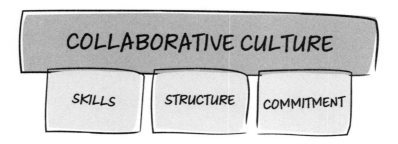

First, they foster commitment to collaboration. For some people, committing to collaboration is as natural as cooperating
on family chores. For other people, collaborative opportunities
resemble a dysfunctional family outing. For some hypercompet-
itive people, collaborative opportunities dissipate because their
ego will not allow others to win. Professor Morten Hansen
of INSEAD studied the challenge of collaboration and noted
that these "lone stars" deliver on their numbers "big-time" but
their "behaviors run counter to the teamwork that the firm is
trying to install."[1]

Second, they ensure they have the right structural elements—or the right soil and seeds to cultivate growth. Structural
elements include making sure the right people are in the room,
securing proper meeting spaces, and creating compelling agendas.

Third, they build and use the right skills. Active listening and empathy are a must, but so are question-asking skills.
Caring leaders ask the right questions at the right time and avoid
the desire to fill silence at the wrong time.[2]

Caring leaders recognize that all three of these building
blocks are necessary and self-reinforcing. For example, leaders
with excellent collaborative skills but without the right people
in the room will become frustrated with the results. Likewise,

assembling the right people, who are not skilled, will be equally infuriating. Integrating these building blocks requires both the visible and subtle strategies discussed next.

VISIBLE PRACTICES FOR COLLABORATION

The visible strategies discussed in this section emerged from our observations and experiences about how to synergize the core building blocks of commitment, structure, and skill (see Figure 11.2).

Figure 11.2

BUILDING BLOCKS FOR A COLLABORATIVE CULTURE: THE NEXT LEVEL

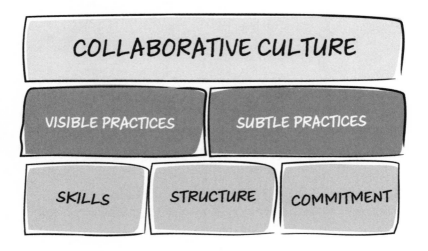

1. **Make sure the right people are in the room and participating at the expected level.** Most collaborative opportunities occur during meetings of various types. But the opportunities are often not realized for a number of reasons.

    First, the right people are not in the room to provide a diversity of viewpoints. This may be the prime factor in setting the stage for groupthink. Decades ago, the insightful social psychologist Irving Janis researched this concept. He defines groupthink as a:

    > ... mode of thinking that persons engage in when concurrence-seeking becomes so dominant in a cohesive ingroup that it tends to override realistic appraisal of alternative courses of action. ... the term refers to a deterioration in mental efficiency, reality testing, and moral judgments as a result of group pressures.[3]

    > Unfortunately, after decades of study, many so-called collaborative groups still suffer from this malady. Caring leaders select the right people so that all points of view are represented—especially the dissenting views.

    Second, even if the right people are in the room, they may be suffering from "collaborative overload," with just too much teamwork, which exhausts employees and saps productivity. According to research cited in *Harvard Business Review*, "over the past two decades, the time spent by managers and employees in collaborative activities has ballooned by 50% or more."[4] This fatigue may manifest itself in the form of faux participation or less thoughtful evaluation of ideas.

    On the surface, auditing participation appears to be a simple matter of determining if the right people are in the room. In practice, though, this proves more challenging, because people fear that being left out of a meeting may signal a loss of status. Likewise, inertia and legacy practices may dictate that certain people attend meetings regardless of the value they might add.

Caring leaders can audit participation by a) inventorying the major meetings in the organization, b) identifying the total number of meetings employees are regularly attending, and c) analyzing the value of each employee's attendance.

In one organization, we identified over thirty major recurring meetings and found that many senior leaders were involved in more than twenty of them, which was gobbling up their strategic thinking time. We did this by asking employees to consider if each meeting was a good use of his or her time based on a five-point scale from one (don't need to attend) to three (like to attend) to five (need to attend). We also asked if there were meetings that they were not currently attending but should be attending. Employees were amazingly candid and readily embraced reconfiguring the organizational meeting structure. Yet, several people expressed concerns and wanted to clarify that rating a meeting low did not indicate a lack of commitment to the organization. The attendees of high numbers of meetings reduced their collaboration load by 10 percent, while several groups added new participants that enhanced a diversity of perspective.

2. **Use personal instruction manuals to jump-start collaboration in newly formed groups.** When you buy a new product, you receive an operating manual with a list of dos and don'ts. Why aren't people equipped with a similar manual? A personal instruction manual can fill this gap. Before a group initially meets, the group facilitator asks each member to prepare a written document outlining key personal attributes that alerts others about how to work with that person

effectively. Group members can use favorite quotes, paintings, critical experiences, or psychological profiles as sources for inspiration. We find instruction manuals particularly helpful in circumventing situations where a team member has been misunderstood in the past. Note in Appendix Two how this person highlighted his debate background to circumvent a possible misimpression. He wanted the group to know that when he argues about an idea, that does not signal his disapproval or even disagreement. Another effective use of the instruction manual is to signal how to best interact with a group member, with a statement like, "Call me rather than email."

After the documents have been generated, the group facilitator can encourage a brief review of each person's instruction manual as a way to lubricate collaborative discussions. In particular, the instruction manuals might point to underlying group dynamics that could influence the degree of cooperation. For example, knowing that four of the five team members were strong introverts might suggest that collaboration should start with team members sharing written documents rather than engaging in oral give-and-take that might be dominated by the one extrovert.

3. **Assess meeting mechanics.** Are meeting facilitators sending out agendas before meetings? Providing information before meetings? Sharing meeting summaries? Routinely evaluating the effectiveness of the meeting? These questions represent the top complaints in many organizations. These comments from one organization are typical of the suggestions offered to improve meetings:

- Use standardized agendas and minutes. Provide regular/timely updates and make sure everyone is properly prepared.

- Have a consistent process and set expectations for all meetings: 1) create an agenda and distribute it ahead of time, 2) appoint someone to take minutes, 3) distribute meeting notes in a timely manner.

- Create a focused, repeatable structure to the meetings that do not focus on reporting but instead focus on sharing and solving problems.

In that same organization, we asked, "What three words best summarize your reactions to most meetings you attend?" As seen in the word cloud, the number one response (largest word) is *informative* (see Figure 11.3). On the surface, that might seem fine, but in the best possible world, the word *collaborative* would be the predominant word, while sentiments like *redundant* and *repetitive* would shrink. It's no wonder that in this organization, only 60 percent of employees felt that "most meetings are a good use of my time."

Agendas and minutes are the primary and most visible way to structure meetings to generate the most value. In the ideal world, a norm like "meetings last until the designated stop time" would be supplanted with "meetings last until the last agenda item is discussed." Likewise, the custom of using meetings to share a great deal of information would be replaced by a practice of using meetings for clarification, analysis, and collaboration. Sharing information that is routine and simple to understand would be done via reports rather than taking up scarce in-person time.

4. **Codevelop meeting ground rules with the team.** Collaborative dynamics are acutely sensitive to the media used for communication—a successful TV advertisement may not play well in print or social media. Likewise, the de facto ground rules of face-to-face communication often do not

Figure 11.3

COLLABORATIVE MEETING?

NON-VALUE-ADDED
TOO-MANY-TALKERS
OVERWHELMED UNNECESSARY
LACK-OF-TOPICS COLLABORATION INFORMATIONAL
TIME-CONSUMING HELPFUL
USEFUL NECESSARY
REPETITIVE
REPORTING FREQUENT
INEFFICIENT UNPRODUCTIVE PROGRESS BENEFICIAL
WASTEFUL OVERWHELMING
LEARNING **INFORMATIVE**
PRODUCTIVE NECESSARY-BUT-TIME-CONSUMING
TOO-MANY
WORTHWHILE CONSUMING LONG RELEVANT
VALUABLE REDUNDANT MANAGEMENT
DISCUSSION DEFINE-PURPOSE COMMUNICATION
ROUTINE
DRAINING COLLABORATIVE UNFOCUSED
OH-MY-GOODNESS

translate well in a Zoom meeting. For example, sensing body language and team dynamics on video can be challenging to some people as well as liberating to others. Jennifer Nason, J. P. Morgan's global chairman of investment banking, noted that "Zoom is the great equalizer. Everyone's box is the same size. It doesn't matter if you are the CEO or the summer intern, your real estate is the same. A box with a name but no title became a tool of empowerment."[5] Yet, to others, video feeds screen out important cues that help form impressions.

Caring leaders recognize these subtle forces at work and take active measures to shape the collaborative dynamics. If these issues are openly discussed up front with the team, people can be remarkably successful at fine-tuning their collaborative ground rules. For example, one organization developed these simple rules:

- When convening a group for the first time, strive to meet face-to-face. Most caring leaders believe collaboration happens best face-to-face. Yet, they recognize that there may be times when workers are remote and timeliness of decision-making is paramount.

- Avoid a meeting where some are face-to-face and others are using a mediated channel. If three people are zooming into a meeting and three others are face-to-face, then natural subgroups start to form that can undermine collaboration.

- Turn off cell phones. This simple courtesy signals to everyone that team members are showing mutual respect and making good use of everyone's time.

- Stay on task by using a "parking garage." A "parking garage" is a storage spot for good ideas brought up that will be covered either later in the meeting or are off-agenda items. The facilitator can note the items on a whiteboard, for example, and return to them at a more opportune, relevant time.

- Solicit everyone's opinion on key collaborative analyses and decisions. In many face-to-face meetings, leaders naturally sense when all the key issues have surfaced without necessarily asking each person in the room. But this is another situation where what works on radio does not work on TV. As one expert explained about virtual collaboration, "You are communicating with blunt tools. Without face-to-face interaction, you spend more time sussing out unspoken expectations, trying to interpret incomplete messages..."[6]

  So, this group decided to be more directive during virtual collaborations than in face-to-face meetings to make sure everyone's voice was heard on key issues. Small tweaks like this may not feel natural at first but will result in collaborative dividends.

- Craft group action lists, between-meeting individual assignments, and follow up on assignments. This process builds virtuous, collaborative loops into the entire meeting structure. It ensures continuity of purpose while jump-starting discussions from one meeting to the next.

In a post–COVID world, technology often comfortably replaces face-to-face meetings. But don't allow it to completely replace face-to-face discussions. Addressing these concerns by codeveloping the team's ground rules provides a simple and effective way to spawn greater collaboration on other, more contentious issues. However, there are times when magical, synergistic discussions occur. At these times, leaders—especially those who embrace uncertainty—allow them to play out, tempering these basic meeting mechanics. One of our favorite cartoons, picturing two employees chatting after a meeting, captures this sentiment best: "That's the problem with epiphanies—you can't schedule them into the agenda."

SUBTLE PRACTICES FOR COLLABORATION

Most of the observable strategies focus on the structural, collaborative building blocks. The subtle strategies seek to build the team's collaborative skill base, strengthen collaborative commitments, and cultivate circumstances for people to respectively express their views. In many ways, this proves far more challenging than dealing with the structural elements, because leaders need to be more attentive to nuances.

1. **Align people on the analysis of the situation before seeking solutions.** Caring leaders envision most discussions as occurring in two distinct phases: 1) analysis and 2) resolution. In the analysis phase, they seek to synthesize information, identify core issues, analyze data, and determine the essence of the challenge. In the resolution phase, the team answers the question of what to do on a strategic and tactical level.

   Many team conversations spin into unnecessary acrimony because people argue over what to do when they don't even agree on the nature of the problem or opportunity. Ideally, consensus would first emerge on the problem or challenge facing the group. Clearly separating the phases helps signal when it's time to debate and when it's time to seek consensus, when it's time to analyze and when it's time to synthesize. Separating the phases helps ensure that the team avoids providing a perfectly wonderful solution to a problem that doesn't really exist.

Think of it this way: many symptoms for the flu mirror those of COVID. You don't want to be treated for COVID when it may be a simple case of the flu. A good doctor, like a good leader, usually spends more time diagnosing than contemplating treatments. To be fair, some mixing of the phases always occurs, but skillful leaders make sure the mixture doesn't become toxic. How? Read on.

2. **Spotlight significant points of agreement and disagreement in both the analysis and resolution phases.** Recording the points can be done on charts or on the wall, for all to see. This exercise begins to bring people together because it demonstrates that leaders are listening and that differences of perspective are not only tolerated but welcomed.

    Of course, this practice implies that leaders can identify salient points of similarity and difference. In some cases, it's simple; in other cases, it can resemble unpacking a tax court's legal opinion. We've all experienced conversations where two parties are engaged in a spirited dispute, but they are using different words to express similar sentiments. Caring leaders discern these implicit unspoken alignments as well as the implicit differences that surface that are worthy of further discussion.

3. **Downplay the formal position and roles of team members.** Everyone in the room knows who has the ultimate power to make the tough calls. Reemphasizing this common knowledge can signal that contrary ideas should not be introduced into the discussion. This is one of the most

---
“

People who are very aware that they have more knowledge than the average person are often very unaware that they do not have one-tenth of the knowledge of all the average persons put together. —THOMAS SOWELL

important ways to ensure all members participate. The responsibility goes far beyond managing the agenda. Caring leaders ensure that all points of view are expressed by asking silent members questions such as, "How are you reacting to this issue?" Caring leaders also look for members who are dominating conversation and ensure there are contributions from all team members.

4. **Pay close attention to the rhythm of the discussion.** Leaders help members embrace the uncertainty while relentlessly searching for the magical and often unspoken moments when views are coalescing. They help the group grab those opportunities to lift themselves to new platforms of agreement, much like we described in Chapter Two.

    If the discussion starts slipping too much off the agenda, then use the "parking garage"—these are good ideas that the facilitator writes down to discuss later. Some leaders use a standard phrase like, "great idea—let's put it in the parking garage and discuss it in more depth later," as a way to pleasantly nudge an out-of-sync comment back into the primary discussion rhythm. Likewise, caring leaders pepper discussions with thoughtful questions to steer the discussions into productive cadences. For example, separating out strategic from tactical solutions proves particularly helpful. Too many groups become mired in arguments over tactical plans rather than making sure the big-picture, strategic decisions address the core challenges. A simple question like, "How does this solution address the core problems?" might be all that's needed to jolt the discussion back in the proper tempo.

5. **Nudge discussions away from premature agreement when signs of groupthink start to emerge.** Detecting signs of groupthink requires sensitivity to clues that people are

self-censoring relevant input. They may be hesitant because of one person's forceful and confident opinion. Or they may fear social disapproval for offering contrary information or views. The former CEO of Boston Consulting Rich Lesser describes this peril as the "CEO bubble." He explains:

> When you become CEO, and you have enormous influence over people's careers, people start sort of screening what they say to you. And the bubble's walls get thicker and thicker. You as CEO have to work so hard to make sure that bubble doesn't grow up around you.[7]

Any leader, not just CEOs, may unwittingly form judgments in these bubbles. Consequently, they may unintentionally stoke the embers of groupthink as "groups focus on shared information—what everybody (in the bubble) already knows—at the expense of unshared information and thus fail to obtain the benefit of critical and perhaps troubling information that one or a few people have."[8] Two thoughtful researchers, Cass Sunstein and Reid Hastie, argue that in some cases, this can result in teams amplifying poor judgments while becoming strongly committed to an ill-advised direction.

Bursting the bubble can be as simple as the leaders asking, "Where could we be going wrong?" or designating someone in the group to act as a devil's advocate. Likewise, one Nobel Prize winner advocates nudging groups to postpone final judgments until everyone has reached independent assessments of more specific issues.[9] Then the team should use those appraisals as a basis for further discussion.

Questions such as, "On a zero-to-ten scale, how important do you see this issue?" can prime the deliberative pump. If team members independently rate the issue before making a final collective judgment, then new concerns and perspectives are more likely to emerge. More importantly, such subtle nudges protect the team from hastily coalescing around ill-informed intuitions, prematurely agreeing, and pushing forward without full consideration of key questions.

THE TOUGH SIDE OF COLLABORATION

Three primary issues hinder collaborative outcomes:

- Getting collaboration confused with negotiation. In this case, one or more members display behaviors associated with bargaining or arbitration, where they give a little to get a little and, as a result, open discussion of issues doesn't happen. Caring leaders should consider taking these members aside and coaching them on the importance of cooperative behaviors.

- A group member routinely obstructs collaborative outcomes. Even after coaching, some members might continue to stand in the way of any progress. They may be clinging to an unwavering opposing point of view. In those cases, leaders might need to remove these members from the collaborative effort. Acting with deliberateness and tact often proves crucial to team dynamics because the personnel shift could be misinterpreted as stifling opposing positions. But most team members who value collaboration recognize the difference between disagreeing and obstructing. And they will look for the leader to act.

- A collaborative result fails to emerge. Sometimes, even after great effort, teams just can't reach consensus or even an accord that all can live with. In short, more time and energy will not solve the problem. Leaders will need to either set aside the issue for a while or make the necessary decision.

Caring leaders transparently take this step while expressing respect for the various points of view and while underscoring the need to move on.

CONCLUSION

In the long run, caring leaders will be respected for their collaborative approach to problem-solving, even if they're not successful in every case. They will also be appreciated for their decisiveness when collaborations fail. Collaboration is much more than people working together; it is building a sense of community with a group of people who respect and trust one other. They support each other and are able to disagree while finding a path forward. They recognize that, together, they find better solutions than anyone individually.

—— **"** ——

Find a group of people who challenge and inspire you, spend a lot of time together and it will change your life.

—AMY POEHLER

End of Chapter 11

COLLABORATION SELF-ASSESSMENT

These questions are designed to provide developmental insights to enhance your effectiveness. Rate yourself, choosing either Improvement Needed, Solid, or Excels.

SELF-REFLECTION QUESTIONS

	IMPROVEMENT NEEDED	SOLID	EXCELS
1. I select collaborative team members who express all points of view, even dissenting ones.	○	○	○
2. I seek to convene face-to-face collaborations.	○	○	○
3. I record points of agreement and disagreement during discussions.	○	○	○
4. I downplay the formal position and status roles of team members (i.e., make everyone an equal partner in the decision).	○	○	○
5. I ensure that all team members are participating in collaborative sessions.	○	○	○
6. I assure people that there are no negative consequences for expressing differences.	○	○	○
7. I create safe environments for discussing opposing points of view.	○	○	○
8. I continually strive to seek consensus.	○	○	○
9. I avoid forcing consensus; instead I allow it to emerge.	○	○	○
10. I'm attentive to signs of groupthink.	○	○	○

*Employees don't leave companies,
they leave people.*

—DALE CARNEGIE

CHAPTER 12
CARING LEADERS CULTIVATE ENGAGEMENT AND DIVERSITY TO BUILD AN INCLUSIVE WORKPLACE

Do you cultivate a diverse, inclusive, and engaging work environment? Of course you do!

In today's working climate, almost every leader embraces engagement, diversity, and team member inclusivity. Certainly, the rhetorical promise of engagement and inclusiveness is unquestionable. After all, who wouldn't want to work at a job they love, doing what they love, with people they love? Who wouldn't want to work in an environment where work hours pass like a contented heartbeat? Engagement, inclusivity, and diversity are fashionable, appealing —and often far from the day-to-day experiences of many people.

———————————————— 66 ————————————————

The only way to do great work is to love what you do.
—STEVE JOBS

In fact, many team members do not feel included and engaged at all. Over the past twenty-five years, we've looked at the underlying patterns of employees who voluntarily leave their organizations. Here's a sampling of their comments:

- I didn't feel appreciated.
- I was talked down to.
- I never really fit in.
- My boss didn't understand what I did and what I contributed.
- I didn't feel valued.
- I only hear criticism, not compliments.
- I work my tail off and seldom get a thank-you.
- I yearn for a deeper connection with my boss.
- My supervisor doesn't take the time to really talk to me.
- I had more to contribute, but no one asked me.
- I had ideas, but they weren't listened to.
- I don't feel part of a greater whole.
- No one asked me how I am really doing.
- I have so much talent to contribute that slips through the cracks.

A deeper dive into these comments reveals five core themes (see Figure 12.1):

1. I'm disconnected from my boss (33 percent)

2. My ideas and input are not valued (24 percent)

3. I don't feel appreciated (19 percent)

4. I don't get enough feedback on how I'm doing (14 percent)

5. I don't feel trusted (10 percent)

Figure 12.1

REASONS EMPLOYEES LEAVE THEIR ORGANIZATIONS

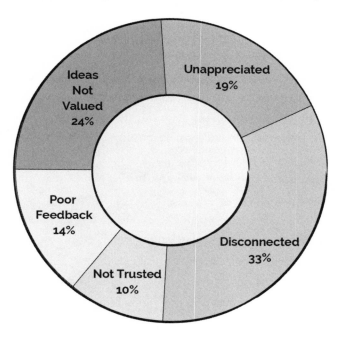

If your heart aches a little after reading these comments, then you have the temperament of a caring leader. However, are you really fostering an inclusive, diverse, engaging work environment?

In fact, when we interviewed the supervisors of some of the people quoted above, none of them felt they created a disengaging workplace. In many cases, they argued just the opposite. We discovered that many people in leadership positions had good intentions but didn't appreciate how their leadership approach unintentionally sabotaged their laudable motives.

UNDERSTANDING DIVERSITY, ENGAGEMENT, AND INCLUSIVENESS

The related ideas of diversity, engagement, and inclusivity float around boardrooms and training sessions with such fluffy, ambiguous meanings that the discussion often undermines the goals of caring leaders. So, let's start by defining these ideas:

What does diversity mean?

The word *diversity* emerged from the Latin expression "diversus," which means "turned in different ways." At its core, the term means "something different in kind and not alike." Applying that concept to people makes perfect sense, because caring leaders believe that every person is different. Even identical twins are different at some level. What a boring world it would be if we were all the same.

The critical question, though, is: What are the dimensions of these differences? The list is long: gender, ethnicity, language, age, race, religion, culture, and countless others. The very effort to make the list is problematic, since it starts to segment the differences in ways that can generate value judgments among team members. Beneath these differences lie three fundamental factors:

- **Culture**: People have different cultural and language backgrounds

- **Beliefs**: People hold different ideas and beliefs

- **Experiences**: People have different defining experiences in their lives

There are, of course, other ways to parse the differences, but this triad proves to be a useful starting point for the deeper discussion. We believe that caring leaders embrace Audre Lorde's sage advice: "It's not our differences that divide us; it's our inability to recognize, accept, and celebrate those differences."[1] In order to do that, we need to understand the concepts of engagement and inclusiveness. Read on.

What does engagement mean?

If you look up "engagement" in a dictionary, you'll find a definition such as, "magical power to attract." Team members who are engaged are motivated, involved, and emotionally committed. Of course, that definition raises a host of other related issues: Motivated by what? Involved to what degree? Emotionally committed to what values, ideas, projects, or people? Discovering the answers to these questions creates the kind of visceral connections that most people yearn for.

After all, engagement benefits both the employee and the organization. Most employees cherish the opportunity to work hard, release their potential, and excel at what they do; it's energizing, motivating, and self-fulfilling. Empowered employees press on during the challenging times. And their spirit is often contagious to those around them.

What does inclusiveness mean?

Our current usage emerged from the medieval Latin expression "inclusivius." Translation: "including a great deal, leaving little out." Caring leaders embrace that sense of the word, because they want everyone on the team to feel included and to feel like their perspective counts. To be fair, caring leaders acknowledge the wiggle room in the definition, because it's impossible to include every idea and perspective in every situation. However, it is possible to listen to multiple views and integrate ideas in respectful ways. You might think, aren't these sentiments the same as we discussed in the chapter about collaboration? There is overlap, but the difference is

———————————— ❝ ————————————

Far and away the best prize that life has to offer is the chance to work hard at work worth doing. —TEDDY ROOSEVELT

that collaboration represents a skill, and inclusiveness represents an outcome.

INCLUSION INTENSITY INDICATOR

The three connected (and often confused) terms above suggest a perspective on these issues we call the Inclusion Intensity Indicator. Our fundamental view is that engaging employees and building diversity generates an inclusive workplace. Diversity without engagement destroys employees' sense of inclusiveness. On the flip side, engagement without diversity undermines inclusivity within the larger community where employees live and work.

The Inclusion Intensity Indicator (see Figure 12.2) highlights the working dynamics that caring leaders seek to avoid as well as foster:

Figure 12.2

INCLUSION INTENSITY INDICATOR

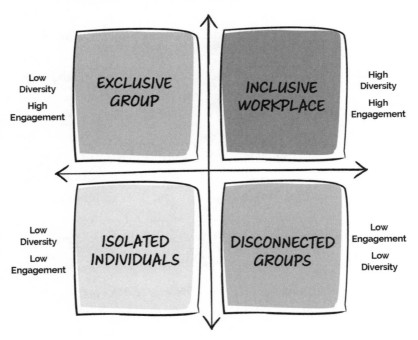

- **Isolated individuals**—If leaders work with people of similar backgrounds while failing to engage them, then the leaders have crafted a team of isolated and disconnected individuals. They lack engagement with the larger workplace. The upside is that some people, like an independent contractor, can be very productive working alone. The downside is that leaders take on the burden of coordination and fail to reap the benefits of team synergy.

- **Exclusive group**—If leaders only hire and interact with like-minded people, then they run the danger of creating an exclusive group. Leaders can easily confuse multiple voices with a diversity of perspectives. The well-documented tendency to hire similar people with similar views cultivates exclusive clans. The upside is that people in an exclusive group can be quite motivated and quick to make decisions and feel quite engaged. They may even feel inclusive. And they are, but only within the narrow confines of their group. The downside is that the team is at high risk for groupthink and could be quickly undermined by competitors with different assumptions and approaches.

- **Disconnected groups**—Historically, people with similarities on any number of dimensions (e.g., religion, ethnicity, profession) tend to clump together in groups. Cops identify with other cops, athletes with athletes, and so on; that's natural. If leaders hire and interact with a diversity of people but fail to engage them, then leaders may unwittingly create inclusive subgroups within their teams. The upside is that the subgroups might be very good at what they do. After all, through shared experiences, they often develop special coded ways to expedite interactions and tasks. They create visceral, unspoken ways of coordinating with one another, much like exclusive cliques. The downside is that this sense of tribal loyalty can inhibit integration into the larger whole and, in some cases, spur deep conflicts between groups. Members of disconnected groups often feel included within their particular group but detached from the whole.

- Inclusive workplace—If leaders engage with a diverse group of people, then they create an inclusive team that reaps the benefits of rich and meaningful collaboration. The benefits of an inclusive team are many: the team is more likely to create an integrated approach to challenging problems and be highly innovative and willing to go the extra mile to implement difficult decisions. The downside is that creating an inclusive team requires time, effort, and the special skill of caring leaders.

SUBTLE PRACTICES FOR BUILDING AN INCLUSIVE WORKPLACE

How do caring leaders cultivate an inclusive workplace, one with high diversity and high engagement? They start by using subtle practices that will be virtually invisible to most people. These are like the heating, plumbing, and electrical systems found in a well-functioning home—they go unnoticed but are immensely important.

1. **Discover the differences that might make a difference on particular issues.** Caring leaders think broadly about the issue of diversity, because the differences that make a difference vary from issue to issue. Consider, for example, the issue of career pathing. Many people overlook generational differences when discussing this particular issue. Different generations experience distinctive, momentous events such as wars, pandemics, and even paradigm-shifting technology advances. These profound events shape each generation's be-

liefs, views, and prospects. Likewise, each generation's daily experiences often differ in profound ways. Older generations routinely listened to radio or TV for their news while entertaining themselves with board games like Monopoly, Clue, and Scrabble. Younger generations relied on social media for news and played video games for entertainment.

These experiences, large and small, influence every generation's beliefs, expectations, and sensibilities. Taking those into account when shaping career-pathing options can prove illuminating. We tackled these influences in a seminar we conducted for a group of thirty human resource managers from around the country. The discussion on generational differences turned to the amount of time young people spent playing video games as opposed to traditional board games. The group noted how the experience of playing video games was so different than that of playing traditional board games; for instance, those who are avid video gamers get accustomed to instantaneous feedback and quick promotion to new levels when challenges are conquered.[2] At one point, we asked, "What would the company's career-pathing options and titles look like if they were structured like a video game?" This question struck a responsive chord, prompting an exuberant discussion. In fact, one of the most senior HR executives in the room remarked, "That would mean we would have to recalibrate almost everything we do on career pathing and performance appraisal!" His startling remark was greeted with a chorus of chuckles, punctuated by an almost universal response of "Exactly!" And, to the company's credit, they did initiate a number of significant changes that have enhanced employee retention to levels higher than the industry average.

Thinking about differences that make a difference, by necessity, means that there will be differences that will not make a difference on particular issues. For example, people have different political beliefs, and those might be influential in crafting certain policies. Yet, this is probably a meaningless difference when crafting a remote work policy. In short, if you're always selecting the same difference, or lens, to view all issues, then you really are not finding the difference that makes a difference.

2. **Select a diverse array of team members.** Caring leaders recognize that they cannot make progress without benefiting from diverse viewpoints. In assembling a team, they look to bring together the right combination of people with differing talents, skills, and viewpoints.

    If they inherit a team lacking appropriate diversity, they act. Sometimes caring leaders recognize that the team needs to enlarge the circle of engagement by adding new people with different experiences, sensibilities, and perspectives. Some teams get stuck in a rut and they just need new blood to move on. This requires team members who are skilled communicators, great listeners, and proficient conflict resolvers and who are comfortable with thoughtful debate. Such skills not only help assimilate new people; they also add new perspectives, ideas, and energy.

    Caring leaders have thick skin and sensitive ears: thick skin because, as they enlarge the circle, they will encounter criticism, often directed at their most cherished ideas. Sensitive ears because, as they enlarge the circle, they need to be attentive to underlying issues that can impede progress while being able to seize on notions that can propel their organizations forward.

3. **Look for signs of subgroup tendencies in your teams—team members align with one another for any number reasons, laudable as well as questionable.** Caring leaders pay partic-

ular attention to subgroup tendencies that will hinder collaborative progress on key issues. Detecting those invisible fault lines in a team often proves crucial. Subgroups of team members often emerge that may be difficult to detect. The subgroups rarely don team jerseys, but an us versus them may take hold. Caring leaders need to detect these signs early in the group process and circumvent these destructive tendencies. Consider some possible signs:

- People who always sit together and routinely joke about some insider incident that's not shared by others.

- Clusters of people who tend to view complex issues from one perspective instead of examining issues from multiple viewpoints.

- Frequent requests for special privileges from a particular subset of people.

Caring leaders look for multiple signs, not just one prime indicator.

Of course, identifying subgroups does not necessarily signal a tribal mentality. Some subgroups, like the offensive and defensive players on an American football team, might be quite natural. As long as these subgroups unite to win the game, then it doesn't really matter. Yet, when subgroups either openly or subtly conflict in ways that hinder progress, caring leaders act.

4. **Model collaborative conversational rules and applaud those who adopt them.** Many people simply don't know how to engage in collaborative discussions focused on others. It's not enough to implore these folks to "collaborate more" or "communicate better." This is like saying to a young driver who just got his temporary license, "Follow the rules of the road," if he never learned the rules in the first place.

Caring leaders encourage others to adopt collaborative conversational rules, such as:

- If someone brings up a compelling story, then avoid playing the "top that story" game. The "top the story" game has only one rule: if someone brings up a topic, another person relays a similar story that is even more outrageous. For example, after someone mentions a gardening mishap, someone else tries to tell another, more calamitous story. It's faux listening, because the new storyteller shifts attention away from the original storyteller. If the game is repeated often enough, most people recognize the pattern and assume that the other person is really not interested in what he or she has to say. It turns into a demoralizing game of one-upmanship.

- If someone brings up a troubling event, probe for more details rather than immediately offering advice. The probing shows respect for the other person and might just provide the relevant details for more candid, caring, and valuable advice.

- If you disagree with someone, paraphrase their position before offering your own. This demonstrates a degree of understanding. Plus, it gives the person the opportunity to clarify if you misunderstood their point. Bottom line: even if you end up disagreeing, at least the other person feels understood and possibly more accepting of a divergent point of view.

5. **Seek the proper balance between harmony and thoughtful debate.** We've all been to meetings where certain people do not freely offer their opinions or insights. That should be a red flag. Of course, at times the number of attendees makes this impossible, but setting aside that circumstance,

caring leaders make sure all viewpoints are heard. If someone remains silent, then the caring leader privately asks for their input depending upon the individual's desires. So, they learn to recognize the danger signs of leaning too far in one direction or the other. The absence of disagreement or serious debate, for example, often signals an overemphasis on relational harmony. Yet groups that constantly bicker and argue may have descended into a struggle for intellectual dominance. Neither extreme engenders lasting progress. Caring leaders are masters at orchestrating this balance of debate and relational communications.

In fact, caring leaders have an intuitive sense about when a team needs to move beyond its current position. Bickering about minor details may signal psychological exhaustion and require the leader's nudge toward the next step. Or the team may experience an uptick in energy as members sense some vague but significant turning point. At this crucial but unstated juncture, caring leaders nudge the group to go beyond the tipping point into genuine, value-adding territory.

VISIBLE PRACTICES FOR BUILDING AN INCLUSIVE WORKPLACE

Let's assume that the leader has in place a solid structure of subtle practices. Now what? Some people may well be impressed with a solid foundation, but most want to see inclusive practices in action, like those we discuss next.

1. **Celebrate differences even as you transcend them.** People of different faiths have different holiday traditions. These are differences that matter to many people, and we should respect them. Which raises an interesting question: Is it okay for someone who doesn't celebrate Christmas to wish "Merry

Christmas" to a teammate who does? Likewise, is it okay for someone of Christian faith to wish someone of Jewish faith "Happy Hanukkah" or "Happy Rosh Hashanah"? Opinions vary on these questions, but in general, we've found that most people, regardless of faith, appreciate these greetings by someone who has different traditions. If done sincerely, it shows respect for the other person and their faith.

Better yet, attending the celebrations of people with different backgrounds can be incredibly educational and enjoyable. Christians who attend bar or bat mitzvahs or Jews who attend Christmas services may feel uncomfortable at times, but they often find special, almost transcendent, bonds of humanity at these moments. Respecting others with different traditions goes a long way to making sure that diversity does not become divisive. Leaders who cannot embrace those differences or wrongly assume everyone celebrates the same holidays fail one of the most basic tests of caring leadership. They will "reap the whirlwind," as the book of Hosea says in the Hebrew scriptures and the Bible's Old Testament.

2.   **Commit to regular "turf talks."** Turf matters. Getting to know people on their turf puts people more at ease, because they feel more control in their own surroundings. Think of it this way: guests who visit someone's home for the first time often react by saying, "They seem like a different person than at the office." Likewise, this simple act of visiting a teammate's space moderates subtle hierarchical cues and encourages more genuine dialogue. Whether this involves walking around the building, stopping by the plant floor, or traveling to remote locations, the objective remains the same: to listen to what people say where they feel most comfortable and the least vulnerable.

Leaders should consider encouraging team members to also visit others on their turf. One leader in the banking industry discovered that team members who worked exclusively remotely had much different perspectives than those working on-site. The remote workers often developed hardened—and sometimes unrealistic—positions on issues that those working on-site thought were simply "nuts." These dueling impressions were fueled by people with distinctively different turf issues (e.g., disconnected groups in the Inclusion Intensity Indicator). So, what to do? The leader dealt with the issue by initiating short virtual tours of the on-site working environment for those virtual employees. This turf tour started to melt away some of the remote workers' hardened attitudes by subtly exposing hidden and errant assumptions about the work site.

3. **Share the results of group members' personality profiles.** Many organizations use personality tests as a tool to prompt greater understanding of other team members. To be sure, many widely used personality profiles, like Myers-Briggs, Caliper Profile, and DISC personality have been fairly criticized by researchers for any number of measurement issues.[3] Even the widely held belief that personality remains stable over situations and time has been challenged. Those are reasonable cautions to keep in mind before adopting this practice. We see these tools much like a physician might use an X-ray—as a useful but not definitive view of what's going on inside someone.

The utility of personality profiles emerges by recognizing, embracing, and utilizing differences on the team. For example, a team member's personality profile, highlighting his extroversion, provided him the catalyst to say in a team meeting, "I know I'm talking too much, so I'm going to shut me up right now." This elicited pleasant chuckles from the more introverted members of the group. The extrovert's willingness to throttle his typical talking tendencies demonstrated not only his self-awareness but also his desire to adapt to the others. The introverts' amusement at his remark expressed both appreciation of his act but also an acceptance of one key team member's personality difference.

4. **Promote formal and more spontaneous, informal get-togethers.** We frequently ask on surveys, "What was the best thing that happened to you at work this past month?" One common theme that regularly emerges is the opportunity to bond with team members outside their formal work environment. Comments such as the following routinely appear:

   • "Gathering workers together and going on an outing outside work to help morale and increase camaraderie"

   • "Some outside-of-work events for fun"

   • "Happy hour with team members"

   • "Participating in the wellness challenge and feeling connected to my colleagues."

   Such gatherings allow people to see dimensions of each other that may not surface in the workplace.

5. **Promote common purpose or mission as a unifying force.** Caring leaders acknowledge that institutions in the United States must reconcile with the historical ugliness of overt and

———————————— 66 ————————————

I know of no single formula for success. But over the years I have observed that some attributes of leadership are universal and are often about finding ways of encouraging people to combine their efforts, their talents, their insights, their enthusiasm, and their inspiration to work together.

—QUEEN ELIZABETH II

subtle racial discrimination. Doing so requires asking some uncomfortable questions and seeking out lessons learned. Much could be gained by discussing what institutions have made the most progress on these issues and how they did it. A good argument could be made that the US military should be near the top of the list. For some perspective, we can look at comments on the subject from former chairman of the Joint Chiefs of Staff and secretary of state Colin Powell:

> As a young black soldier, I looked for inspiration to the few senior black officers in the Army, and back in history to the black soldiers who had always served the nation proudly, even if the nation would not serve them. I had an obligation to stand on their shoulders and reach higher. I had to let my race be someone else's problem, never mine. I was an American soldier who was black, not a black American soldier.[4]

Such sentiments, no doubt, became part of his legendary "Thirteen Rules" for leaders. One of those rules, "Have a vision. Be demanding," proves particularly helpful to building an inclusive, high-performing workplace (see Figure 12.2). Noble missions cultivate resiliency, determination, flexibility, and the creative oomph to make progress together. Caring leaders promote a common purpose, personalize the mission's relevance, and frame the significant challenges in terms of the mission. They invoke shared core values as a bonding agent through the tough times.

MANAGE THE TOUGH SIDE OF ENGAGEMENT

Cultivating an engaged team requires mastery of visible and subtle practices. However, you will inevitably run into tough situations, which will require specific attention.

How do you manage a team member who doesn't really want to be engaged? Step back and ask, "Am I really sure that this person is disengaged?" Oftentimes leaders find it difficult to clearly identify a person's underlying motivations. In fact, it might take multiple interactions to discover this, because the employee may not be able to articulate his or her motivations particularly well. By observing the person in action and finding those activities or situations that seem to bring the employee enjoyment, you may glean insights into how to properly engage them.

How do I handle a team member who is engaged but headed in the wrong direction? This is the time to talk about creatively merging an employee's passion with the organization's needs. It will take coaching and guidance, which is the focus of Chapter Six. In fact, coaching provides team members with the right guardrails to guide the pursuit of their passions.

I'm a problem solver; how do I develop the patience that engagement requires? This is a natural temptation, because good leaders are usually great problem solvers. Sometimes, however, the problem is that you are trying to solve problems rather than listen to the problems presented. Creating a truly engaged work environment often requires that leaders shift their focus away from solving specific problems to concentrating more on team member development. This may be the only way to truly start reaping the benefits of engagement. In short, the dedicated problem solver needs to reframe the problem as one of employee development (e.g., equipping them to solve their own problems) rather than a specific issue to resolve.

CONCLUSION

The central tenet of this chapter can be stated in one sentence: caring leaders recognize the things that might separate people but connect them with the things that can unite. This presents a quandary: if leaders dwell too heavily on the things that separate, they risk alienating certain groups of people while empowering others (i.e., an exclusive group or disconnected groups). Yet, if leaders lean too heavily on the things that unite people, they risk overlooking important tensions that need resolution and collaborative opportunities ripe for innovation.

Reconciling the tension between things that might separate and things that might unite requires special leadership insight, creativity, and persistence. Leaders need insight to define the things that might separate and unite. Creatively and expansively searching for those things represents a fundamental leadership responsibility, which naturally prompts leaders to develop messaging and build relationships around robustly resonating ideas to developing messages and building relationships around strongly resonating ideas. Of course, insight and creativity are not enough; leaders need to persistently advocate for inclusive workplaces and communities. Civil rights leader Martin Luther King Jr. may have captured these sentiments best when he said, "An individual has not started living until he can rise above the narrow confines of his individualistic concerns to the broader concerns of all of humanity."

End of Chapter 12

BUILDING AN INCLUSIVE WORKPLACE SELF-ASSESSMENT

These questions are designed to provide developmental insights to enhance your effectiveness. Rate yourself, choosing either Improvement Needed, Solid, or Excels.

SELF-REFLECTION QUESTIONS

	IMPROVEMENT NEEDED	SOLID	EXCELS
1. I'm effective at selecting the right team members for particular issues.	◯	◯	◯
2. I'm good at spotting subgroup tendencies.	◯	◯	◯
3. I routinely model collaborative conversational rules.	◯	◯	◯
4. I'm effective at promoting common purpose and shared values.	◯	◯	◯
5. I know how to celebrate differences even as I transcend them.	◯	◯	◯
6. I visit employees where they work.	◯	◯	◯
7. I promote both formal as well as informal opportunities for team member get-togethers.	◯	◯	◯
8. I routinely ask for the input of others even if I think I might disagree.	◯	◯	◯
9 I can spot things that might separate people but connect people with things that can unite.	◯	◯	◯
10. I understand the relationship between diversity, inclusion, and engagement.	◯	◯	◯

Millions of businesspeople are constantly forced to choose between their desire not to be viewed as a bad person and their desire to be a good businessperson.

—MOKOKOMA MOKHONOANA

CHAPTER 13
CARING LEADERS PRIORITIZE SUSTAINABLE FINANCIAL PERFORMANCE

Previously, we discussed how caring leaders adeptly transform pushback into progress (see Chapter Nine). Here's some pushback we received from an executive after a recent "leading with care" discussion:

> I've spent my whole career believing in all of this stuff—the development of people, high involvement of members, transparent communications—all of it. It's all great and necessary. But my experience has been, when the money gets tight, when a business goes south, and when profits turn to losses, a few enlightened people hunker down in a secluded conference room and determine how much cost they can cut and how many bodies they can get rid of. That experience is demoralizing to the entire

team, and the care for the "softer stuff" is out the window. That's the "real world."

Other people express similar apprehensions in less cynical terms, but this executive's underlying sentiments reflect a typical concern about leading with care. Bluntly stated, reconciling the tension between caring about financial performance and caring about people poses a unique challenge. It is one, though, that we directly address in this chapter. Much has been written elsewhere about adroitly managing finances and investment strategy.[1] We use a wide-angled lens to view a broader set of issues facing caring leaders that receives far less attention.

SUSTAINABLE FINANCIAL PERFORMANCE

Sustainable financial performance appears to be an easy idea to understand and embrace—over time, your organization should generate more revenue than it spends. What's not quite so simple is identifying all the potential costs and revenues that could occur over time. For example, on the cost side, many organizations fail to recognize the threats of cybertheft and the possibility of paying ransom for their digitized data. On the revenue side, investments in innovative ideas may or may not pay off in the long run.

Caring leaders think of sustainable financial performance in terms of three interrelated elements: 1) investments, 2) operating costs, and 3) revenues (see Figure 13.1).

Investments: capital devoted to projects expected to produce a positive return over the long term. This might include financing technology intended to deliver a service more efficiently and training designed to maximize the effectiveness of people, as well as funding innovative endeavors. All investments represent calculated bets to increase revenues or cut costs. Funding innovations

Figure 13.1

STRATEGIC ELEMENTS OF SUSTAINABLE FINANCIAL PERFORMANCE

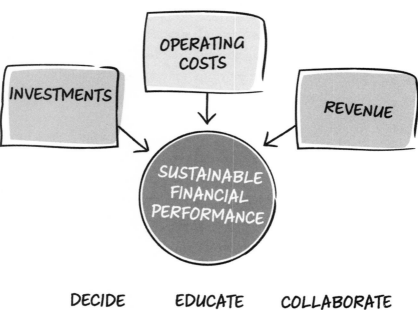

DECIDE   EDUCATE   COLLABORATE

represents a special set of challenges, which we address in the next chapter.

Operating costs: generally recurring expenses to cover the day-to-day operations of the organization. These might include electricity to run the office as well insurance to protect from certain kinds of losses.

Revenues: the total amount of income generated by the service or good. This might include the sales of a widget for a particular price or a donation received by a nonprofit. Both represent positive additions to the ledger.

Obviously, investments and operating costs represent negative items on the ledger, while revenues represent positives. Leaders are tasked with generating more pluses than minuses in the long run. Doing so embodies the idea of sustainable financial performance.

Caring leaders construct a lattice of commitments to investments, operating costs, and revenues. These interconnected commitments help to reconcile the tension between caring for people and caring for results:

1. **Caring leaders exercise good strategic judgment when making decisions about investments, operating costs, and revenues.** The shortest word in this commitment—*and*—makes it a particularly thorny pledge to honor. Unfortunately, some leaders act like the statement contains the shorter word *or.* That's a big mistake.

   In the long run, leaders must concentrate on all three elements to create sustainable financial performance. For instance, a myopic focus on just slashing operating costs may well generate positive results, but it may do so only in the short term. Without investments in the future, particularly innovations, the balance sheet may only look good in the short term. Strategically balancing short-term and long-term interests requires great decision-making skills. And caring leaders gladly accept that learning challenge.

2. **Caring leaders educate their team about the organization's investments, operating costs, and revenues.** Leaders are often dismayed by many employees' lack of knowledge about the basics of their organization's financial performance. In fact, we've often advised organizations to create a simple, five-item quiz to gauge employees' knowledge of their organization's financial position. Consider the questions in Table 13.1. How many of your team members could correctly answer them?

Table 13.1

FINANCIAL QUIZ

QUESTION	CATEGORY
1. What are the top 3 sources of revenue for our organization?	**Revenue**
2. What is our largest operating expense?	**Operating costs**
3. What are the top 3 investments we're making for the future?	**Investments**
4. Who are our top customers/donors?	**Revenue**
5. How do we rate against the competition in terms of net profit margin?	**Revenue, Operating costs, Investments**

3. **When possible, caring leaders collaborate with team members on investments, operating costs, and revenue decisions.** For instance, involving team members in decisions regarding investment opportunities educates team members in a more profound way than even the glitziest financial presentation or expertly delivered training session. Ditto for committees tasked with cutting operating costs. Why? Because it reveals the underlying complexity and difficulty of these decisions. It forces team members to reconcile the inherent trade-offs between investments, operating costs, and revenue. And it sensitizes people to the inherent uncertainties surrounding any investment or cost-cutting measure.

Caring leaders honor these three commitments by using the subtle and visible practices discussed next.

SUBTLE PRACTICES TO PRIORITIZE SUSTAINABLE PERFORMANCE

The subtle practices discussed below provide the backdrop for the visible practices. Leaders who use the subtle practices provide a foundation for thinking about finances while minimizing team member stress and unpleasant surprises.

1. **Set responsible budgets and live within the guidance of those budgets.** Making the numbers work is a tough part of leadership; after all, people rely on organizations to be economically vibrant. Shareholders, for example, expect financial performance for their ownership participation. In nonprofit organizations, caring leaders ensure that the costs of programs and services do not outstrip the funding sources.

Caring leaders may use debt, but at levels appropriate to the circumstances. By avoiding excessive debt, they do not impose burdens on those who would face future obligations too large to handle. In short, caring leaders operate within their means while planning for the inevitable cycles of business growth and decline.

Caring leaders master the continuous balancing act between investments, operating costs, and revenues. For example, they learn to properly fund and balance investments in people, technology, communications, innovations, and a host of other areas. Social responsibility issues are also part of the financial equation, signifying leaders' responsibilities to society at large. They understand that these investments need to increase during times of growth and decrease during difficult times.

2. **Support people as they navigate through the uncertain financial times.** It's easy to talk about financial results when economic conditions are good but far more difficult when financial conditions shift downward. When financial conditions cycle down, caring leaders avoid promises about ultimate outcomes, such as, "I assure you, these problems will be behind us in three months." Instead, they speak transparently about the conditions and give their best assessment of cause. They outline actions being taken, the status of previous actions that worked or didn't work, and further corrective measures being considered. Frequent and transparent communication helps team members deal with the inherent uncertainties of business cycles and the accompanying stress.

3. **Show respect for team members' personal financial hardships.** During difficult financial times, leaders need to make hard decisions to lower costs, eliminate programs, or reduce the number of team members. Caring leaders understand these are high-stress times. Nobody is happy. Caring leaders treat team members with empathy for the hardships they face. They communicate often and listen to concerns, even offering

counseling services to help people through the difficulty. This empathy does not stop leaders from taking appropriate actions, but it does cause leaders to act in compassionate ways. Perhaps leaders can take a page from the playbooks of NFL and NBA coaches about how to handle such situations with compassion—after all, they routinely cut or trade players. We know that some coaches excel at this gut-wrenching task, because, when circumstances change, some of those same players return to play for those very same coaches.

4. **Discourage a gig mentality.** Historically, the word *gig* meant a light carriage pulled by one horse, not a team. Today, we use the word to describe temporary workers seeking additional income or opportunities. In some cases, organizations thrive on gig workers.[2] After all, where would Uber and Lyft be without them? Gig workers often ask themselves a simple cost/benefit question: "Is it worth my time and effort to do this gig?" Repeatedly asking this question shapes a mentality focused on the task at hand to secure quick income and an attitude of "I just do what I'm contracted to do." Those with an extreme gig mentality rarely entertain questions like, "What do our customers or clients need?" "Can I contribute now for something more important in the future?" or "Am I acting in accordance with the organization's brand or values?"

    Allowing some workers to adopt this mentality may be necessary. Yet, if too many employees adopt this perspective, it will undermine sustainable financial performance. Why? Because there will not be enough of the right people who will think and collaborate about creating a sustainable future by decreasing costs, making better investments,

———————————— 66 ————————————

Rarely does a corporation have a comprehensive approach to the management of its most used and most important asset: information. —JAMES W. CORTADA

and securing new revenue sources. When caring leaders spot a "Just do what I'm contracted to do" mentality, they seek ways to reach out to that person's latent insights, creativity, and problem-solving abilities. (See Figure 13.2.) Caring leaders embrace the totality of as many people as possible. It's the right thing to do and it's the smart thing to do to secure the long-term viability of the organization.

Figure 13.2

SIGNS OF A GIG MENTALITY

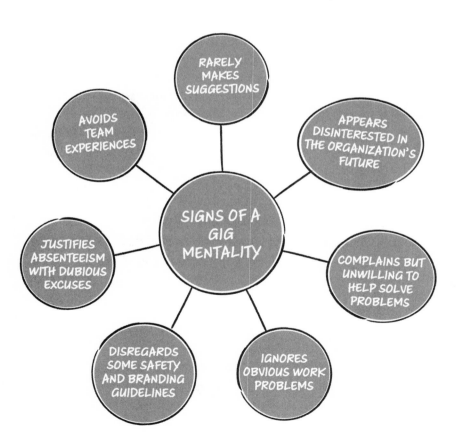

VISIBLE PRACTICES TO ENSURE SUSTAINABLE FINANCIAL PERFORMANCE

Communicating and collaborating, when possible, maximizes the potential of all employees and may well be the best medicine for those suffering from the gig mentality. We provide some helpful practices next.

1. **Publicize a list of ten financial facts that everyone on the team should know.** The list should contain at least one fact from each financial category of investments, costs, and revenues. These items should be the major drivers of the organization's financial positioning. The purpose: provide a broad overview of the organization's short- and long-term financial situation.

    Caring leaders artfully construct the list of financial facts to not only educate but focus attention on issues that will propel the team or organization to excel (see Table 13.2). While the facts may include some pertinent income statement items (e.g., revenues hit $1 billion this year), they might also address percentages emphasizing areas of shifting sources of revenue. One executive, for example, compared the change in percentage of revenues generated by certain market sectors over time to explain the rationale for reallocating resources (e.g., in 2010, 60 percent of our revenues were generated in the manufacturing sector; today that represents 20 percent of our revenues). Likewise, a nonprofit executive used a financial fact about the percentage of revenues generated by grants to emphasize the unique funding opportunity for this chamber music group. Some financial facts may not contain a number or statistic at all—noting the names of the largest donors (i.e., revenue sources) of a nonprofit should prompt all members of the organization to enrich and extend those relationships. This fact has as much significance to the organization's financial health as any dollar amount or percentage.

Table 13.2

EXAMPLES OF FINANCIAL FACTS

NONPROFIT	FOR-PROFIT	FINANCIAL CATEGORY
We invested $10,000 for a new sound system to replace the old one.	We invested $5M in a new production line.	
We allocated $5,000 to recruit a new development person to head up our fundraising efforts.	We allocated $3.5M in next year's budget for a new business venture.	Investments
We allocated $8,000 to a study to determine the feasibility of owning our premises vs. leasing.	We allocated $50,000 to investigate opportunities in a new geographical market.	
We spend 20% of our annual budget on securing performance venues.	We spend 75% of our annual budget on people resources.	
We spend 5% of our annual budget on advertising.	We spend 10% of our annual budget on research for new projects and services.	Costs
We spend 60% of our annual budget on salaries and benefits.	We spend 8% of our annual budget to repair equipment.	
Our top donors are Betty Brice, Andrew Adams, Charles Cartwright, & Hillary Harris.	40% of our annual revenue comes from the industrial sector.	
Grants represented 20% of our income.	Our top 10 target customers make up 70% of our revenue.	Revenue
Our annual donor renewal rate was 4.6% compared to the national average of 5%.	Our largest customer nationally is Alliance logistics.	
On average, each fundraising meet-and-greet event we held generated 10 new donors.	The overall net profit margin on our business is 10%.	Revenue & Cost

2. **Educate team members about the organization's financial performance.** A thoughtfully prepared list of financial facts may well inform people, but it's not the same as educating them. Information represents the raw material used in the education process. The stories behind the numbers enrich understanding about both financial performance and future organizational direction.

     Educating team members requires the kind of robust communication advocated in Chapter Eight. Additionally, it often means grappling with pushback in ways proposed in Chapter Nine. As caring leaders educate about sustained financial performance, they pay particular attention that they broadcast on both the WIFO (What's In it For the Organization) and WIFM (What's In it For Me) channels:

     > WIFO—Consider a CEO who explained the shifts in the customer mix by sharing underlying economic data and emergent trends. He noted that while the company had lost some customers, it also gained new customers that were not even on the radar screen ten years prior.

     By noting both the upside and downside of this particular financial fact, he shaped employee understanding on two levels: first, his evenhanded discussion helped explain major decisions and future directions. After such explanations, team members almost magically aligned and positioned themselves for their own best interests as well the organization's. Second, it fostered a mind-set that every financial trend, regardless of direction, has both positive and negative implications. That mind-set cultivates dispassionate analysis, dynamic learning, progress, and a spirit of resiliency.

     > WIFM—Educating about a trend needs to extend to the personal level. Answering, "How will the

financial trend affect individual team members?" often does the trick. Even if the leader does not know the answer, the mere acknowledgment of the issue strengthens trust and perhaps sparks illuminating dialogue about issues not even on the leader's radar screen. Such discussions can only occur when the leader embraces uncertainty, as we described in Chapter One.

Bluntly stated: leaders who fail to broadcast on both channels are not educating their team members or demonstrating care for them. As Anna Bernasek noted in her book *The Economics of Integrity*, "Once a relationship of trust and integrity exists, remarkable efficiencies result. Pervasive integrity is fundamental to our enormous, fast-moving economy. Integrity isn't something that's nice to have. It's something we have to have."[3]

3. **Calibrate the right tempo of financial communications to the needs of team members and the organization.** Asking about the right tempo of financial communication resembles asking a physician about how often patients should measure their blood pressure. It depends, of course, on the patient: for some, once a year will work; for others, a daily reading may be necessary. Likewise, the tempo of financial communication can range from a yearly check-in to a daily reading. For example, many public institutions, like universities, may only need an annual or semiannual report. Most for-profit organizations may consider following the rhythm of the market and share results on a quarterly basis. Some organizations take this one step further and treat financial results like a rolling set of critical football game stats. That's exactly what an innovative dental supply company, Dental City, does with its sales results: it displays them on large

monitors, in real time, for all to see. Dave Withbroe, one of the owners, noted that these scoreboards signal that "every day represents a new game while also building sales reps' accountability and friendly competition."[4]

Just as physicians recommend monitoring based on a patient's health condition, caring leaders set the tempo to reflect the needs of team members and the organization. Tempo decisions determine how quickly organizations detect challenges and opportunities. At Dental City, the "game day" sales statistics send a powerful message. Yet, thoughtful leaders recognize that quicker is not always better. For example, a fast-paced tempo may prompt overcorrection and oversensitivity to occasional blips. Of course, a dirgelike pace may provide perspective but miss important red flags until challenges have metastasized.

That's why thoughtful leaders carefully ponder the Goldilocks problem of finding just the right tempo—not too fast, not too slow. The right tempo reconciles the tensions between the short-term versus long-term, oversensitivity versus undersensitivity, and reactive versus proactive responses. The objective: avoid over- and underreacting to daily setbacks or triumph. Some leaders resolve the Goldilocks tempo challenge by providing short monthly reports on key indicators, holding quarterly meetings to review current trends, and hosting a major state-of-the-company event at the end of the fiscal year.

4. **Transparently communicate about the big three financial elements—investments, operating costs, and revenues.** When leaders communicate matters. That's why we highlighted tempo above. What leaders communicate matters, as well. Caring leaders update and educate employees about these three financial elements while paying particular attention to WIFO and WIFM issues. How leaders communicate may matter the most.

Team members want to hear directly and transparently from their leaders about financial performance—the good, the bad, and the ugly. Openly harvesting dissenting views may be the most important way to demonstrate honesty and transparency. Some team members may raise difficult questions, while others may criticize major decisions. Caring leaders embrace and kindheartedly respond to these questions and dissenting views to build deeper understanding, if not necessarily agreement.

Sincerely communicating and legitimizing dissent builds goodwill, augments the leader's credibility, and usually cultivates a willingness to consider alternative views. Sometimes, though, employees fixate on a minor flaw or area of disagreement, failing to see the bigger picture of trade-offs that leaders face. This may be unavoidable. Yet, caring leaders minimize the probability that one employee's unhealthy fixation becomes disruptive to the entire team by spotlighting issues across the spectrum of financial performance. Doing so brings a sense of context and proportionality to the issue as it is weighed against other, more pressing concerns. Using the planning checklist in Table 13.3 provides a helpful reminder about the proper balance between all the elements of sustained financial performance.

5. **Offer personal finance training for team members.** Most organizations offer a host of benefits to employees, but often without the necessary training on how to make these decisions within the realm of their personal finances. The University of Wisconsin system, for example, provides employees with a wide range of benefit options, ranging from dental insurance to participation in various supplemental retirement plans. New employees are often bewildered

Table 13.3

FINANCIAL REVIEW CHECKLIST

MAJOR ISSUES	CHECKLIST
Discuss Investments	Notable issues WIFO WIFM
Discuss Operating Costs	Notable issues WIFO WIFM
Discuss Revenues	Notable issues WIFO WIFM
Outline General Financial Health	Comparisons to similar organizations WIFO WIFM
Entertain Questions	What issues can I clarify? What concerns do you have? How do you see your role in each of these areas?

by the array of possibilities and the decisions they need to make in a short period of time. It often boils down to a lack of knowledge about the basics of personal finance. In fact, regardless of the economic sector, we have discovered a surprising number of employees are unaware of how to incorporate into their personal situation some fundamental personal financial activities, like setting budgets, dollar cost averaging, and diversifying investments. They may have heard about these principles, but they are unaware of how to go about employing them. As Morgan Housel, a former columnist for the *Wall Street Journal* and the *Motley Fool*, put it, "People do some crazy things with money. But no one is crazy."[5] People may not be "crazy," but they are often undereducated. Training can stop some of the ill-advised craziness, particularly of less financially savvy employees.

While this practice is highly visible, the benefits tend to be far more subtle. Team members who follow even the most basic personal financial guidelines gain greater control over their financial situations. This allows them to weather the inevitable ups and downs of business cycles with less anxiety and more optimism. The benefits to the organization or team may be subtler, but they are equally important. A firm foundation in personal finance helps employees better understand the leadership challenges of reconciling the tensions between investments, cost management, and revenues. In fact, with a well-informed audience, skillful executives can use personal finance principles to explain major organizational decisions.

6. **Engage a diverse group of team members in financial communication and action planning.** For example, developing the list of ten financial facts with a collaborative team often proves educational, as people sift through all the potential items to

emphasize. The constraint of only selecting ten facts promotes focus while providing a tangible way to honor a basic communication principle: you can communicate about almost anything, but you can't communicate about everything.

Additionally, strive to hear multiple voices when developing financial action plans. Avoid leaning too heavily on financial people. Nonfinancially oriented team members often discover creative ways to reduce costs, pause spending for less essential investments, improve efficiencies, or uncover creative ways to improve sources of funds. The bonus: such actions boost morale while enhancing financial sensitivity across the entire team.

THE TOUGH SIDE OF SUSTAINABLE FINANCIAL PERFORMANCE

The subtle and visible practices build relationships based on honesty, transparency, and integrity. But what about when financial situations deteriorate? Even then, respectful, caring relationships moderate further damage. After all, well-informed and educated team members typically detect shifting trend lines well in advance of an organization resorting to cost-cutting measures. They should not be surprised by these unfortunate but necessary organizational responses.

When finances tighten, losses loom, and budgets shrink, caring leaders take the necessary and difficult actions for the long-term viability of the organization. However, if these reductions are not done with care, they will cause damage to morale, engagement, and confidence that lasts far beyond the time frame of the actions. In such difficult times, caring leaders treat all people with dignity and respect. For people asked to leave, caring leaders provide financial and counseling resources as bridges to new employment opportunities. Ironically, researchers have found that many employees laid off in the proper way experience better psychological health than those who remain behind. Some psychologists note these feelings parallel survivor guilt for those who survived a horrific accident or natural disaster.[6] That's one reason why caring leaders robustly communicate with the remaining employees about the economic realities while outlining a path forward to brighter days.

CONCLUSION

Some leaders who embrace the caring leadership approach sideline financial issues until a crisis hits. Others, like the executive at the beginning of the chapter, abandon caring leader sentiments in a favor of the cold, hard economic realities.

Neither reaction syncs up with the leading-with-care approach we've advocated throughout this book. Instead, we embrace those realities by transparently, frequently, and robustly communicating about the organization's strategy for investments, operating costs, and revenues. Such actions minimize unpleasant financial surprises while maximizing opportunities for imaginatively addressing financial challenges. In short, following through on the commitments to exercise good judgment, communicate results, and involve team members provides a hedge against the bad times while maximizing growth possibilities.

End of Chapter 13

SUSTAINABLE FINANCIAL PERFORMANCE SELF-ASSESSMENT

These questions are designed to provide developmental insights to enhance your effectiveness. Rate yourself, choosing either Improvement Needed, Solid, or Excels.

SELF-REFLECTION QUESTIONS

	IMPROVEMENT NEEDED	SOLID	EXCELS
1. I know the three most important metrics associated with revenues, costs, and investments for my team/organization.	◯	◯	◯
2. I'm routinely briefing my team on financial performance.	◯	◯	◯
3. I encourage employees to shape financial decisions as much as possible.	◯	◯	◯
4. I help team members understand that returns on any investment are uncertain.	◯	◯	◯
5. I can explain how the organization balances the tensions between costs, investments, and revenues.	◯	◯	◯
6. I seek to become more skilled at making financial decisions.	◯	◯	◯
7. I'm comfortable discussing financial issues (good and bad) with team members.	◯	◯	◯

If I had asked the public what they wanted,
they would have said a faster horse.

—HENRY FORD

CHAPTER 14

CARING LEADERS EAGERLY IMAGINE AND PIONEER THE FUTURE

Consider these questions:

- Why didn't Sears morph into Amazon.com? After all, Sears perfected mass catalog selling and countrywide distribution networks.

- Why didn't Random House explicitly secure the digital rights of their top titles and instead ended up suing a start-up company that did? After all, it would have been easy to amend the authors' contracts.[1]

- Why didn't taxicab companies build in technical and service delivery models like Uber and Lyft have done? After all, mobile phone apps were widely available.

Caring leaders ponder dilemmas like these because they reveal latent issues they must master.[2] Each of these questions highlights how innovations can rapidly change the competitive landscape. On the surface, it may appear like leaders of Sears, Random House, and a slew of taxicab companies simply failed to properly envision the future. Fair enough, but it goes much deeper. In all likelihood, there were at least a few employees at Sears, Random House, and the cab companies that did, indeed, visualize the future delivery of their products and services. Yet, those voices were either marginalized or silenced in some way. Organizational inertia abounds with thinking like, "If it ain't broke, don't fix it." In essence, the prevailing operating models in these industries trumped any attempt to develop new models.[3]

Caring leaders recognize these tendencies and take active steps to counteract the inertia of tradition and raise the voices of innovators who create the future. Caring leaders do so because they recognize the future begins at the edge of everyone's comfort zone and materializes in the uncertainties beyond. Caring leaders lead in ways that trigger innovation, because they spark and embrace innovative pursuits by individuals and teams. Growth will not occur simply because leaders set aggressive targets; instead, growth emerges when new ideas are surfaced, incubated, and put into action.[4] Doing so requires a firm grasp of the innovation process, which we discuss next.

THE INNOVATION PROCESS

People often equate creativity or invention with innovation. It's easy to do, because these ideas are closely related. In contrast, caring leaders think of innovation as a developmental process, best represented in three major phases (see Figure 14.1).

It all starts with conceiving a new approach and ends when the mainstream of the organization or society assimilates the idea into everyday life.

Figure 14.1

THE INNOVATION PROCESS

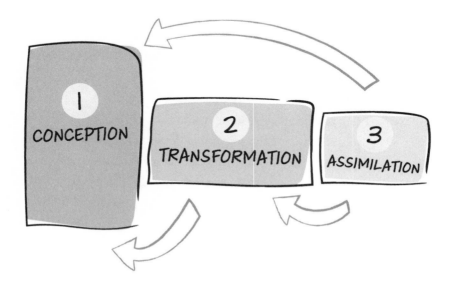

Phase 1: Conception—The innovation process begins with conceiving a new idea.[5] The novel spark might be how to improve something that already exists, like adding a pull-down step to the bed of your favorite pickup truck. In the progress model, we described such actions as tweaking an existing platform (see Chapter Two).

Or it could be something entirely novel, like the Moderna and Pfizer COVID vaccines, which relied on mRNA technology. (Note: The Johnson & Johnson COVID vaccine was also innovative but relied on traditional vaccine technology.) In the progress model, we described these rarer activities as "exploring to create a new platform."

Phase 2: Transformation—Transforming an idea into a practical reality represents the second crucial step in the innovation process. This means moving the idea off the mental or actual drawing board into a prototype to analyze, test, and critique. Orville and Wilbur Wright transformed the idea of human flight into reality by solving some major engineering problems—wing design, power, and steering. They had help. They studied and critiqued the concepts of da Vinci, Galileo, and many others. Those early ideas, coupled with years of experiments, resulted in the famous flight at Huffman Prairie near Dayton, Ohio, in 1905.[6]

Some new ideas, like the Wright brothers' planes, take years of testing and development to move from the conception to the transformation phase. Other sparks of imagination can move through these phases in a matter of hours. For example, skilled social media managers can conceive of a new stream of postings, develop samples, and test them—all within one day.

Phase 3: Assimilation—Widespread public acceptance of air travel occurred decades after the wonders of winged flight emerged. We call this the assimilation phase, where most people learn to embrace the benefits of the innovation, while managing the risks. The rapid conception and development of the COVID vaccines (i.e., Operation Warp Speed) ran into some challenges at this stage with many members of the public. That's to be expected with any innovation, because unique individual objections and circumstances play a larger role at this stage. In other words, innovation does not stop once a beautiful and compelling idea has been transformed into an effective prototype. Cost could be a factor, but so could other social, political, or religious issues. Electric-powered vehicles, for instance, clearly have moved beyond phase two but have not yet been fully assimilated into many people's lives.

Innovation Principles

Three key innovation principles emerge from this framework.

First, caring leaders cultivate innovative climates. The beliefs we highlighted in the first section of the book prove vital in creating innovative climates:

- Innovative leaders must embrace uncertainty—People who are certain undermine the innovative spirit of others, because they frequently undercut or even challenge new ways of thinking. As Chip Gaines, arguably the second most famous "fixer-upper" and cofounder of the Magnolia Network, disclosed, "When we become insistent on certainty, conformity becomes the most probable outcome."[7] Innovative leaders are the first to greet a new and often unformed idea with a hearty "That sounds interesting—let's develop that notion." This kind of inquisitiveness sets the tone for discovery, invention, and progress. In fact, the Wright brothers were often touted as examples of the uniquely American success narrative because they were raised with no "special advantages." Intriguingly, Orville emphatically retorted, "The greatest thing in our favor was growing up in a family where there was always much encouragement to intellectual curiosity."[8]

- Innovative leaders inspire progress making by encouraging others to tweak existing practices or leap to new approaches. Encouraging experimentation on both a large and small scale builds the foundation for continued performance excellence.[9] Caring leaders think of innovation as an elastic process. Some innovations are small, like just tweaking an existing procedure. Other innovations are large and platform shifting, requiring years of development and countless iterations.

- Innovative leaders have the right values. The values of patience, respect, and humility play large roles in cultivating a sustainable innovative climate throughout the three phases.

  - It requires patience to allow ideas to be nurtured through the transformation phase, because of the inevitable setbacks.

  - It requires a deep respect for others to allow them the freedom to try new things; they may fail from time to time but will learn important lessons as a result.

  - And it requires humility for the leader to recognize that they don't have all the answers.

Likewise, many of the practices discussed in Section Two promote an innovative climate. Robust conversations and related pushback can often spark innovative impulses. In particular, thoughtful communication often proves essential during the assimilation phase—people won't assimilate something new just because a leader suggests it. People want their questions answered so they can properly weigh the costs and benefits of the innovation. Building strong, dynamic relationships serves as a never-ending source of inspiration for new ideas in both the conception as well as transformation phases of the innovation process. Likewise, collaborative and engaged teams can break logjams in the transformation or assimilation phases.

Second, caring leaders envision an iterative process rather than a checklist approach. Some people perceive a one-two-three checklist after looking at the figure describing the innovation process (see Figure 14.1). That is, they expect the process to work exactly like the main features of the diagram—first, conceive of an innovation, then transform it into reality, and finally deploy it. Innovation rarely works that way; it's usually far messier. That's why the diagram also includes some smaller arrows pointing in the opposite direction from the primary arrows. These represent iterative loops, where ideas move back through the process for refinement or reconsideration. Sometimes, this might involve making a small tweak to enhance acceptance. Adding an eraser to the pencil proved crucial to widespread acceptance of this unique innovation.[10] At other times, it might be a total reimagining of the concept. For example, credit for inventing the potato chip is widely attributed to George Crum, a chef at a New York lodge, after customers complained about the thickness of his French fries in 1853.

Third, caring leaders attend to the unique challenges of each phase. Some organizations struggle with the conceptualization stage. In other words, they are not entertaining enough new ideas. Caring leaders diagnose the underlying reasons: it could be cultural; it could be the organizational structure or even the natural proclivities of the employees. Other organizations grapple with gaining acceptance of new ideas (i.e., assimilation) for similar reasons. Regardless, caring leaders seek to understand the underlying issues and address them.

Caring leaders are mindful that each stage in the process represents a different set of challenges. Typically, there are far more ideas to pursue than resources to deploy for the transformation and assimilation phases. That's why we adjusted the size of the boxes in the illustration. That's appropriate as long as leaders don't undermine the spirit of people through the winnowing process. Caring leaders recognize that some people are naturally better suited to one part of the process than to others. Highly creative people thrive when conceiving new ideas and resourcefully transforming those ideas into prototypes. They may then lose interest in pushing for assimilation. Other, more pragmatic, people excel in the transformation and assimilation stages. They know how to get things done and gain others' acceptance.

VISIBLE PRACTICES FOR INNOVATION

Caring leaders use the innovation framework and principles to guide their visible practices and help their teams courageously imagine the future.

1. **Frame broad challenges, rather than suggest specific solutions.** When leaders consistently frame issues more broadly, they create a viewpoint that implicitly focuses employee energy, helping them make sense of the chaos and confusion. A proper frame allows employees to see the big picture amid the day-to-day complexities. It spotlights the grand challenge while diverting the gaze from specific solutions. For example, during the COVID pandemic, nonprofit organizations around the world were asking pressing questions, such as, "How can we make our workplace safe?" and "How do we maintain fund-raising in this environment?" These kinds of operational questions were pressing and important. Yet, queries like these do not really frame the innovative opportunities forced on leaders. But Oliver Zornow, the executive director of the Building for Kids Children's Museum in Appleton, Wisconsin, recognized the opportunity and expanded the frame of the challenge by asking, "How can we deliver the experiences for children that we pride ourselves in creating within this restrictive environment?" Such framing led to some impressive, innovative results. The team created take-home art studio kits that parents could pick up at curbside for their antsy, homebound kids. It was a spectacular success, as the first set "sold out" in hours. Such are the innovative successes of properly framing innovative opportunities, even in the most challenging of circumstances.

A frame provides the lens through which people view situations, highlighting certain features while deflecting attention from others. Leaders need to be particularly sensitive to how they present innovative challenges and push for resolution of problems. The way a leader presents the opportunity often has a disproportionate influence on the eventual innovation or solution. The reason is simple: people often want to please their leaders, and if their leader advocates for a particular solution, then they will strive to deliver that result—often regardless of other, more optimal possibilities. That's the genius behind the famous Henry Ford quote at the beginning of the chapter: "If I had asked the public what they wanted, they would have said a faster horse." Developing new platforms like horseless carriages—or automobiles—requires a more expansive view of the innovative opportunity.

2. **Establish an innovation studio.** We once heard a painter discuss her craft. She started by highlighting what creating is not. It's not an exercise in painting by the numbers; rather, painters view their craft as a deliberate attempt to match color with shape and texture that reveal the artist's conception. She continued,

> My craft starts with a blank white canvas. I have blobs of different colored paints on a palette next to me, which I can use or mix in a rainbow of hues. I have a selection of brushes, large and small, stiff and soft, narrow and wide. I have a vision in my mind of what I want to create. I start with a first brushstroke, then another, and then another color, then another brush as I start to create the vision that's in my mind.
>
> What about mistakes?

> I make all kinds of mistakes. I can't erase the paint.
> I put another brushstroke over the bad one. If the
> developing picture does not match my vision, I re-
> stroke, recolor, and blend previous mistakes in to
> perfect my creation.

If the mistakes are too large, she trashes the canvas and starts again, learning from the "failure." That's the life of a potter, sculptor, or innovator.

So it is with caring leaders as they encourage their team to select a brush, mix colors, and make the early brushstrokes on their clean, blank canvas. Caring leaders establish innovation studios for experimentation while embracing the inevitable mistakes as an opportunity to learn. The studio of innovation must push beyond what everyone else does or what is considered typical or standard practice. Innovators don't paint by the numbers; they start with a blank sheet of paper and paint outside the lines. The choice is simple: you have a chance to do more of the same or make a new brushstroke.

The studio itself can be a physical or a virtual space, with a dedicated slot in team members' schedules to allow for innovative thinking. Make the studio safe for people to raise new ideas, with no repercussions. For example, few people know where the first man on the moon's spacesuit was originally imagined and developed. Answer: Playtex, a women's bra company.[11] Making the studio safe requires that leaders applaud reactions like "Maybe there are other possibilities," "Very interesting," and "Is there another way we can look at this issue?"

3. **Vary the speed of the clock.** Historically, clocks have been used as instruments of control to induce order, conformity, and compliance to convention. For instance, when England

was colonizing countries in the world, a top-priority infrastructure task was building highly visible and architecturally dominating clocks.[12]

But rigid timetables can undermine the innovative spirit. This is particularly true during the conception and transformation phases. Committing to a timetable for creativity rarely works, at least for very long. Calling a time-out and reevaluating the timetable may be the best way to successfully develop and deploy an innovative idea.

Issues of great complexity often require a great deal of time to truly understand. Sometimes by sleeping on an idea, an unconscious reconciliation of conflicting ideas can emerge.[13] Shifting the speed of the clock to allow time to ponder cultivates flexibility necessary for genius to emerge. Consider the pressure that Leonardo da Vinci was under when painting the "Last Supper." His patron was frustrated by da Vinci's lack of progress on the painting, as every brushstroke was completed except the face of one disciple. For months, da Vinci did not visit his studio, further delaying painting the last face. Yet, when pressed on the issue, he replied that he had been working on the face for two hours every day. The duke could not understand how the artist could be working on a painting he had not seen in months. Leonardo responded:

> Your Excellency is aware that only the head of Judas remains to be done, and he was, as everyone knows, an egregious villain. Therefore he should be given a physiognomy fitting his wickedness. To this end, for about a year if not more, night and morning, I have been going every day to the Borghetto, where Your Excellency knows that all the ruffians of the city live. But I have not yet been able to discover a villain's

face corresponding to what I have in mind. Once
I find that face, I will finish the painting in a day.[14]

Da Vinci shrewdly slowed a ticking clock by noting that if
his facial scavenger hunt proved fruitless, he would use the
face of the person who complained to the duke in the first
place. His Excellency's pressure ceased, and the masterpiece
was eventually completed. These are not the mere musings
of an eccentric artist; they are, in fact, the sentiments of one
who recognized the artistic element in all kinds of endeavors. After all, Leonardo was also a skilled architect, inventor,
scientist, and engineer.

4. **Entertain different models of the situation.** If you are expe-
    riencing knee pain, you might go to your family physician.
    She could conduct a physical exam on your knee, gently
    bending it, checking for the point of pain. She might also
    request an X-ray, which could reveal other underlying issues.
    Then an orthopedic surgeon might get involved and even
    request an MRI of your knee. Each one of these steps rep-
    resents different models of the underlying condition—physi-
    cal exam is one model, X-ray another, and MRI still another.
    Each successive model helps refine the diagnosis before any
    treatments or surgery might be prescribed.

    This kind of care makes perfect sense in the medical en-
    vironment. Each successive model provides another layer of
    understanding of the underlying condition. Innovation in
    challenging environments can be looked at in the same way.
    Each new model of the underlying circumstances augments
    understanding and allows for more focus on the challenge at
    hand.[15] A simple query by the leader, such as, "Before moving
    forward with this idea, could we look at the situation in a dif-
    ferent way?" or "Could we use a different metaphor to describe
    the situation?" will almost magically surface differing models.

Innovation often emerges as the models of the situation shift. For example, innovative treatments for heart disease could only emerge after the "heart as a furnace" model was replaced by the "heart as a pump" model. Subsequent discussions based on the new model have a way of generating dialogue based on different perspectives. Consequently, they provide various explanations and yield unique predictions. At the very least, debating those differences creates an awareness of viable alternatives at every stage in the innovation process. Without such a shift in perspective, heart patients today would have few, if any, treatment options.

5. **Seek out and resolve implicit organizational barriers to the innovation process.** As we noted above, each innovation phase can present different organizational challenges. Some organizations seem hobbled in creating new ideas worth pursuing (phases one and two), while others struggle with the assimilation stage (phase three).

Some rigid, top-down organizational cultures subtly stymie the conception phase (phase one) developments even as they excel at the assimilation phase (phase three) activities. In other words, the implicit norm is that all the good ideas come from the top. Sometimes structural issues stand in the way of innovation. For example, cumbersome proposal and review procedures can hinder innovation at any of these phases. In general, roadblocks typically fall into one or more of these three categories: people, culture, and structure. Caring leaders are attentive to these kinds of systematic challenges and take steps to address them.

SUBTLE PRACTICES FOR INNOVATION

Properly pairing more visible practices with subtle ones often ignites innovative thinking at all three phases. Caring leaders master many of the behind-the-scenes practices discussed below.

1. **Encourage spontaneous brainstorming.** Innovation thrives in informal networks, because people can serendipitously encounter new connections or ideas that spur novel thinking. Universities, with liberal travel policies, open sabbatical processes, and transparent publishing norms, set the gold standard for cultivating these kinds of informal networks that rapidly ricochet ideas across information silos. That's one reason why universities, at least traditionally, have been great incubators for new ideas and transformative thinking. Caring leaders can stimulate these informal brainstorming climates through random encounters in hallways and offices. Likewise, showcasing new ideas at company gatherings has proven quite effective in sparking innovative ideas.

    Caring leaders embrace the spontaneity of unplanned collaborations. They convene discussions at the spur of the moment to gather new ideas and to brainstorm new approaches, using questions like:

    - What are your thoughts about…?

    - What would happen if…?

    - Could we use another metaphor to describe the situation?

    - What other perspectives should we consider?

    - What are your intuitive reactions to…?

    These types of questions signal that new ideas are welcomed. Save the evaluation for phases two and three in the innovation process. Meanwhile, let the brainstormers' imaginations take over for a while.

    At some point the energy diminishes and it's time to end the brainstorming phase; then it's time to move on to the transformation and assimilation phases.

2. **Communicate with innovative language and tools.** Great innovators not only embrace experimentation, they also de-

light in the process. Why? Because they know the experiments supply insights that no amount of grand planning can ever yield. Yet, many leaders discourage an experimental mentality by the language they use, with words like, "Bring me results" or "I want something you can guarantee will work." Clearly, in some cases that mentality might make sense, but it also hinders innovation.[16]

Caring leaders sprinkle their conversations with words and phrases designed to spawn innovation, like *experiment, ponder, sketch, visualize, play with, noodle on,* and *start with a clean sheet of paper.* These exploratory words invite people to clear their minds from existing paradigms and stretch new frontiers. If you talk that way, people will start to think that way. This language legitimizes the idea of experimentation, encouraging learning from trial and error, and celebrates that it's okay to be wrong in the pursuit of innovation.

Experimental ideas often emerge from pictures and roughly sketched diagrams. These images release intuitions, helping us to articulate something hidden in the unconscious. They also highlight associations and relationships. After sketching out the ideas, prompt everyone to step back, ponder, and then continue to noodle on! At some point, a sense of closure will emerge, and the team can move on.

The communicative tools you place around the workplace and routinely use can also spur an experimental mind-set. Flip charts, sketch pads, Post-it notes, and whiteboards often do the trick. These tools allow people to quickly sketch and amend ideas in the flow of conversation. Some electronic tools are available that offer the same feel, but they have not quite captured all the nuances of fluid thinking derived from quick sketching. That said, if electronic tools represent the only option, then go ahead and use them! Still, for our money, pencils with large erasers always trump pens when brainstorming innovative ideas. The pencil allows everyone to rapidly erase and experiment, and no one loses face for penning a "dumb idea."

3. **Embrace fun and serendipitous moments.** Tourists who visit the beautiful Door County, Wisconsin, peninsula known as the Cape Cod of the Midwest will encounter someone who will recommend checking out the restaurant with the goats on the roof. Al Johnson's Swedish Restaurant overlooks the idyllic waters of Green Bay, and goats often graze on the restaurant's grassy rooftop. Whoever thought to put goats on the roof? It was not the founders, Al or his wife, Ingert. It all started as a practical joke by Al's friend Winkie Larson, who herded them up there on a whim. They soon became the talk of the town, then the region, and today the goats are a must-see—and even if you can't visit, there is a goat cam available on their website.[17]

   We find this incident instructive on several levels. First, no one ever convened a marketing committee to dream this idea up; it happened on a whim. Second, Al was brilliantly perceptive by recognizing the potential of the goats to draw tourists to this bucolic peninsula. He could have just shrugged it off and continued to engage in tit-for-tat practical jokes with his friend. Third, he reoriented the restaurant and other businesses around these iconic goats. The company even trademarked "Goats on the Roof," which ended up in lawsuit settled in Al's favor by the US Supreme Court. In short, by embracing the fun and serendipity, Al and his goats deserve to be in the greatest of all time marketing success stories.

4. **Depersonalize your critiques by focusing on specific issues.** Consider this situation: a web designer presented a client with an idea based on their previous discussion. The client was not thrilled with the proposal and was tempted to say,

"This is not what I had in mind; try again," but resisted that visceral, gut reaction. Instead, the client responded, "Here's what I like about this idea, and here are some features that I think we could tweak to give it a little more pizzazz."

Note the depersonalization with "this idea," rather than "your idea," and how the client focused on attributes to retain as well as those to change. Critiquing in this manner encourages tweaking, further developing the concept, and maybe even reimagining the idea. In this case, the client was blown away by the next draft and used it to launch a successful promotional website.

Leaders often precipitously dismiss new ideas based on an all-encompassing, intuitive reaction like, "That won't work—try something else." Such reactions create a hit-or-miss dichotomy in the minds of team members. That's a mistake, because new ideas are rarely fully formed and require many developmental cycles in order to be ready for prime time. Moreover, summarily dismissing a new idea undermines timid or young innovators' confidence. They may simply give up and deliver what the boss wants. Caring leaders use a more encouraging, nuanced approach when voicing concerns by focusing attention on specific issues, attributes, or even dimensions of the challenge, rather than an overly broad assessment.[18]

5. **Cultivate a working climate that embraces focused flexibility.** Caring leaders cultivate a focused-flexibility working climate. They learn to quickly inspire others to shift focus with little loss in productivity. On a practical level, it translates into making others comfortable with sidelining the old ways of doing things while maintaining those memories in the event they are needed in the future. Above all, it means artfully reconciling the trade-offs between focus and flexibility. Too much focus destroys flexibility; too much flexibility crushes the capacity for focus.

THE TOUGH SIDE OF INNOVATION

Like the painter, sometimes you place the wrong brushstroke on the canvas. Not all ideas turn out to be good ideas or doable in the face of current conditions. By being tolerant of mistakes without being naive or too permissive, and by not passing blame for mistakes or bad ideas, a caring leader creates a safe environment for idea generation. And the input and opposing views of critics are important, as they bring seemingly undoable ideas into better focus. And the leader's role in all this? They legitimize the full circle of ideas and then manage the dynamics of the conversation to keep the energy building rather than allowing critiques to undermine the spirit and the progress the team is making. Why? Because great ideas may emerge from anyone at any time, as long as caring leaders create a welcoming climate for conjecture, spontaneity, and novelty.

CONCLUSION

We started this chapter by asking you to ponder three situations where innovators beat the traditionalists of the day. Lurking in the background is another, even more fundamental question: What can leaders guarantee with certainty? Certainty and innovation have an uneasy relationship. Can leaders guarantee that what is currently successful will remain so? No.[19] Can leaders guarantee that a new idea will become successful? No. Those are the fundamental uncertainties facing innovative leaders. Yet, there is one certainty that all caring leaders instinctively recognize: if we don't seek to imagine and create the future, someone else will. That's why caring leaders invest so much time in mastering innovative thinking and practices. They want their employees and organizations to be trailblazers, regardless of the circuitous route that might entail.

End of Chapter 14

INNOVATION SELF-ASSESSMENT

These questions are designed to provide developmental insights to enhance your effectiveness. Rate yourself, choosing either Improvement Needed, Solid, or Excels.

SELF-REFLECTION QUESTIONS

	IMPROVEMENT NEEDED	SOLID	EXCELS
1. I have created an Innovation Studio, a physical or virtual space, with a dedicated slot in team members' schedules to allow for innovative thinking.	○	○	○
2. I foster safe environments for new ideas to surface.	○	○	○
3. I use innovative language in my everyday vocabulary.	○	○	○
4. I often start with a "clean sheet of paper" to sketch new ideas and ask my team to do the same.	○	○	○
5. I encourage spontaneous, unplanned brainstorming sessions.	○	○	○
6. I'm patient with my team members as they grapple with new perspectives.	○	○	○
7. I liberally sprinkle the work environment with innovative tools like whiteboards, sketch pads, and pencils.	○	○	○
8. I actively refine divergent ideas to develop new platforms of thinking.	○	○	○
9 I don't place blame for mistakes; rather, I help my team learn from missteps.	○	○	○
10. I actively manage the dynamics between critique and criticism to allow progress to emerge.	○	○	○

PART 3

CONCLUSION

The summit is what drives us, but the climb itself is what matters.

—CONRAD ANKER

CHAPTER 15
BEYOND SERVANT LEADERSHIP

In 1970, Robert K. Greenleaf, an executive at AT&T, launched a leadership thought revolution with an essay provocatively titled "Leader as Servant." At the time, this was a revolutionary idea, because other, more authoritarian, charismatic, and expertise-driven leadership models dominated thinking (e.g., leader as commander, leader as prophet, and leader as authority). The idea caught the imagination of many, because it stood in sharp contrast to the experience of countless employees and team members.

The fundamental tenet of servant leadership, as it came to be called, was that "the great leader is seen as servant first."[1] Anyone reading through the essay today would warm to the thoughts, as they possess a timeless resonance. Greenleaf's "Leader as Servant" essay was liberally sprinkled with poetic, spiritual, and philosophical references (e.g., Robert Frost, William Blake, Saint Francis, Rabbi Heschel, and Albert Camus).

Such an orientation inspires, yet may gloss over important but complex issues. If we consider Greenleaf's servant-leadership idea as a seed, then the main branches would be the five beliefs we've highlighted in the first section of the book: uncertainty, progress, values, learning, and kindness. The caring leader's practices emerge as secondary branches and leaves to these fundamental leadership beliefs.

Greenleaf's ideas launched a new leadership platform (1.0), subsequently developed and tweaked by many others. We wrote *Leading with Care in a Tough World* with the intent of honoring his legacy while launching a new stream of leadership thought (platform 2.0). We sought to answer three nagging and often unstated questions in the servant-leadership movement:

- How can leaders reconcile the tension between the organizational mission and caring for people?

- Can leaders possess caring leadership beliefs without the ability to practice what they preach?

- Can leaders use caring practices without embracing fundamental beliefs and sentiments?

CARING FOR THE PERSON AND CARING FOR THE MISSION

People in leadership positions have missions, goals, and expected outcomes. Some authors who embrace the servant-leadership philosophy overlook those realities and focus almost exclusively on serving others. This approach is at best naive and at worse subtly manipulative. Even Greenleaf acknowledged that "part of our dilemma is that all leadership is to some extent, manipulative."[2] The leading-with-care philosophy directly faces that dilemma and does not try to marginalize it. In fact, we devoted an entire chapter to how caring leaders prioritize sustainable financial performance.[3]

Leading with care means caring about people AND about the mission, but it starts with people. That's one reason why we added the phrase *in a tough world*, because achieving the mission can be quite challenging. Caring leaders offer people realistic choices and then collaboratively set expectations about priorities. Leading with care does not gloss over the mission and related difficulties; rather, it embraces them while placing team members' aspirations front and center.

Think of it this way: assume that you want to lead a mission to climb a mountain. The caring leader would say up front to anyone who joins the expedition that the mission will be challenging and potentially dangerous. But the leader would hasten to add, "My first obligation is to the team members. We collaborate to help each other and make difficult decisions. We seek to develop every person's full potential and realize their dreams. If that's what you want, then tether up to our team and let's start climbing."

BELIEFS WITHOUT PRACTICES

Is it possible for leaders to possess leading-with-care beliefs but stumble with the actual practices? Yes. And that can be problematic. If leaders can't translate their ideas and sentiments into effective action, then many employees may become confused, and some may even question the leader's sincerity and honesty.

For example, leaders who preach about the value of lifelong learning but fail to make opportunities available to themselves or their team members will be viewed as disingenuous at best and hypocrites at worse. Ditto for leaders who trumpet progress making but never approve reasonable tweaks from their team members.[4]

The disconnect between leaders' beliefs and practices can occur for several reasons. First, the leader may see their role as prophet and seer and simply want to avoid the details, muckiness, and complexity of becoming a skilled practitioner. Sadly, many people in academia and some thought leaders seem to live by this creed. It's doubly sad, because those same people could enrich their inspirational and often compelling thoughts through conceiving and testing new practices. Second, a leader may need to preach a bit as a self-motivation tactic to learn about new practices. After all, it's one matter to embrace uncertainty in concept; it's another matter to learn how to do that in your leadership role.[5] Learning to do so may require many cycles of trial and error before the actions sync up with the aspirations. Third, the leader may need guidance and coaching on how to practice what they preach. That's one reason why we wrote this book. We wanted to provide more specific guidance to leaders about how to act on critical leadership beliefs.

PRACTICES WITHOUT BELIEFS

Could someone embrace leading-with-care practices but not the leading-with-care beliefs? Yes. In fact, aspiring leaders might find that this is the best place to start, because the beliefs may appear more abstract upon first reading. Yet, over time, embracing practices without the beliefs undermines a leader's effectiveness. Many people yearn for off-the-shelf how-tos or practices free of richer explanations about the rationale and philosophy behind the practical recommendations. That's fine for connecting your TV, but you can't connect with people in that way.

Leaders need a profound understanding of what they are seeking to accomplish. Without the richness of perspective offered by core beliefs, people soon realize the thinness of leaders' commitment to any laudable sentiment. For example, leaders can follow a good, visible communication practice like "frequently update people" in one of two ways: they can be a) truly transparent or b) merely faux transparent.[6] After all, most politicians provide frequent updates—they like to talk—but it's quite another issue if they are candidly updating people on the things that really matter. The faux transparency of many politicians, no doubt, explains why so many are held in such low esteem. Ditto for a visible collaborative practice like seeking input from others: some leaders genuinely seek ideas from others and use them to shape policies and decisions, while others just go through the motions, not really listening. They are checking the get-input-from-others box on their to-do list. These kinds of disconnects undermine inspiring practices like coaching, communication, and collaboration. No wonder subterranean rivers of employee cynicism and disillusionment flow whenever practices stray too far from beliefs.

MUTUALLY ENRICHING BELIEFS AND PRACTICES

Leading with care means that leaders' core beliefs about fundamental issues enrich their day-to-day practices, even as the visible and subtle practices enhance understanding of their beliefs. Separating leading-with-care practices from fundamental beliefs would be like separating bees and flowers—they both need and enrich one another.

Up to this point, we've hinted at the power of this symbiotic relationship. (See Figure 15.1.) Consider these examples:

- The progress-making framework described in Chapter Two orients the coaching practices discussed in Chapter Six. For instance, coaches need to recognize that progress can occur by tweaking an employee's existing project management platform or leaping to a new one. The costs of tweaking are less than those of leaping, but the benefits might be greater. The thoughtful coach uses that framework in the background to guide the employee and discuss options. Without that framework to weigh

Figure 15.1

BELIEFS AND PRACTICES SYNERGY

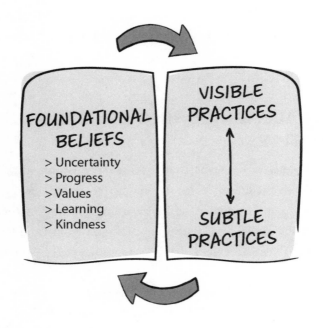

the costs and benefits, the coach may just adopt a tweak-or-leap approach without much thought. On the flip side, working through day-to-day coaching decisions can enrich the leader's understanding of the nuances of the progress-making model that can be applied to countless other issues.

- Strongly believing in the power of embracing uncertainty enriches a leader's collaborative practices.[7] Leaders who wholeheartedly believe that there are far more uncertainties than certainties in life would eagerly embrace efforts to seek perspectives and ideas from a wide range of people. Caring leaders also recognize that many people crave authoritarian-decreed certainties (i.e., "Just tell me what to do, now!"), but it's not ideal for problem-solving. So, caring leaders seek alignment on the analysis of the situation before creating consensus around solutions. On the flip side, working through the practicalities of collaboration helps leaders better understand the meaning of embracing uncertainty and how difficult it really is!

- Advocating core values like trust and respect orients leaders as they nudge employees into the actualized performance zone, where they realize their full potential.[8] As leaders demonstrate trust and respect to their team members, they will minimize the need for direct oversight and supervision. On the flip side, helping teammates become passionate high performers renews any leader's understanding of the importance of values.

We could provide many more examples, but we will leave the joy of discovering other connections to our readers. As you grow as a leader, you will revise some of the practices and add others. Experimenting, thinking, and tweaking these practices build leaders' skill sets while augmenting their core beliefs about uncertainty, progress, values, learning, and kindness.

Effective leadership requires understanding and grappling with a diverse range of variables.[9] We've discussed how caring leaders craft an architecture of networks to propel progress, build the right coaching routines into their relationships, and promote motivating cultural values. The magic emerges as leaders blend the visible and subtle practices across these dimensions, producing synergistic dynamics throughout their organizations.[10]

Doing so will take any leader beyond servant leadership, into their own distinctive and compelling leadership style that unleashes the latent energy of people and their organizations. This is exactly what people yearn for in their leaders. Now you have a guidebook for that trek. We believe that *Leading with Care* provides the next platform (2.0) of leadership thinking. Explore, enjoy, and grow as you ascend to new leadership vistas. The climb can be tough. Even though the view from the mountaintop shifts as clouds gather from time to time, it never ceases to amaze.

— **66** —

I've learned...

- That being kind is more important than being right.
- That under everyone's hard shell is someone who wants to be appreciated.
- That opportunities are never lost; someone will take the ones you miss.
- That one should keep his words both soft and tender, because tomorrow he may have to eat them.
- That everyone wants to live on top of the mountain, but all the happiness and growth occurs while you're climbing it.

—ANDY ROONEY

Appendix I

PERFORMANCE DISCUSSION QUESTIONS

Using the "Performance Discussion Items," what are your strengths and how do they apply to your performance during the past year?

-
-
-

Using the "Performance Discussion Items," what are your areas of improvements for the coming year?

-
-
-

What are your most significant learnings during the past year and how have you applied them?

-
-
-

What are your learning/training plans for the coming year?

-
-
-

Describe/update your career path aspirations

-
-
-

Appendix I

PERFORMANCE DISCUSSION ITEMS

	IMPROVEMENT NEEDED	SOLID	EXCELS
Ability to Motivate and Inspire: The skill involved in perceiving and reacting sensitively to the needs of others so that there is an effectiveness in bringing an individual or a group to accomplish a task and in getting ideas accepted.	◯	◯	◯
Adaptability: The ability to maintain effectiveness in different situations and in being able to handle changing responsibilities including the capacity to live and work in different areas under different circumstances.	◯	◯	◯
Aspiration: The level of importance that one attaches to their work accomplishments and the desire that they possess to achieve a high level of reward and recognition for their efforts.	◯	◯	◯
Charismatic Leadership: The ability to generate in others a strong sense of affiliation and participation where the intensity of feelings has a strong emotional overtone.	◯	◯	◯
Communication: The ability to clearly discuss and write about the "things that matter" and transform pushback into progress.	◯	◯	◯
Comprehensiveness: The ability to bring all relevant information and ideas to bear upon a particular problem situation so that all attendant factors may be taken into account as a solution or approach is generated.	◯	◯	◯
Confidence: The ability to convey a sense of self-assurance and the idea that things will get done in a positive fashion. The ability to convey a sense of assertiveness and the capacity to take advantage of opportunities as they arise.	◯	◯	◯
Cooperation: The ability to effect a cooperative set of relationships with other people and to stimulate a sense of participation and involvement.	◯	◯	◯
Customer Relationship Development: Personally maintains strong customer relationships and leads customer relationship management in areas of responsibility.	◯	◯	◯
Deductive Reasoning: The ability to draw conclusions from given premises, to infer from general principles and arrive at specifics.	◯	◯	◯
Determination: The ability to maintain effectiveness in different situations, including where one has to handle disappointments and rejections. The capacity one has for working their way through and/or around a variety of obstacles.	◯	◯	◯
Development of People: Relates to the efforts one puts forth to maximize the human potential of other people through training and development activities related to their current and future job responsibilities.	◯	◯	◯
Drive Level/Energy: The ability to be self-starting and to achieve a high activity level where one is concerned with the attainment of personal and professional goals.	◯	◯	◯

Appendix I

PERFORMANCE DISCUSSION ITEMS

	IMPROVEMENT NEEDED	SOLID	EXCELS
Flexibility: The ability to modify behavioral style and management approach to reach a goal.	○	○	○
Follow-Through: The ability to finish what one starts in a logical fashion which will also convey a sense of completion and accomplishment.	○	○	○
Imagination/Creativity: The ability to come up with imaginative and innovative solutions in business situations.	○	○	○
Impact: The ability to create a good first impression, to command attention and respect, to show an air of confidence, and to achieve personal recognition.	○	○	○
Inductive Reasoning: The ability to reason and generate a whole concept and/or general principles as a result of the observation and analysis of specific parts or particulars.	○	○	○
Integrity: This relates to an individual's maintenance of societal, ethical, and organizational norms in business practices.	○	○	○
Intuitive Judgment: The ability to react instinctively to problems and to develop a sense of appropriate action where hard facts or evidence are not readily available.	○	○	○
Loyalty to Others: The capacity to generate and maintain a sense of participation and a high level of personal integrity in dealing with others. The ability to convey a sense of loyalty and continuing responsive obligation where others are concerned.	○	○	○
Objective Insight: The ability to perceive oneself in a clear perspective and to objectively evaluate the impact and influence they have upon others. The ability to be sensitive and aware of the factors and individuals who in turn affect and influence oneself.	○	○	○
Organizational Sensitivity: The skill required in order to perceive the impact and implications of decisions on other components of the organization. It also includes recognizing how the various areas and functions must interrelate for effectiveness.	○	○	○
Perceptiveness/Listening: The ability to pick out important information in oral communications and to develop an awareness and sensitivity to the needs, feelings and motivations of others.	○	○	○
Perseverance: The ability to persevere and to act in a very responsible and concerned manner so that one conveys a sense of real determination and tenacity.	○	○	○
Practicality: The ability to reach logical conclusions based on the evidence at hand so that the solutions or actions will not only accomplish a given objective but will also be viewed by others as showing good common sense and application.	○	○	○

Appendix I

PERFORMANCE DISCUSSION ITEMS

	IMPROVEMENT NEEDED	SOLID	EXCELS
Range of Interests: This relates to the breadth and diversity of interests, concern for personal and organizational environment, and a desire to participate actively in events of both a personal and professional nature.	O	O	O
Realistic Judgment: The skill one has to perceive the impact and implications of decisions made by themselves and by others on other components of the organization, as well as upon their own activities and functions.	O	O	O
Resilience: The ability to handle disappointments and rejection while maintaining effectiveness in a variety of situations and under diverse conditions.	O	O	O
Risk Taking: The ability to weigh alternatives and make decisions in which a calculated risk is taken to achieve maximum benefits from the decision.	O	O	O
Sales Ability/Persuasiveness: The ability to organize and present material in a convincing manner to gain agreement or acceptance of an idea, product or service.	O	O	O
Sense of Priority: The capacity to effectively seek out pertinent data and determine the order in which various elements must be tackled and dealt with in order to effectively accomplish a goal or objective.	O	O	O
Sensitivity: The skill in perceiving and reacting to the needs of others. This includes both objectivity in perceiving the impact of oneself on others and the impact or influence that the actions and words of others will have on oneself.	O	O	O
Stress Tolerance: The stability of performance under pressure, opposition, or confrontation.	O	O	O
Thoroughness: The ability to include all relevant information and factors in a given task or function so that there is documentation to describe and support all alternatives and subsequent actions.	O	O	O
Time Efficiency: The capacity to schedule one's time and efforts in a logical and sequentially relevant fashion so the work flows smoothly and meets the time constraints that are applicable to any given situation.	O	O	O

Appendix 2

PERSONAL INSTRUCTION MANUAL

Almost every new product you buy has an instruction manual. Why doesn't someone issue a similar manual for the people we work with most frequently? In an attempt to bridge the gap, I've constructed a manual of tips for working with me.

CHARACTERISTICS	SO WHAT?
I'm a thinker. ("T" on the Myers-Briggs scale)	• I like to hear both sides of an issue before making a decision. • Link your rationale to enduring principles.
I'm an innovator. ("P" on the Myers-Briggs scale)	• Show me new ideas based on sound principles. • Expand on pre-existing ideas and avoid repeating exactly what I say in a lecture or article
I focus on the big picture. ("N" on the Myers-Briggs scale)	• Talk to me about strategy and then discuss your tactics. • Show me the links between your main points or ideas (e.g., illustrations, diagrams etc.) • Occasionally I get impatient with too many details.
I'm a former debater.	• Show me a clear organizational structure. • Give me evidence to back up your claims. • Don't assume that because I make a counterargument that I disagree with you. • Don't assume that if I push you to defend your ideas, I disagree with them.
I read a lot.	• Be ready to answer questions about links to current events and ideas (i.e., *Wall Street Journal, Fortune, Forbes, Harvard Business Review*). • I appreciate well-written papers and clever phrases.
I have some introvert characteristics.	• Give me some time to get to know you. • Sometimes I may seem standoffish, but that will disappear in time.
I'm busy.	• Come prepared to meetings. • Focus your communication on high-value items. • If the matter can be handled through lean channels, then use them. • Email is often the best way to make initial contact with me or give me project updates. • Don't assume that time constraints mean I'm uninterested.
I like to have fun and be challenged.	• Sometimes I'll spontaneously veer off track, for a moment, in a lecture. • I get bored quickly. • I'll often joke around with people.

ACKNOWLEDGMENTS

BOB'S ACKNOWLEDGMENTS

I have learned from many, but I can point to a few people from whom I have learned the most. There are many special people who have guided my development.

When I was growing up, I remember vividly my mother saying, "Bob, you can accomplish anything you put your mind to, and your dad and I are here to support you." She was telling me to have high aspirations and constantly push to achieve them.

My father would quickly add, "Son, as you achieve these things, you will work with many people. They will all have different ideas and responsibilities, and they are all very important. Remember, you put your pants on one leg at a time, just like everyone else." He was telling me to always be humble and recognize the work of many. Humility is an essential quality in leadership.

I attended a great liberal arts university, Lawrence University. Although my degree was in a technical discipline, I used the opportunity to embrace a broader liberal arts education. I learned that there were many points of view that come together to reach great outcomes. I learned the skills of open communication to come to common ground. And I learned the critical nature of intense investigation and critical thinking to uncover underlying causes. This learning process has become a lifelong passion.

During my early years in business, I met a professor who helped me develop my leadership skills. He would coach, "As you work with people and help groups strive to make a difference, always do it with care." In other words, do it with respect and regard for every individual. Thank you, Professor C. Y. Allen.

I owe many thanks to Robert McKee, the world-renowned screenwriter, author, teacher, and coach of all things story. I befriended Robert several years ago, as he made valiant attempts to teach a businessman how to tell stories. I fondly remember many hours spent in his New York City office, overlooking Central Park—a stunning setting for intense learning. He hammered away, "What's the inciting incident?" "What's the crisis?" "Where's the climax?" "What's the resolution?" "Give up the rhetoric!" I zealously tried to translate these learnings into actionable, everyday business life. I learned it was essential for leaders to communicate through stories. Thank you, Robert.

Over the last thirty years, I've worked with a very important colleague who has contributed greatly to my development as a leader. His name is Dr. Phil Clampitt, and he is the Blair Endowed Chair of Communication at the University of Wisconsin at Green Bay. We've written three books together, along with many articles. We've studied, collaborated, and innovated around all things leadership and communication. This experience has been irreplaceable; it's been much like going through a continuous doctoral education over my entire career. This has been an experience and commitment to lifelong leadership learning.

For over fifteen years, I had the privilege of working alongside Kathi Seifert, a Kimberly-Clark senior executive, professional board member, and nonprofit leader. Together, we spearheaded and cochaired a regional economic development corporation in northeastern Wisconsin, called the New North. We brought together many public and private sector leaders, which was a grand collaborative effort. We had tremendous respect for our mutual strengths, and we worked to lead for the good of the people and organizations that we served. Together we learned a lot about regional collaboration, barrier busting, and progress making. We think we made a difference.

During the past twenty-plus years, I worked with Oscar C. Boldt (1924–2020), for whom I had the utmost respect. Oscar was the chairman and the third-generation family patriarch of the Boldt Company. I learned endless things from him, but at the top of that list was his often-repeated mantra "Values are everything. If you get those right, everything else follows." He ran his family business that way, and I learned, even more profoundly, how an organization lives its values every day that emanate from its leaders. Thank you, Oscar.

Lastly, and perhaps most importantly, are all the colleagues, peers, and team members I have worked with over these years. I have learned many things about leadership as a result of my work with them. For that, I thank them and congratulate them for the great things we have accomplished together.

PHIL'S ACKNOWLEDGMENTS

C. S. Lewis keenly recognized that "Two heads are better than one, not because either is infallible but because they are unlikely to go wrong in the same direction." Many wise minds guided me throughout the research and writing of this book. In particular, I would like to thank one of my mentors, Dr. M. Lee Williams, and one of my most valued colleagues, Dr. James Barker of Dalhousie University. This book could not have been completed without social and professional relationships with colleagues like Danielle Bina, Shauna Froelich, Terri Pawer, Alida Al-Saadi, Rick Fantini, Ron Reed, Dan Resop, Joan Nellen, Jim Nellen, Jordan Lorenz, Phil Salem, and George Reed. Thank you to the numerous thoughtful students who have challenged and improved my thinking in countless ways. Finally, I want to thank my wife, Laurey, who tirelessly worked on making this book more accessible, readable, and understandable. She has an amazing capacity to bring out the best in dogs, people, and my books. Bob and I couldn't have completed this manuscript without her.

BOB & PHIL'S ACKNOWLEDGMENTS

Successfully approaching the publishing market is very challenging. We thank Mark Malatesta for his guidance. Writing, editing, and producing a good book requires an incredible team. We had one! Thanks to Amanda Lorge, Laurey Clampitt, Amy Copeland, and Coalesce Marketing for your talents, encouragement, and support. We owe a special thanks to all the wonderful professionals at Rodin Books, including Arthur Klebanoff, David Wilk, Michelle Weyenberg (a former student of Phil's), and the great copy editor Sara Brady.

ABOUT THE AUTHORS

Bob DeKoch has devoted his entire career to leadership roles, refining his own skills, and mentoring hundreds of aspiring leaders. His passion for people and for extraordinary outcomes is what drives him. Rising to senior executive roles in numerous organizations, Bob has developed and put into practice the many teachings in his books. He has over four decades of experience across major market sectors: the construction services industry and real estate development business, the pulp and paper industry, the beverage industry, and the chemical industry. He has served on boards of US organizations—for-profit and nonprofit—including a major international corporation. This diverse experience has helped him develop unique insight into inspired leadership.

Bob is currently the president of his leadership consulting firm, Limitless, whose services are described at www.lmtlss.biz.

Bob is the past president of the Boldt Company, a major US construction services and real estate development company. Over a twenty-year period, Bob and his leadership team grew

Boldt's revenue by three times to a $1 billion platform—all through organic growth.

Prior to this role, Bob spent twenty years in management and leadership positions in the pulp and paper industry.

Bob is an authority in areas of economic development. He was the start-up executive and cochairman of the board of New North, a regional economic development corporation, focused on attracting and retaining companies and jobs to an eighteen-county region in northeastern Wisconsin. His passion for leadership and collaboration brought together corporate leaders, public-sector leaders, and government leaders to increase business activity in the region.

Bob has a liberal arts undergraduate degree from Lawrence University and holds an MBA from the University of Wisconsin at Oshkosh. He also was recognized with an honorary doctorate degree from the University of Wisconsin at Oshkosh for his work in economic development.

Phillip G. Clampitt (PhD, University of Kansas) is the Blair Endowed Chair of Communication at the University of Wisconsin at Green Bay. He was previously designated the Hendrickson Named Professor of Business. Phil has won numerous awards for his teaching and scholarship. His students started calling him "Dr. So What" because he asked, "So what?" so often, as a prod to encourage them to think about the implications of their ideas. He embraced the moniker and created a website devoted to improving critical thinking (see www. DrSoWhat.com).

The *Wall Street Journal* and *MIT Sloan Management Review* highlighted his work on decision downloading, which details how companies can effectively communicate decisions to those not involved in the decision-making process. His book *Communicating for Managerial Effectiveness* (sixth edition), is a Sage Publications best-seller (see www.mycmebook.net). He also authored the book *Social Media Strategy: Tools for Professionals and Organizations* (see www.amazingSMstrategy. com). His most recent book, *Clear Thinking in an Age of Hype, Nonsense, and Anxiety*, is available on iBooks or Amazon Kindle (see clearthinkingtoday.com).

In addition to many guest speaking opportunities in the United States, he has also been invited to speak internationally at the University of Pisa, the University of Aberdeen, the University of Ulster, and numerous multinational businesses and professional organizations. As a principal in his firm, Metacomm, he consults on communication issues with a variety of organizations, such as PepsiCo, Manpower, Schneider National, American Medical Security, Dean Foods, the Boldt Company, Thilmany Papers, Dental City, Prevea, the US Army War College, Appleton, and Nokia (see www.imetacomm.com).

DeKoch and Clampitt have worked in a partnership for over thirty years. They have coauthored *Transforming Leaders into Progress Makers: Leadership for the 21st Century* (see www.progressmakers.net) and *Embracing Uncertainty: The Essence of Leadership* (see www.imetacomm.com/eu). They have a passionate interest in helping others become successful leaders. Their research, writing, and mentoring have helped thousands of people become better leaders.

REFERENCES

PREFACE AND INTRODUCTION

Insert 1 See https://blog.smarp.com/employee-engagement-8-statistics-you-need-to-know.

Insert 2 See https://blog.smarp.com/employee-engagement-8-statistics-you-need-to-know.

Insert 3 See https://www.gallup.com/workplace/283985/working-remotely-effective-gallup-research-says-yes.aspx.

CHAPTER 1

1. R. Feynman, *Surely You're Joking, Mr. Feynman!* New York: W. W. Norton & Company, 1985, p. 343.

2. P. Clampitt and R. DeKoch, *Embracing Uncertainty: The Essence of Leadership.* Armonk, NY: M. E. Sharpe, 2001.

3. R. Sobel, *When Giants Stumble.* Paramus, NJ: Prentice Hall Press, 1999.

4. C. M. Christensen, *The Innovator's Dilemma.* Boston: Harvard Business School Press, 1997, p. xii.

5. R. Matthews, "The Science of Murphy's Law." *Scientific American* 276 (4), 1997, 88–91, p. 91.

6. J. E. Russo and P. J. Schoemaker, "Managing Overconfidence." *Sloan Management Review* 33(2), 1992, p. 7-17.

7. D. Terry, "7 Chicago Officers Indicted in Extortion Scheme." *New York Times*, 21 February 1996, p. 12.

8. A. Slider, "What Happened When United Stopped Trying to Predict the Pandemic." *Wall Street Journal*, 21 October 2021.

9. David McCullough interview by Brian Lamb in *Booknotes: America's Finest Authors on Reading, Writing, and the Power of Ideas*. New York: Times Books, 1997, p. 6.

10. L. LaFreniere and M. Newman, "Exposing Worry's Deceit: Percentage of Untrue Worries in Generalized Anxiety Disorder Treatment." *Behavior Therapy* 51(3), 2020, 413–423.

11. J. Dean, P. Brandes, and R. Dharwadkar, "Organizational Cynicism." *Academy of Management Review* 23 (2), 1998, 341–352, p. 346.

12. Reichers, J. Wanous, and J. Austin, "Understanding and Managing Cynicism About Organizational Change." *Academy of Management Executive* 11(1), 1997, 48–59.

13. E. Langer, *The Power of Mindful Learning*. Reading, MA: Addison-Wesley, 1997, p. 15–16.

14. "Innovative Design to Improve the Shopping Cart." *ABC Nightline*, 9 February 1999, program no. N990209-01.

15. A. Hargadon and R. I. Sutton, "Building an Innovation Factory." *Harvard Business Review* 78(3), 2000, 157–166.

CHAPTER 2

1. R. Leighton, *Tuva or Bust! Richard Feynman's Last Journey*. New York: Norton, 2000.

2. R. Feynman, *The Meaning of it All: Thoughts of a Citizen-Scientist*. New York: Basic Books, 2005, p. 28.

3. E. Dane and M. Pratt, "Exploring Intuition and Its Role in Managerial Decision Making." *Academy of Management Review* 32(1), 2007, 33–54; C. Miller and D. Ireland, "Intuition in Strategic Decision Making: Friend or Foe in the Fast-Paced 21st Century?" *Academy of Management Executive* 19(1) 2005, 19–30; G. Gigerenzer, *Gut Feeling: The Intelligence of the Unconscious*. New York: Viking, 2007.

4. H. Judson, *The Eighth Day of Creation: Makers of the Revolution in Biology*. New York: Cold Spring Harbor Laboratory Press, 1996.

5. J. D. Bernal, "Dr. Rosalind E. Franklin." *Nature*, 19 July 1958, p. 154.

6. B. Maddox, *Rosalind Franklin: The Dark Lady of DNA*. New York: HarperCollins, 2002.

7. J. March, "Exploration and Exploitation in Organizational Learning." *Organizational Science* 2(1) 1991, 71–86, p. 71.

8. J. March, "Exploration and Exploitation in Organizational Learning." p. 73.

9. Personal interview with Mike Cowen, 22 June 2009.

10. See http://www.sportablescoreboards.com/index.php?option=com_conte nt&task=view&id=371&Itemid=159. Accessed 24 June 2009.

11. J. Lindsay, *Conquering Innovation Fatigue: Overcoming the Barriers to Personal and Corporate Success*. New York: Wiley, 2009.

12. G. Moskowitz and H. Grant, *The Psychology of Goals*. New York: Guilford Press, 2009.

13. F. Scott Fitzgerald, "The Crack-Up." *Esquire* magazine, February 1936. Republished as part of a book of essays and other writing, also called *The Crack-Up*, 1945.

CHAPTER 3

1. T. Leahy, *Management in 10 Words*. New York: Crown Publishing, 2012.

2. See R. Krznaric, *How Should We Live? Great Ideas From the Past for Everyday Life*. New York: BlueBridge Press, 2011.

3. J. Bronowski, *Science and Human Values*. New York: Perennial Library, 1965.

4. J. Clarke and J. Nicholson, *Resilience: Bounce Back From Whatever Life Throws at You*. Richmond, Surrey: Crimson Publishing, 2010.

5. A. Zolli, *Resilience: Why Things Bounce Back*. New York: Free Press, 2012, p. 59 of 1016.

6. J. Gitomer, *The Little Teal Book of Trust*. New Jersey: FT Press, 2008.

7. Adapted from the *Oxford English Dictionary*.

8. Proverbs 11.2 (New International Version)

9. S. Bok, *Lying: Moral Choice in Public and Private Life*. New York: Pantheon Books, 1978.

10. H. Frankfurt, *On Truth*. New York: Knopf, 2006.

11. See C. Porath, *Mastering Civility: A Manifesto for the Workplace*. New York: Grand Central Publishing, 2016.

12. Consider the case of a newly appointed director of the CDC during the pandemic. See S. Toy and S. Siddiqui, "CDC Director Says She's Struggling to Communicate With Americans About COVID-19 Amid Politics, Mistrust." *Wall Street Journal*, 13 August 2021.

CHAPTER 4

1. T. Hanson, *Hurricane Lizards and Plastic Squid: The Fraught and Fascinating Biology of Climate Change*. New York: Basic Books, 2021.

2. B. Staats, *Never Stop Learning: Stay Relevant, Reinvent Yourself, and Thrive*. Boston: Harvard Business Review Press, 2018, p. 3.

3. S. Carey and reported in an article "The Child as Word Learner" published in *Linguistic Theory and Psychological Reality*, edited by M. Halle, J. Bresnan, and G. Miller. Cambridge, MA: MIT Press, 1977.

4. G. Miller, *The Science of Words*. New York: Scientific American Library, 1991.

5. J. Allen and J. Macomber, *Healthy Buildings: How Indoor Spaces Drive Performance and Productivity*. Cambridge: Harvard University Press, 2020.

CHAPTER 5

1. J. Gay, "What Simone Biles Was Saying." *Wall Street Journal*, 29 July 2021, p. A15.

2. See https://archive.fortune.com/galleries/2008/fortune/0804/gallery. bestadvice.fortune/7.html.

3. M. Loon, "Practices for Learning in Early Careers." *Learning & Education* 20(2), 2021, 182–202.

4. C. D'Este, *Eisenhower: A Soldier's Life*. New York: Henry Holt and Company, 2002, p. 99.

5. J. C. Humes, *Confessions of White House Ghostwriter*. Washington, DC: Regnery, 1997, p. 39.

6. P. Bloom, *Against Empathy: The Case for Rational Compassion*. New York: HarperCollins, 2016.

7. S. Kotkin, *Stalin: Waiting for Hitler*. New York: Penguin Books, 2017, p. 57 of 3386.

8. J. Patterson, J. Connolly, and T. Malloy, *Filthy Rich: The Jeffrey Epstein Story*. New York: Little Brown, 2016.

9. D. Couch, *The Warrior Elite: The Forging of SEAL Class 228*. New York: Crown Publishing, 2001, p. 274.

10. D. Couch, *The Warrior Elite: The Forging of SEAL Class 228*. New York: Crown Publishing, 2001, p. 292.

11. G. Chapman and P. White, *The 5 Languages of Appreciation in the Workplace*. Chicago: Northfield Publishing, 2019, p. 38 of 654 (ebook).

12. J. Petrocelli, *The Life-Changing Science of Detecting Bullshit*. New York: St. Martin's Press, 2021.

13. E. Bernstein, "Your B.S. Detector Is Rusty." *Wall Street Journal*, 14 July 2021, p. A11.

14. D. Sarasohn, "How Kindness Appreciates—How a Gracious Act Can Resonate for a Lifetime." *The Rotarian Magazine*, November 2019.

15. P. Cappelli, "Stop Overengineering People Management." *Harvard Business Review*, 2020 September–October, 56–63.

CHAPTER 6

1. See for example, C. D'Este, *Patton: A Genius for War*. New York: HarperCollins, 1993.

2. W. Manchester, *American Caesar: Douglas MacArthur 1880–1964*. New York: Dell Publishing, 1978.

3. K. Marton, *The Chancellor: The Remarkable Odyssey of Angela Merkel*. New York: Simon & Schuster, 2021, p. 24 of 1126 (ebook).

4. M. Hallsworth and E. Kirkman, *Behavioral Insights*. Cambridge, MA: MIT Press, 2020, p. 2.

5. Personal interview with A. Al-Saadi, January 2021.

6. J. Liker, *The Toyota Way: 14 Management Principles*. New York: McGraw-Hill, 2020, p. 263–265.

7. K. Grind, J. Hagerty, and K. Sayre, "The Death of Zappos's Tony Hsieh: A Spiral of Alcohol, Drugs, and Extreme Behavior." *Wall Street Journal*, 7 December 2020.

8. K. Marton, *The Chancellor: The Remarkable Odyssey of Angela Merkel*. New York: Simon & Schuster, 2021, p. 962 of 1126 (ebook).

CHAPTER 7

1. V. Vroom, *Work and Motivation*. San Francisco: Jossey-Bass, 1995.

2. P. Cappelli, "Stop Overengineering People Management." *Harvard Business Review*, 2020, September–October, 56–63.

3. R. Goffee and G. Jones, *Clever: Leading Your Smartest, Most Creative People*. Boston: Harvard Business School Publishing, 2009. B. Cohen, "Stephen Curry's Quest for the Perfect Shot." *Wall Street Journal*, 21 November 2021, p. A16.

4. M. Csikszentmihalyi, *The Evolving Self: A Psychology for the Third Millennium*. New York: HarperCollins, 1993.

5. M. Csikszentmihalyi, *The Evolving Self: A Psychology for the Third Millennium*. New York: HarperCollins, 1993.

6. F. Luntz, *Words That Work: It's Not What You Say, It's What People Hear*. New York: Hyperion, 2007.

7. S. Lund, A. Madgavkar, J. Manyika, and S. Smit, "What's Next for Remote Work: An Analysis of 2,000 Tasks, 800 Jobs, and Nine Countries." McKinsey Global Institute white paper, 2020.

8. I. Nooyi, *My Life in Full: Work, Family, and Our Future*. New York: Portfolio/Penguin, 2021, p. 516 of 593 (ebook).

9. A. Beaton and J. Robinson, "Chess Grandmasters Obsess Over Gambits, Endgames—and Chairs." *Wall Street Journal*, 28 April 2021, p. A1, 8.

10. G. Hamel and M. Zanini, *Humanocracy: Creating Organizations as Amazing as the People Inside Them*. Boston: Harvard Business School Press, 2020.

11. M. Meyer, and L. Zucker, *Permanently Failing Organizations*. Newbury Park, CA: Sage Publications, 1989.

12. P. Lawrence and J. Lorsch, *Organization and Environment: Managing Differentiation and Integration*. Homewood, IL: Richard D. Irwin, 1969.

CHAPTER 8

1. P. Clampitt and M. Williams, "Decision Downloading." *MIT Sloan Management Review* 48 (2), Winter 2007, 77–82.

2. Y. Lee, "Dynamics of Symmetrical Communication Within Organizations: The Impacts of Channel Usage on CEO, Managers, and Peers." *International Journal of Business Communication* 59(1), January 2022, p. 3–21.

3. R. Rostow and G. Fine, *Rumors and Gossip: The Social Psychology of Hearsay*. New York: Elsevier, 1976.

4. See I. Engleberg and J. Daly, *The Norton Field Guide to Speaking*. New York: W. W. Norton & Company, 2022.

5. H. W. Brands, *Reagan: The Life*. New York: Doubleday, 2015.

6. For the complete speech, see https://www.ff.org/ronald-reagans-farewell-address/.

7. P. Smith, *Lead With a Story: A Guide to Crafting Business Narratives That Captivate, Convince and Inspire*. New York: AMACOM, 2012.

8. P. Noonan, *On Speaking Well: How to Give a Speech With Style, Substance, and Clarity*. New York: HarperPerennial, 1999.

9. R. McKee, *Story: Substance, Structure, Style, and the Principles of Screenwriting*. New York: Regan Books, 1997.

10. A. Kraut, *Organizational Surveys: Tools for Assessment and Change*. San Francisco: Jossey-Bass, 1996.

11. See related story: https://www.etalk.ca/celebrity/dave-chappelle-new-comedy-special-major-backlash-dababy-caitlyn-jenner-jokes.html.

12. J. Rauch, *The Constitution of Knowledge: A Defense of Truth*. Washington, DC: Brookings Institution Press, 2021, p. 240 of 566 (ebook).

13. P. Clampitt, *Social Media Strategy: Tools for Professionals and Organizations*. Thousand Oaks, CA: Sage Publications, 2018.

14. See S. Covey tweet, https://twitter.com/stephenrcovey/status/1186644009210515458.

15. M. Burley-Allen, *Listening: The Forgotten Skill*. New York: John Wiley, 1982, p. 16.

CHAPTER 9

1. J. Grimaldi, "Millions of Fake Comments on FCC Plan." *Wall Street Journal*, 7 May 2021, p. A5.

2. See J. Carreyrou, *Bad Blood: Secrets and Lies in a Silicon Valley Startup*. New York: Knopf, 2018.

3. S. Nadler and L. Shapiro, *When Bad Thinking Happens to Good People: How Philosophy Can Save Us From Ourselves*. Princeton, NJ: Princeton University Press, 2021.

4. T. Gooley, *How to Read Water: Clues and Patterns From Puddles to the Sea*. New York: The Experiment, 2016, p. 11.

5. J. Kassing, *Dissent in Organizations*. Cambridge, UK: Polity Press, 2011.

6. E. Schein, *Humble Inquiry: The Gentle Art of Asking Instead of Telling*. San Francisco: Berrett-Koehler, 2013.

7. W. Bennis, D. Goleman, and J. O'Toole, *Transparency: How Leaders Create a Culture of Candor*. San Francisco: Jossey-Bass, 2008.

8. See https://apple.news/AC0pCc_msTWCGP22iyXRprA.

CHAPTER 10

1. R. Dunbar, *How Many Friends Does One Person Need?* Cambridge, MA: Harvard University Press, 2010.

2. R. Dunbar, *Grooming, Gossip, and the Evolution of Language*. Cambridge, MA: Harvard University Press, 1988, p. 77.

3. See https://www.npr.org/templates/story/story.php?storyId=18255131.

4. See https://www.wsj.com/articles/can-spa-resorts-still-be-relaxing-during-covid-11609524093.

5. S. Oliver, "Close Colleagues, Even on Zoom." *Wall Street Journal*, 29 November 2021, p. R3.

6. D. Akst, "The Hidden Costs of Remote Work." *Wall Street Journal*, 1 November 2021, p. R4.

7. E. Kross. *Chatter: The Voice in Our Head, Why It Matters, and How to Harness It*. New York: Crown, 2021.

8. See https://www.forbes.com/sites/carminegallo/2014/05/31/the-maya-angelou-quote-that-will-radically-improve-your-business/?sh=2bee85eb118b.

CHAPTER 11

1. M. Hansen, *Collaboration: How Leaders Avoid the Traps, Create Unity, and Reap Big Results*. Boston: Harvard Business Press, 2009, p. 95.

2. F. Gino, "Cracking the Code of Sustained Collaboration." *Harvard Business Review* 97(6), 2019, November–December, 73–81.

3. I. Janis, "GroupThink: The Problems of Conformity." In G. Morgan (ed.) *Creative Organization Theory: A Resource Book*. Newbury Park, CA: Sage, 2006, p. 225.

4. R. Cross, R. Rebele, and A. Grant, "Collaboration Overload." *Harvard Business Review* 94(1), 2016, January–February, 74–79, p. 76.

5. J. Nason, "The Zoom Revolutions Empowers Women to Speak Up." *Wall Street Journal*, 6 July 2021, p. B3.

6. "Virtual Collaboration" in 20 Minute Manager series. Boston: Harvard Business Review Press, 2016, p. 7.

7. R. Lesser, "The CEO Whisperer." *Wall Street Journal*, 26–27 June 2021, p. B8.

8. C. Sunstein and R. Hastie, *Wiser: Getting Beyond Groupthink to Make Groups Smarter*. Boston: Harvard Business Review Press, 2015, p. 51 of 491 (ebook).

9. D. Kahneman, O. Sibony, and C. Sunstein, *Noise: A Flaw in Human Judgment*. New York: Little, Brown Spark, 2021.

CHAPTER 12

1. See https://www.writergirl.com/its-time-to-recognize-accept-and-celebrate-our-differences/.

2. J. McGonigal, *Reality Is Broken: Why Games Make Us Better and How They Change the World*. New York: Penguin Books, 2011.

3. M. Emre, *The Personality Brokers: The Strange History of Myers-Briggs and the Birth of Personality Testing*. New York: Doubleday, 2018.

4. C. Powell, *It Worked for Me*. New York: HarperCollins, 2012, p. 341 of 372 (ebook).

CHAPTER 13

1. For one of the best sources, we suggest S. Maital, *Executive Economics: Ten Essential Tools for Managers*. New York: Free Press, 2011.

2. J. Woodcock and M. Graham, *The Gig Economy*. Cambridge, UK: Polity Press, 2022.

3. A. Bernasek, *The Economics of Integrity.* New York: HarperCollins, 2010, p. 11.

4. Personal interview with Dave Withbroe, 14 January 2022.

5. M. Housel, *The Psychology of Money.* Hampshire, UK: Harriman House, 2020, p. 11.

6. P. R. Breggin, *Guilt, Shame, and Anxiety: Understanding and Overcoming Negative Emotions.* New York: Prometheus Books, 2014.

CHAPTER 14

1. J. Thompson, *Book Wars: The Digital Revolution in Publishing.* Cambridge, UK: Polity Press, 2001.

2. P. Aghion, C. Antonin, and S. Bunel, *The Power of Creative Destruction: Economic Upheaval and the Wealth of Nations.* Cambridge, MA: Belknap Press, 2021.

3. T. McCraw, *Prophet of Innovation: Joseph Schumpeter and Creative Destruction.* Cambridge, MA: Belknap Press, 2007.

4. M. Dodgson and D. Gann, *Innovation: A Very Short Introduction.* Oxford, UK: Oxford University Press, 2010.

5. N. Wiener, *Invention: The Care and Feeding of Ideas.* Cambridge, MA: MIT Press, 1993.

6. D. McCullough, *The Wright Brothers.* New York: Simon & Schuster, 2015.

7. C. Gaines, "Chip Gets the Last Word." *Magnolia Journal*, Fall 2021.

8. D. McCullough, *The Wright Brothers.* New York: Simon & Schuster, 2015, p. 32 of 551 (ebook).

9. R. Foster, *Innovation: The Attacker's Advantage.* New York: Summit Books, 1986.

10. D. Baron, *A Better Pencil: Readers, Writers, and the Digital Revolution.* New York: Oxford University Press, 2009.

11. K. Marcal, *Mother of Invention: How Good Ideas Get Ignored in an Economy Built for Men.* New York: Abrams Press, 2021.

12. D. Rooney, *About Time: A History of Civilization in Twelve Clocks.* New York: W. W. Norton & Company, 2021.

13. S. Ribeiro, *The Oracle of Night: The History and Science of Dreams.* New York: Pantheon, 2019.

14. S. Bramley, *Leonardo: Discovering the Life of Leonardo da Vinci.* (Translated by S. Reynolds.) New York: Edward Burlingame Books, 1991, p. 295.

15. K. Borner, *Atlas of Forecasts: Modeling and Mapping Desirable Futures.* Cambridge, MA: MIT Press, 2021.

16. L. Marquet, *Leadership Is Language: The Hidden Power of What You Say—and What You Don't*. New York: Portfolio/Penguin, 2020.

17. See https://aljohnsons.com/goat-cam/.

18. L. Weinzimmer and J. McConoughey, *The Wisdom of Failure: How to Learn the Tough Leadership Lessons Without Paying the Price*. San Francisco: Jossey-Bass, 2013.

19. P. Aghion, C. Antonin, and S. Bunel, *The Power of Creative Destruction: The Economic Upheaval and the Wealth of Nations*. Cambridge, MA: Belknap Press, 2021.

CHAPTER 15

1. R. Greenleaf, *Servant Leadership: A Journey Into the Nature of Legitimate Power & Greatness* (twenty-fifth anniversary edition). Mahwah, NJ: Paulist Press, 1977, p. 21.

2. R. Greenleaf, *Servant Leadership: A Journey Into the Nature of Legitimate Power & Greatness* (twenty-fifth anniversary edition). Mahwah, NJ: Paulist Press, 1977, p. 55.

3. See Chapter 13.

4. See Chapters 2 and 4.

5. See Chapter 1.

6. See Chapter 8.

7. See Chapters 1 and 11.

8. See Chapters 3 and 7.

9. J. Roberts, *The Modern Firm: Organizational Design for Performance and Growth*. New York: Oxford University Press, 2004. Note: Roberts advocates looking at organizations as composed of people, architecture, routines, and culture (PARC). *Leading with Care* provides important ideas about all four variables that are sprinkled throughout the book.

10. M. Mayfield, J. Mayfield, and R. Walker, "Leader Communication and Follower Identity: How Leader Motivating Language Shapes Organizational Identification Through Cultural Knowledge and Fit." *International Journal of Business Communication* 58(2), 2021, 221–253.

INDEX

Page references in italics indicate figures, and t *indicates a table.*